ABANDONED ROADSIDE ATTRACTIONS

UNDER A SOUTHWEST MOON

KEN LEE

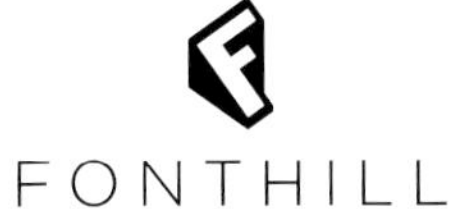

FONTHILL

Fonthill Media Inc.
www.fonthillmedia.com
office@fonthillmedia.com

First published 2024

ISBN 978-1-62545-147-7

Typeset in Trade Gothic 10pt on 15pt
Printed and bound in England

CONTENTS

ACKNOWLEDGMENTS

Special thanks to night photography friends and traveling mates Tim Little, Mike Cooper, George Loo, Ron Pinkerton, Dave Dasinger, Tony Donofrio, and more.

Lance Keimig and Troy Paiva for your pioneering work, friendship, and inspiration.

Bobbie and Shauna Werling of Nelson Ghost Town, Linda Speckels of Bedrock City, and Bill Johnson of Santa's Village for their kindness.

Thank you to Lisa Kelly for your editorial help.

For books, photos, night photography workshops, and general weirdness, visit www.kenleephotography.com

INTRODUCTION

The USA's love affair with car culture may have begun with the 1926 construction of Route 66, which connected Chicago and Los Angeles and all the small towns in between. Regardless, we love our four million miles of roads. Entrepreneurs and artists alike understood that we needed to get out of our cars and stretch our legs. Roadside attractions began to spring up. Whether it was real-life replicas of a cartoon city from *The Flintstones*, vehicles jammed into the ground at unnatural angles and painted with fascinating figures, or immense life-sized metal statues of dinosaurs rising up from the desert floor, their creativity knew no bounds.

Still others constructed a Santa's Village on the way to Lake Arrowhead or sprawling waterparks with death-defying stand-up slides in the desert. One family turned an old, dusty mining ghost town into a fantasy version of one, featuring fields of abandoned, rusty automobiles, kludging some into post-apocalyptic "Burning Man" creations.

Not all these oddities of the road remain. Some were banished to the elements. Some have even created attractions from that abandonment.

I photographed their ghosts—cartoon cities, enormous dinosaurs, bizarre car art installations—in the dark of night. To do this, I set my camera on a tripod, then held the camera shutter open for long periods of time while illuminating the weather-worn subjects with a handheld light.

I feel that night photography with light painting is the most actively creative form of photography. I am able to move freely, unencumbered by light stands, choosing angles of lighting, colors, what to illuminate, and what to keep in shadow. This approach can produce a rather surreal, dreamlike appearance.

I am fortunate to have shared these experiences with friends along the way. You'll discover some of our adventures and encounters on these trips. I also value the deeper connection I experience when spending so much time in a location due to long exposure night photography, a slower, more deliberate form of art. This unusual book focuses on these cast-off roadside attractions beneath the starry canopy of the moonlit American Southwest.

1

INTERNATIONAL CAR FOREST OF THE LAST CHURCH, NEVADA

Navigating the hilly dirt paths in the Car Forest at night in summer 2014, I saw a shadowy figure walking in the dark. Killing the headlights, I slowed and rolled down the window. We introduced each other.

"Ken? Ken Lee?"

How did he know my name? I was momentarily apprehensive. However, he said that he had seen my photo of Trona Pinnacles at night in the *Los Angeles Times* when I won Photo of the Year in their travel section.

This person was Ron Pinkerton, a masterful night photographer. Later that evening, Ron showed me an incredible handheld light he was using: a ProtoMachines LED2. George Loo had designed this light specifically for light painting subjects. Up to this point, I had been illuminating my subjects with a $30 Streamlight LED flashlight. If I wanted to add color with my light, I either grabbed Roscolux gels or colored plastic bags and held them over the front of the flashlight. After Ron's brief demonstration, I laughed and said, "You just cost me $500!" I purchased it six months later and have used it ever since.

At that time, little did I know that I would become friends with Ron and George and go on future night photography adventures with them.

For now, though, I was here because I had recently heard about the Car Forest, a place where approximately forty vehicles were jammed into the earth at unlikely angles, then painted with colorful skulls, ants, devils, words, and other fantastic images. Mark Rippie owned eighty acres of land next to Highway 95 in Goldfield, which itself has a plethora of fascinating abandoned buildings. He enlisted the help of Bay Area artist Chad Sorg to set the record for the most upturned cars in an art installation. His mission was to beat Carhenge in Alliance, Nebraska. Rippie owned over forty cars, trucks, and buses. Work began in the early 2000s, using a backhoe and a lot of work to "plant" the vehicles. Sorg was so taken with it all that he moved there in 2004.

The two had a falling out a bit later. The reason? A difference in vision. Sorg wanted to create a more artistic vision at the Car Forest. Rippie just wanted to break the Guinness World Record. I doubt that Rippie going to prison for two years for improperly possessing and attempting to purchase firearms helped them come any closer to a consensus.

I contacted Sorg in spring 2014, asking if it would be okay to photograph the Car Forest at night. Although I realized that I didn't really require permission, I preferred to make contact regardless. I felt especially strong about this since Rippie had been arrested again the previous year for having fifteen firearms, including assault-type rifles and a ridiculous amount of ammunition. But Sorg said that all was well and encouraged me to take photos and share them.

I had not been doing night photography for very long. In fact, the Car Forest would be only the third time I had ever photographed vehicles at night. The strangeness and absurdity of the Car Forest screamed, "Use color!" I was only too happy to oblige. Sure, I used warm white light. But I also used vivid red, blue, green, and yellow colors to further emphasize the cars.

No one lives there. It's been abandoned for years. People have smashed the cars, lit them ablaze, and painted them over and over. It's a fascinating roadside attraction in a town that is on the brink of being abandoned as well.

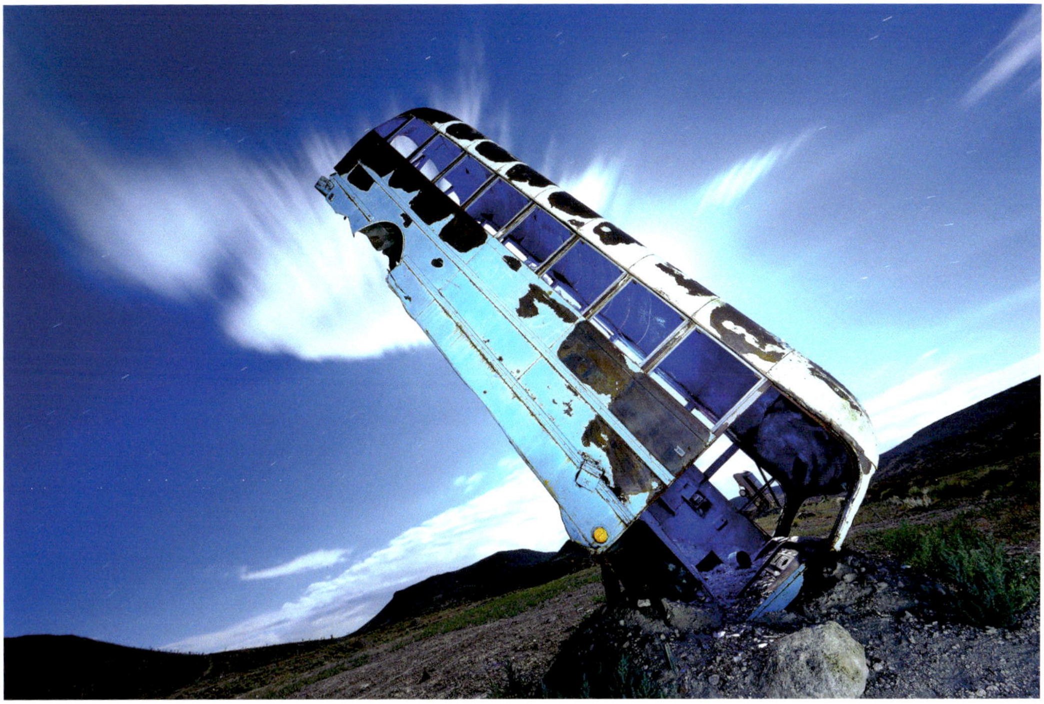

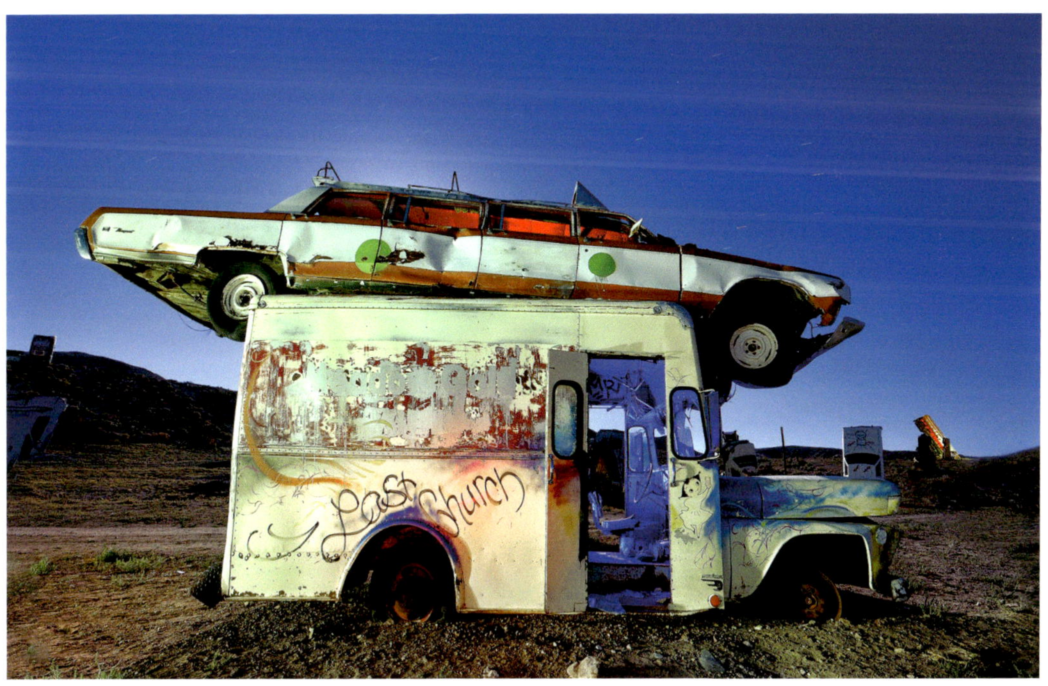

Big Blue Bus Burrowing Bottomward · Car Forest, Nevada · Nikon D610/14-24mm f/2.8G ED lens. 146 second exposure, f/8, ISO 400. July 2014 · Full moon, Dorcy LED flashlight with blue plastic bag, Nikon SB-600 flash with blue colored gel.

Double Scoop, Double Scoop · Car Forest, Nevada · Nikon D610/14-24mm f/2.8G ED lens. 227 seconds f/8 ISO 200. July 2014 · Full moon, Streamlight LED flashlight with natural white light, red colored gel.

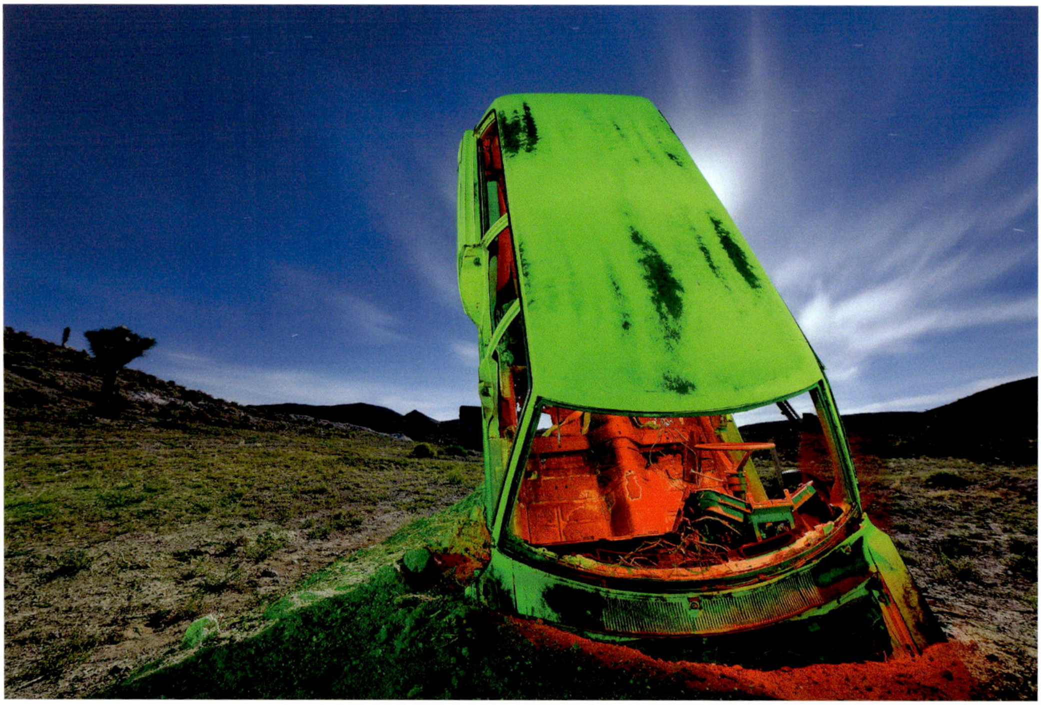

Grinch · Car Forest, Nevada · Nikon D610/14-24mm f/2.8G ED lens. 164 seconds f/8 ISO 200. July 2014 · Full moon, Streamlight LED flashlight with green colored gel, Nikon SB-600 flash with red colored gel.

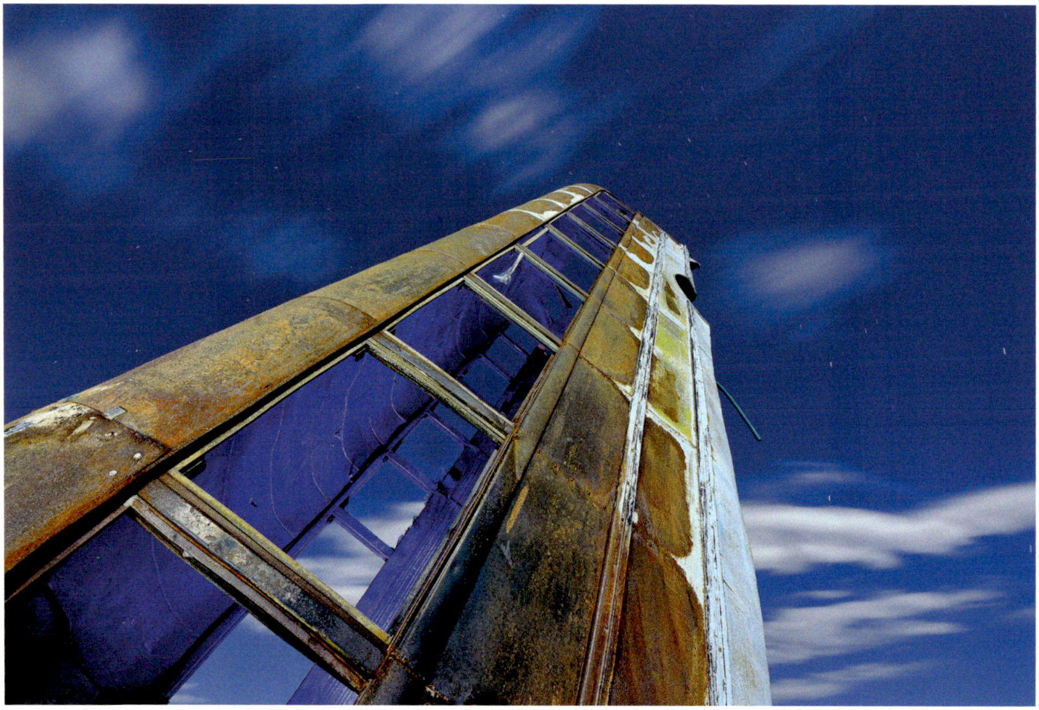

The New FlyAway Bus · Car Forest, Nevada · Nikon D610/14-24mm f/2.8G ED lens. 134 seconds f/8 ISO 320. July 2014 · Full moon, Streamlight LED flashlight with natural white light, Nikon SB-600 flash with blue colored gel.

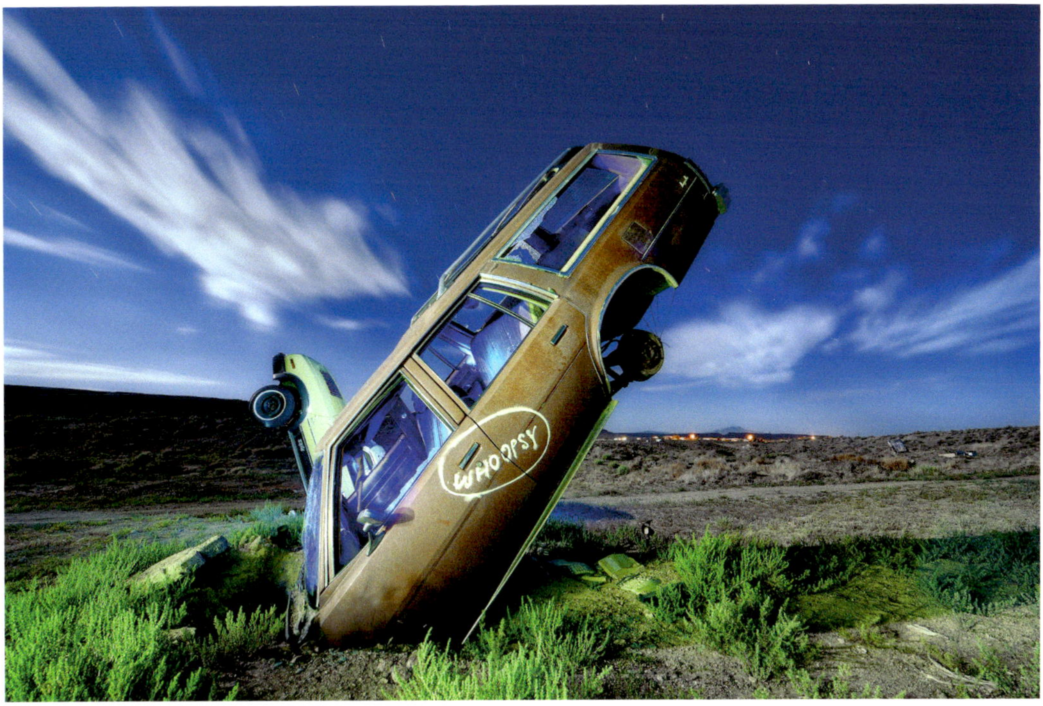

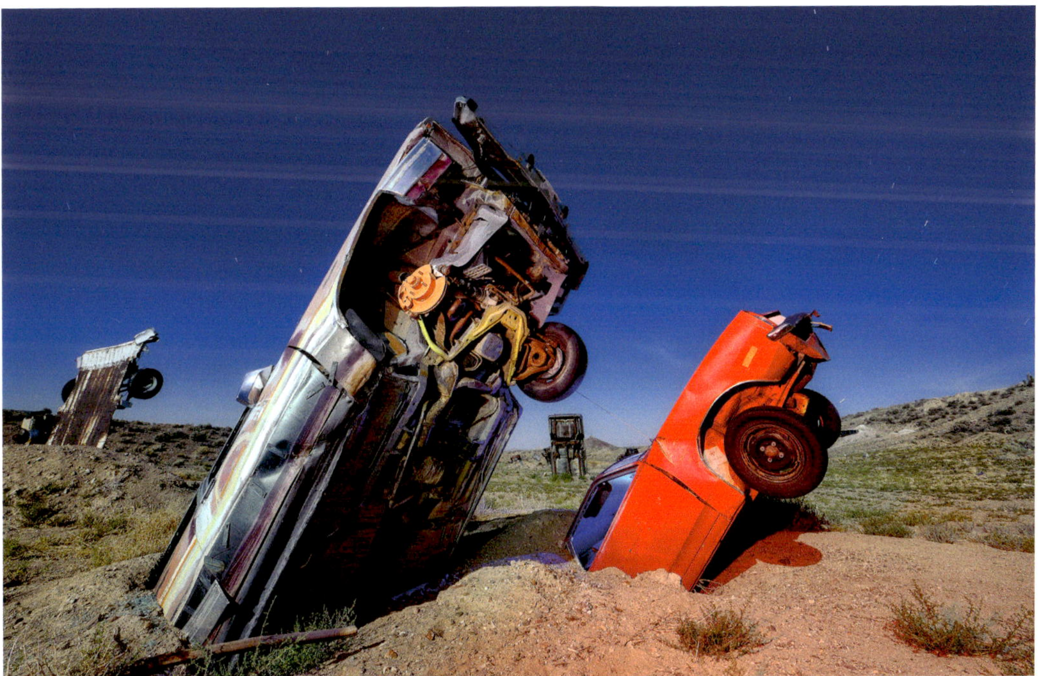

Whoopsy · Car Forest, Nevada · Nikon D610/14-24mm f/2.8G ED lens. 270 seconds f/8 ISO 200. July 2014 · Full moon, Streamlight LED flashlight with natural white light, Nikon SB-600 flash with blue colored gel.

Salute · Car Forest, Nevada · Nikon D610/14-24mm f/2.8G ED lens. 182 seconds f/8 ISO 200. July 2014 · Full moon, Streamlight LED flashlight with natural white light and red colored gel, Nikon SB-600 flash with blue colored gel.

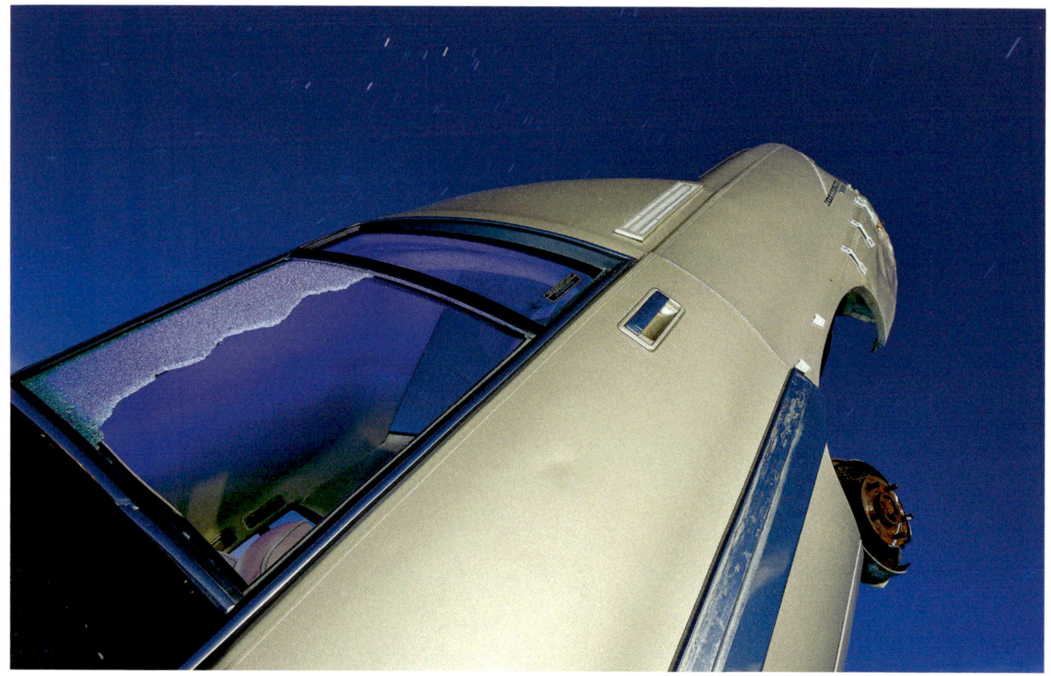

Crystal · Car Forest, Nevada · Nikon D610/14-24mm f/2.8G ED lens. 314 seconds f/8 ISO 200. July 2014 · Full moon, Streamlight LED flashlight with natural white light, Nikon SB-600 flash with blue colored gel.

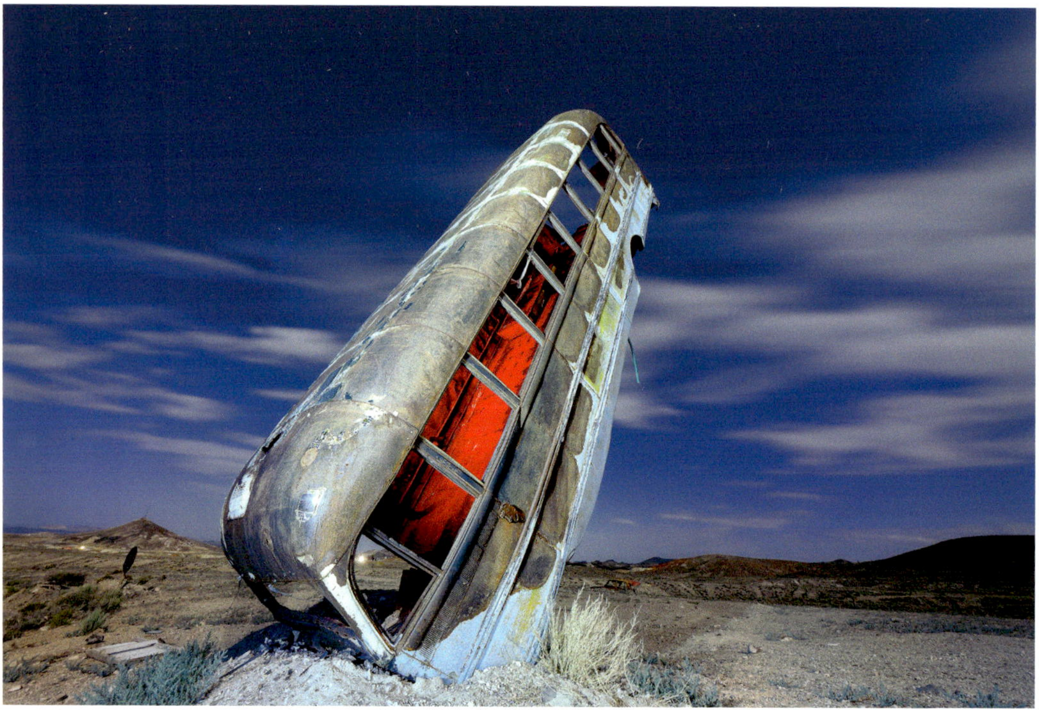

Red Ride Rolls Wrong Way · Car Forest, Nevada · Nikon D610/14-24mm f/2.8G ED lens. 190 seconds f/8 ISO 250. July 2014 · Full moon, Streamlight LED flashlight with natural white light, Nikon SB-600 flash with red colored gel.

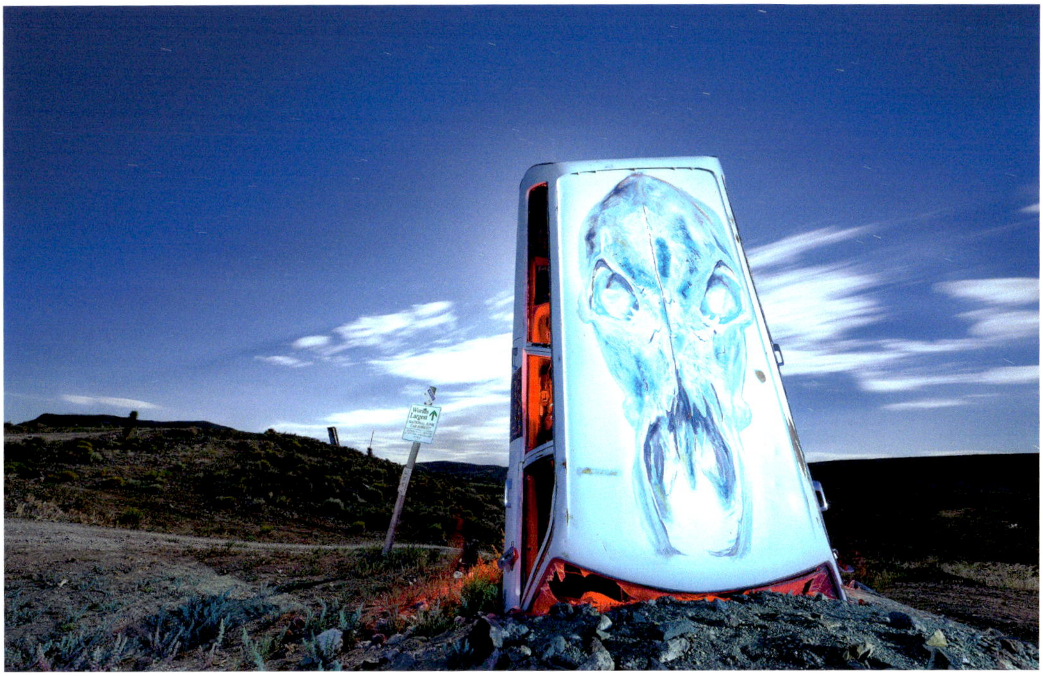

Skull · Car Forest, Nevada · Nikon D610/14-24mm f/2.8G ED lens. 178 seconds f/8 ISO 250. July 2014 · Full moon, Streamlight LED flashlight with natural white light, Nikon SB-600 flash with red colored gel.

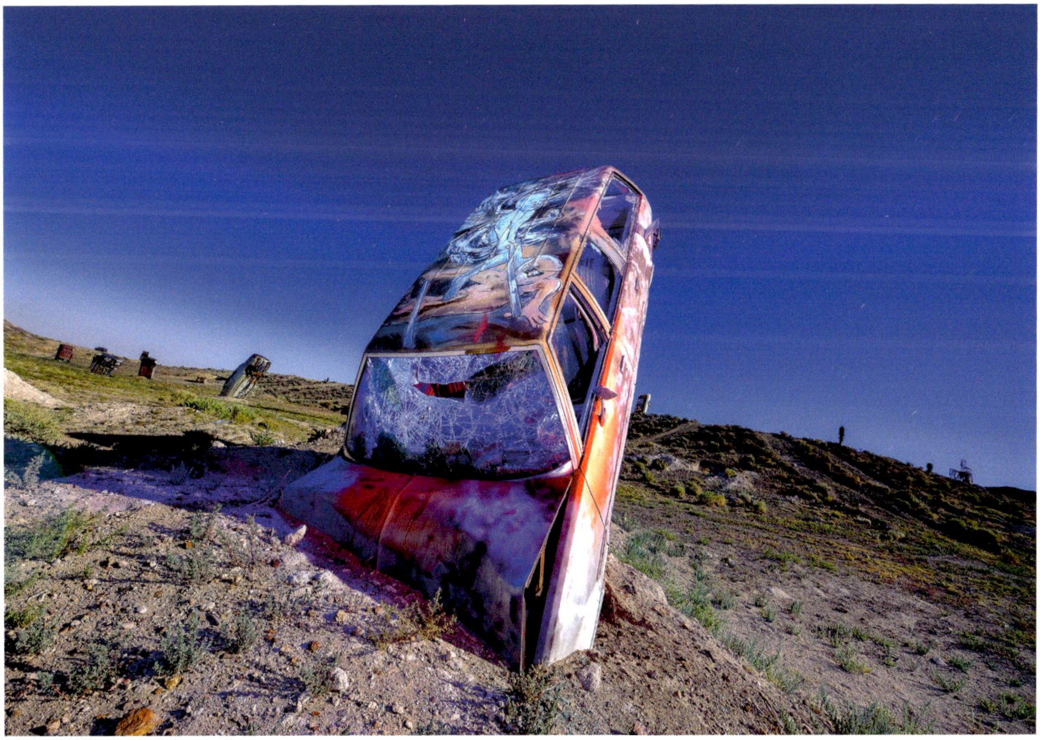

Alien Blue · Car Forest, Nevada · Nikon D610/14-24mm f/2.8G ED lens. 128 seconds f/8 ISO 250. July 2014 · Full moon, Streamlight LED flashlight with natural white light, Nikon SB-600 flash with blue colored gel.

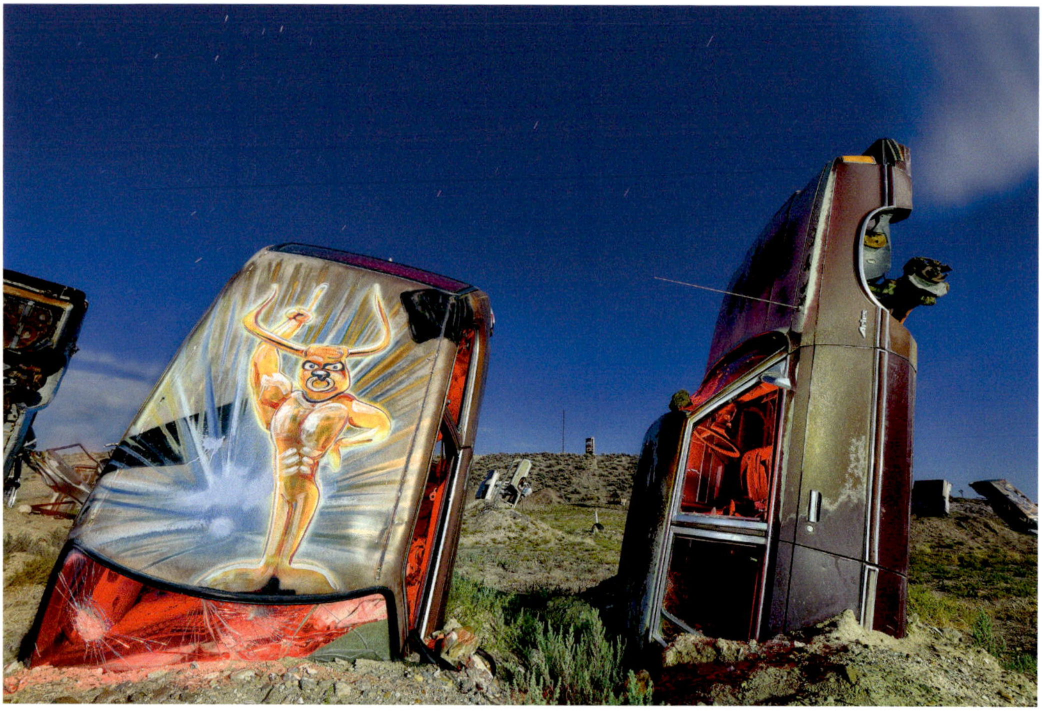

Diablo · Car Forest, Nevada · Nikon D610/14-24mm f/2.8G ED lens. 184 seconds f/8 ISO 200. July 2014 · Full moon, Streamlight LED flashlight with natural white light, Nikon SB-600 flash with red colored gel.

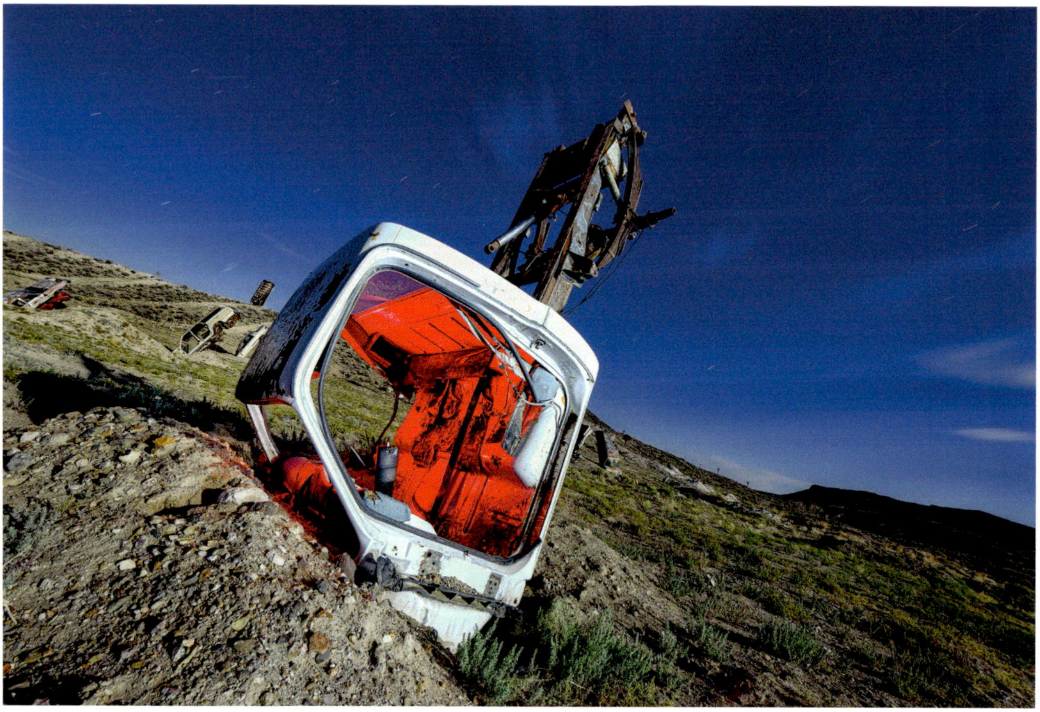

Space Truckin' · Car Forest, Nevada · Nikon D610/14-24mm f/2.8G ED lens. 231 seconds f/8 ISO 200. July 2014 · Full moon, Streamlight LED flashlight with natural white light, Nikon SB-600 flash with red colored gel.

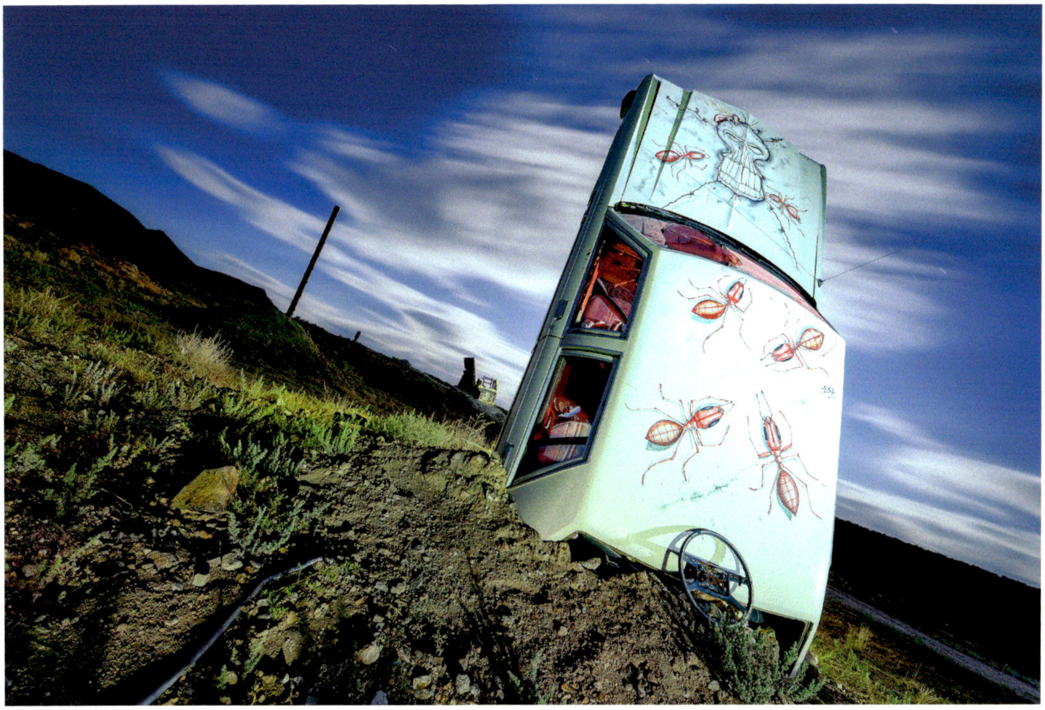

Picnic · Car Forest, Nevada · Nikon D610/14-24mm f/2.8G ED lens. 190 seconds f/8 ISO 200. July 2014 · Full moon, Streamlight LED flashlight with blue plastic bag, Nikon SB-600 flash with red colored gel.

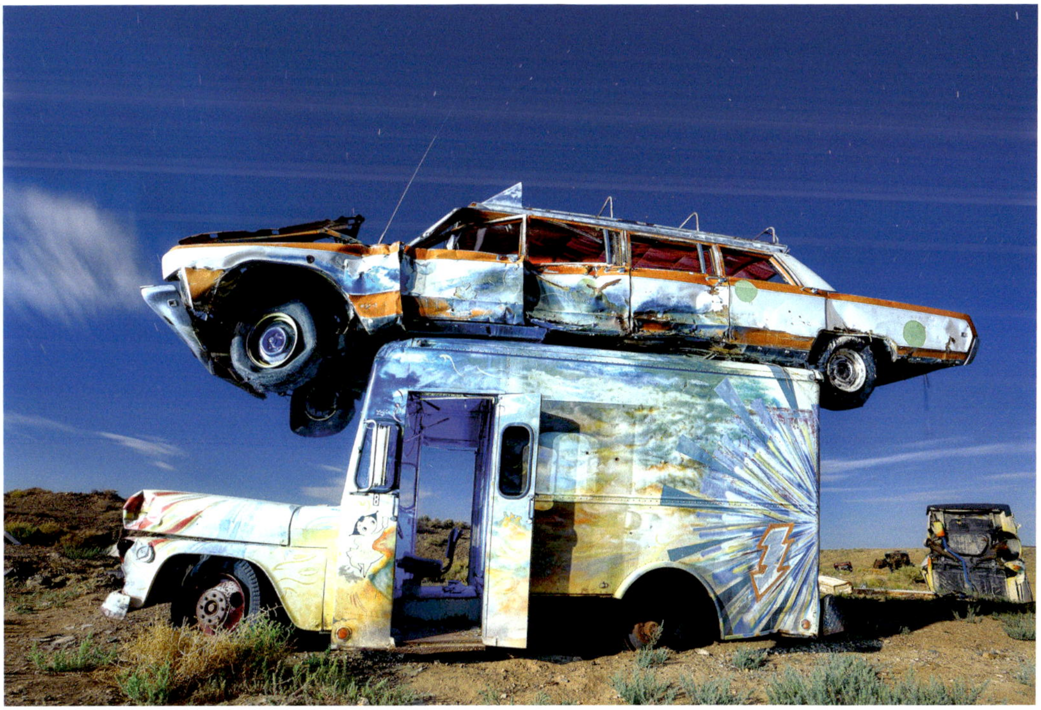

Spumoni · Car Forest, Nevada · Nikon D610/14-24mm f/2.8G ED lens. 225 seconds f/8 ISO 200. July 2014 · Full moon, Streamlight LED flashlight with natural white light, Nikon SB-600 flash with red and blue colored gel.

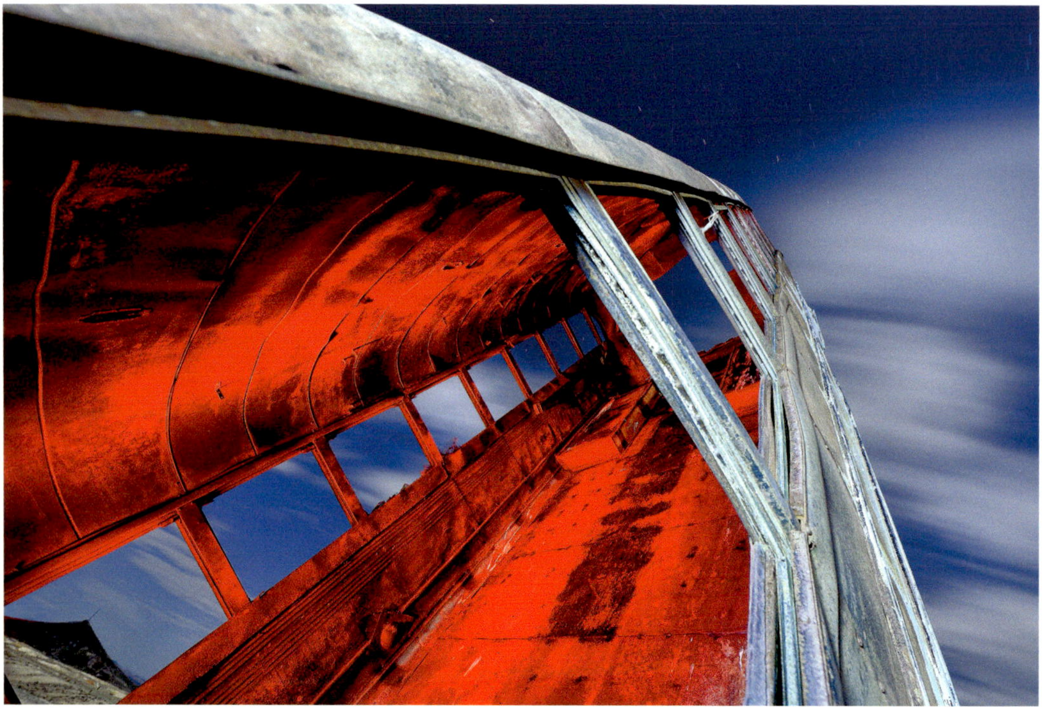

Redshirt · Car Forest, Nevada · Nikon D610/14-24mm f/2.8G ED lens. 186 seconds f/8 ISO 250. July 2014 · Full moon, Streamlight LED flashlight with natural white light, Nikon SB-600 flash with red colored gel.

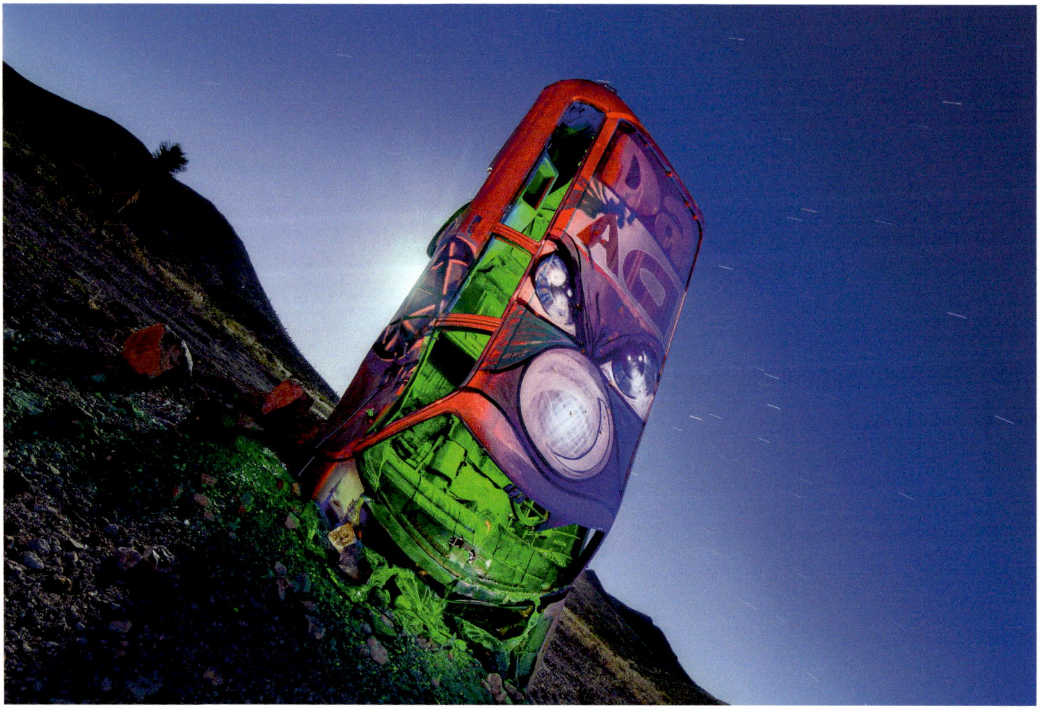

Dada · Car Forest, Nevada · Nikon D7000/Tokina 11-16mm f/2.8 lens. 355 seconds f/8 ISO 200. June 2017 · Full moon, ProtoMachines LED2 with warm white, red, and green light.

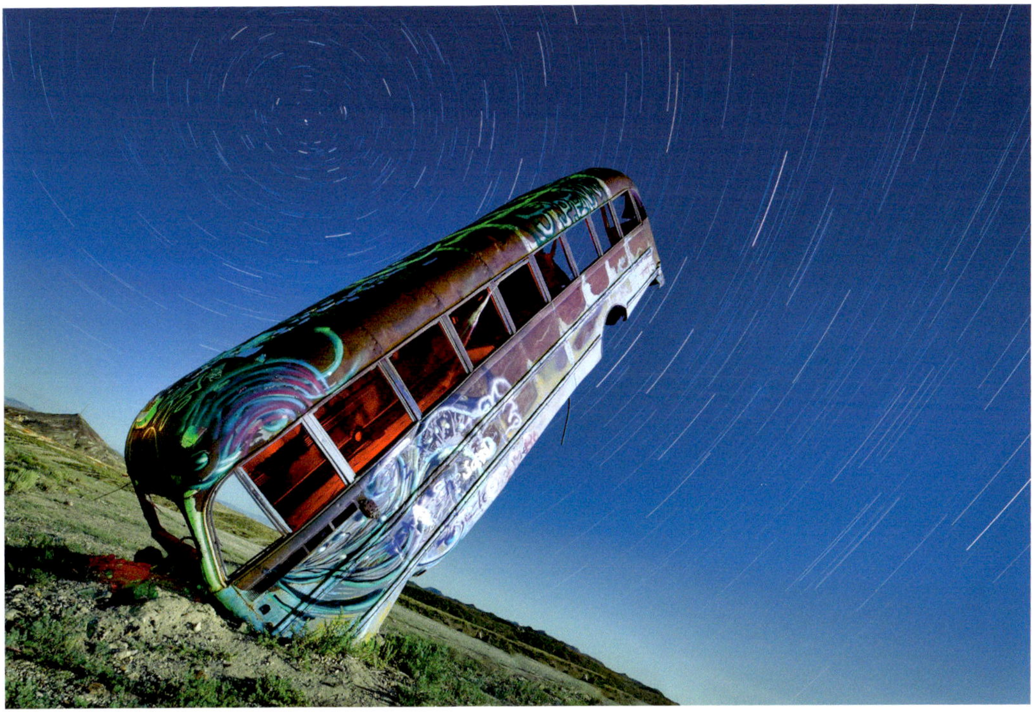

Hurtling Through Time · Car Forest, Nevada. This 49-minute exposure shows the perceived movement of the stars due to the rotation of the earth while facing north · Nikon D610/14-24mm f/2.8 lens. 49 minutes total "stacked". Each photo 7 minutes f/8 ISO 200. June 2017 · Full moon, ProtoMachines LED2 with warm white and red light.

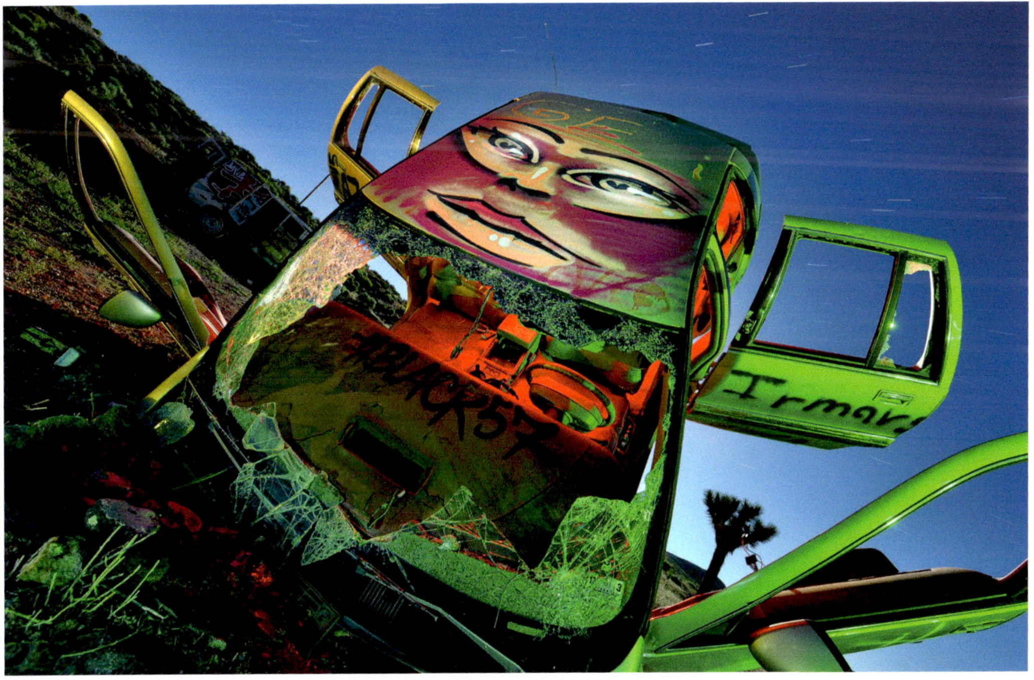

Girlfriend · Car Forest, Nevada · Nikon D610/14-24mm f/2.8 lens. 7 minutes f/8 ISO 200. June 2017 · Full moon, ProtoMachines LED2 with warm white and red light.

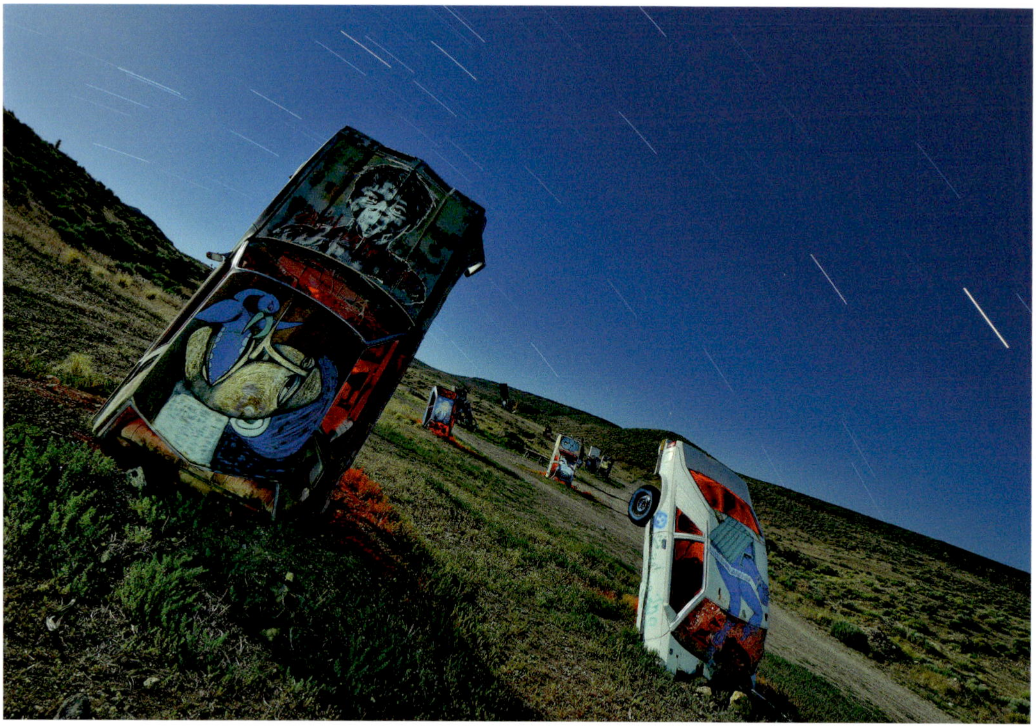

Saluting the Night Sky · Car Forest, Nevada · Nikon D610/14-24mm f/2.8 lens. 21 minutes total "stacked." Each photo 7 minutes f/8 ISO 200. June 2017 · Full moon, ProtoMachines LED2 with warm white and red light.

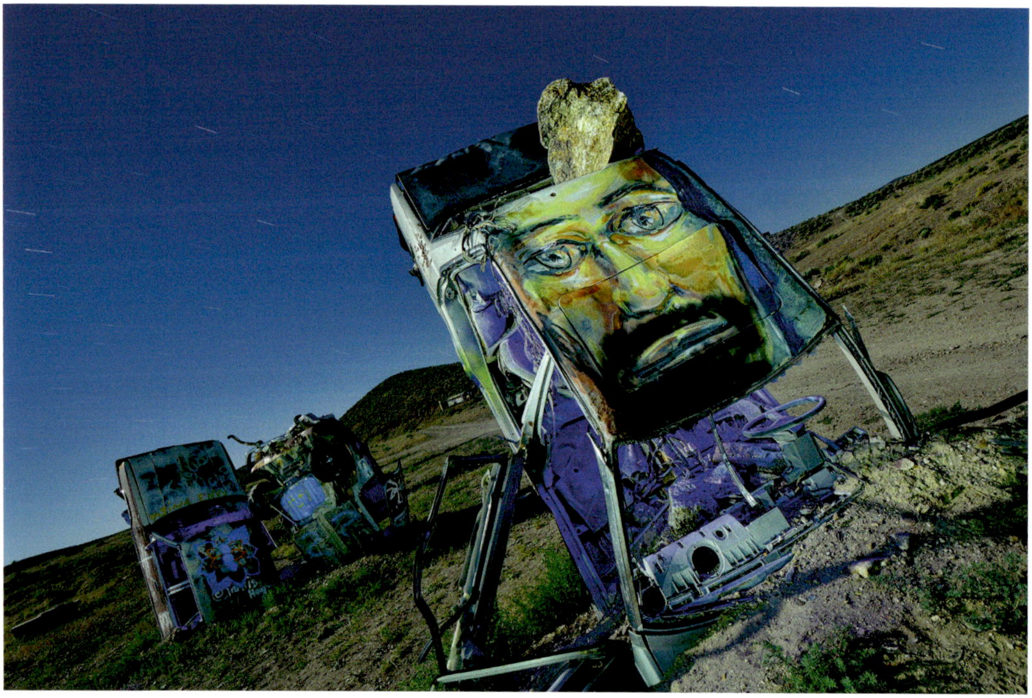

Stonehead · Car Forest, Nevada · Nikon D610/14-24mm f/2.8 lens. 7 minutes f/8 ISO 200. June 2017 · Full moon, ProtoMachines LED2 with warm white and blue light.

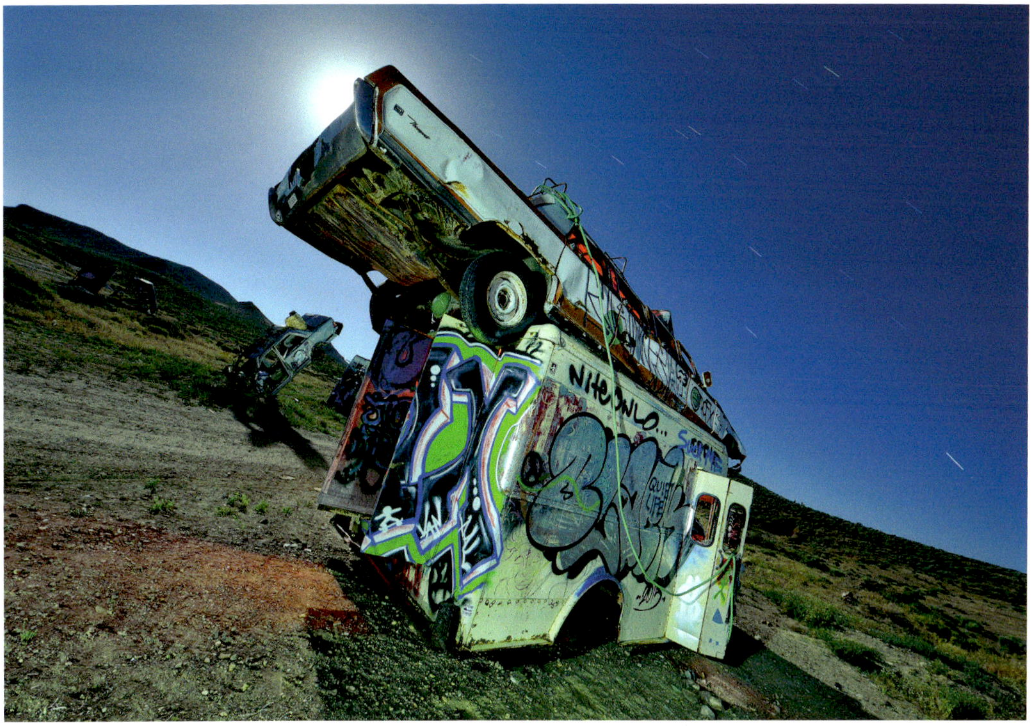

Lunar Ice Cream · Car Forest, Nevada · Nikon D610/14-24mm f/2.8 lens. 7 minutes f/8 ISO 200. June 2017 · Full moon, ProtoMachines LED2 with warm white and red light.

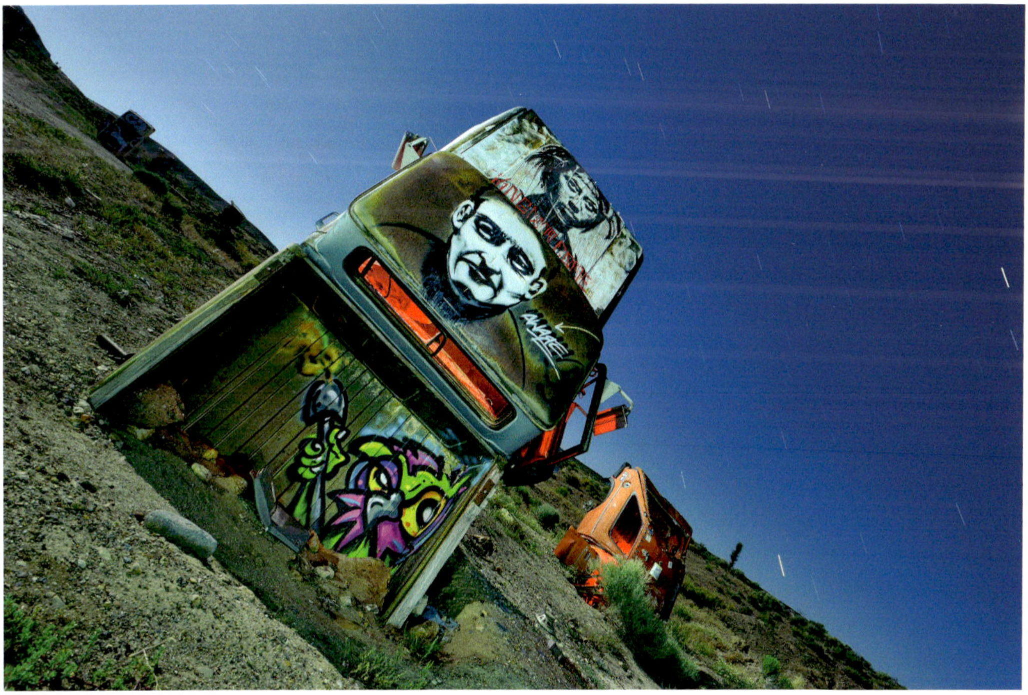

Aware/Unaware · Car Forest, Nevada · Nikon D610/14-24mm f/2.8 lens. 7 minutes f/8 ISO 200. June 2017 · Full moon, ProtoMachines LED2 with warm white and red light.

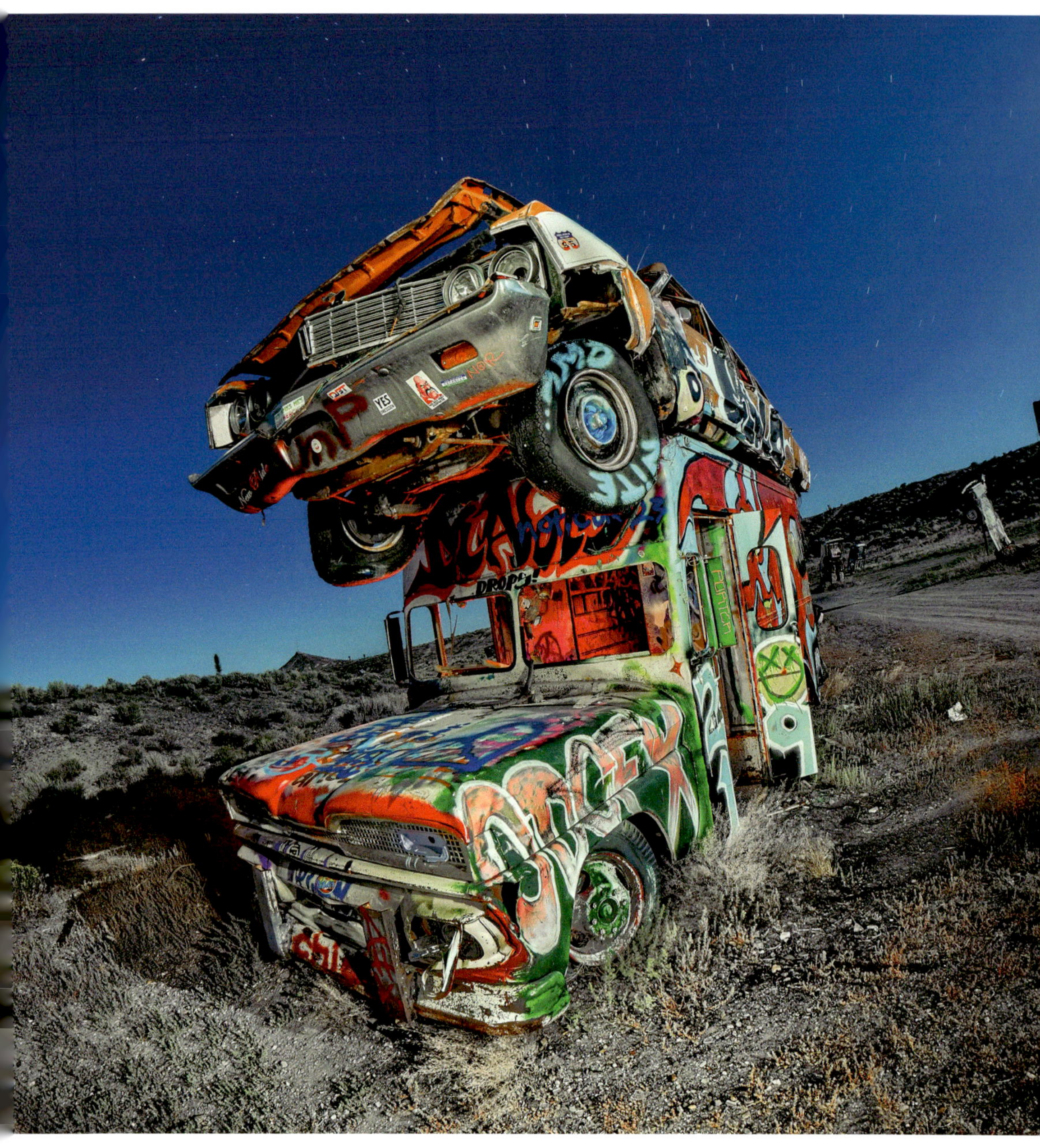

Gonna Hitch a Ride, Head for the Other Side · Car Forest, Nevada. These and other July 2019 photos were photographed during a ten-day, 2,559-mile night photography road trip with Mike Cooper and Tim Little · Nikon D610/Rokinon 12mm f/2.8 fisheye lens. 176 seconds f/8 ISO 200. July 2019 · Full moon, ProtoMachines LED2 with warm white and red light.

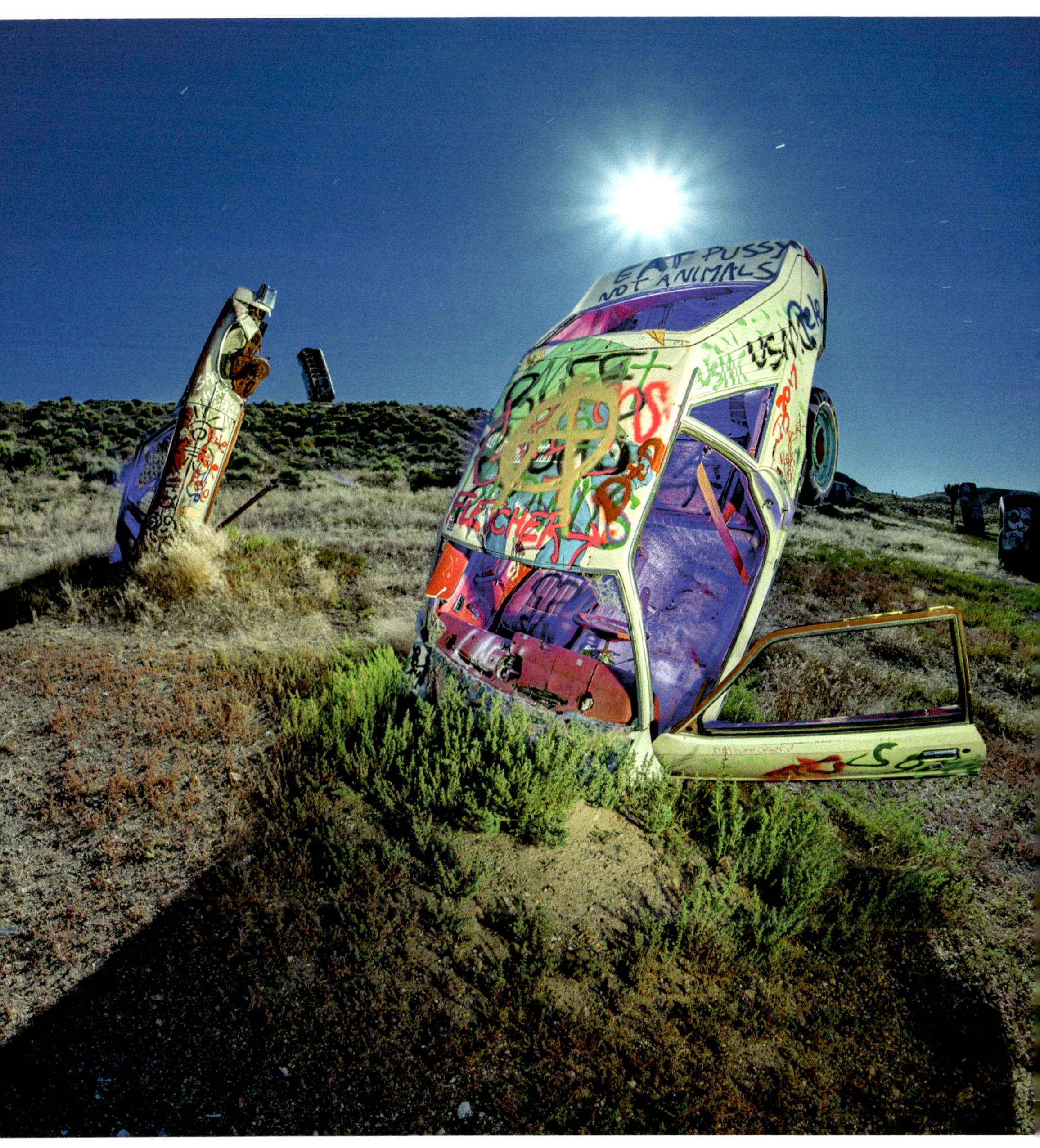

Anarchy Blue · Car Forest, Nevada. Fisheye view of a rather strange garden in the Mojave Desert · Nikon D610/ Rokinon 12mm f/2.8 fisheye lens. 197 seconds f/8 ISO 200. July 2019 · Full moon, ProtoMachines LED2 with warm white and blue light.

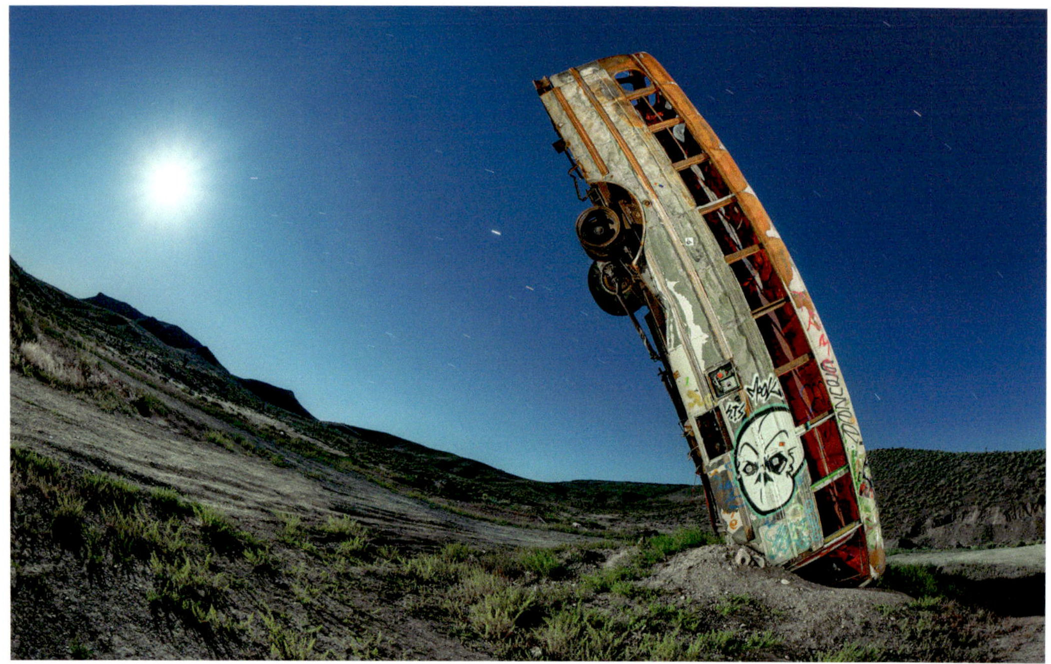

Bending to its Will · Car Forest, Nevada. Strangely bent by my fisheye lens · Nikon D610/Rokinon 12mm f/2.8 fisheye lens. 3 minutes f/8 ISO 200. July 2019 · Full moon, ProtoMachines LED2 with warm white and red light.

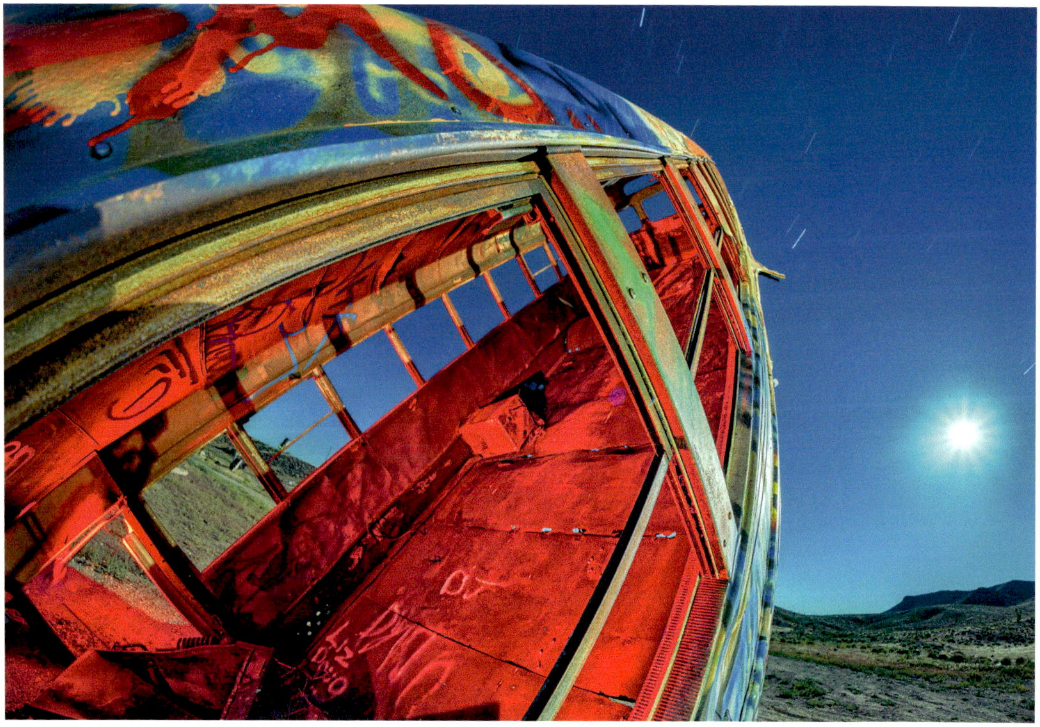

My Red Ride · Car Forest, Nevada. Strangely bent by my fisheye lens · Nikon D610/Rokinon 12mm f/2.8 fisheye lens. 12 minutes total "stacked." Each photo 3 minutes f/8 ISO 200. July 2019 · Full moon, ProtoMachines LED2 with warm white and red light.

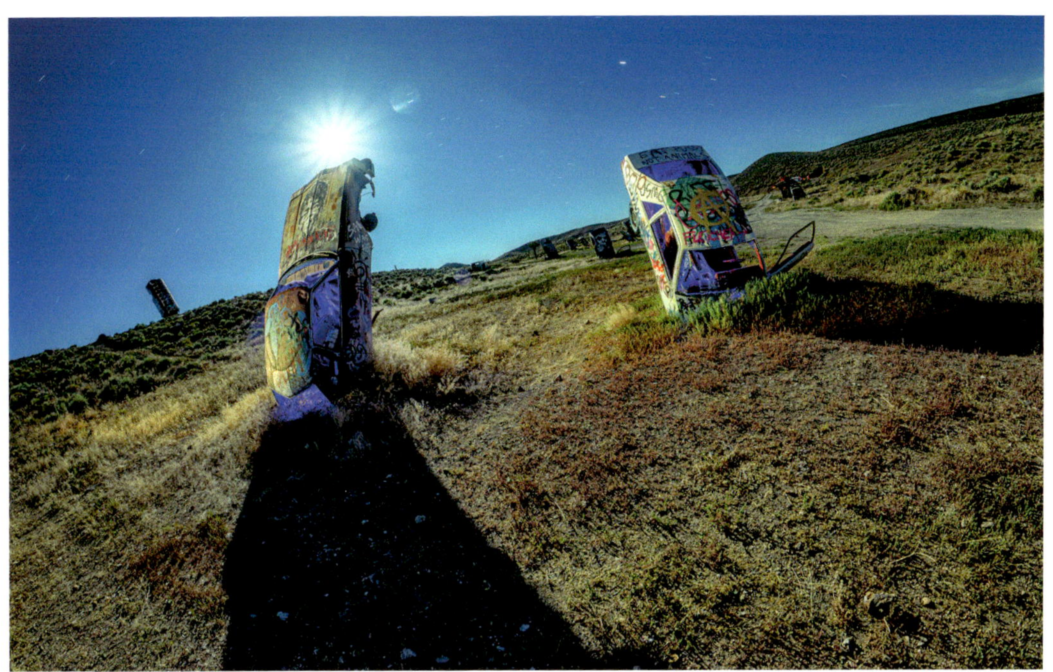

I've Got the Moon on my Shoulders · Car Forest, Nevada. Fisheye view of a rather strange garden in the Mojave Desert · Nikon D610/Rokinon 12mm f/2.8 fisheye lens. 3 minutes f/8 ISO 200. July 2019 · Full moon, ProtoMachines LED2 with warm white and blue light.

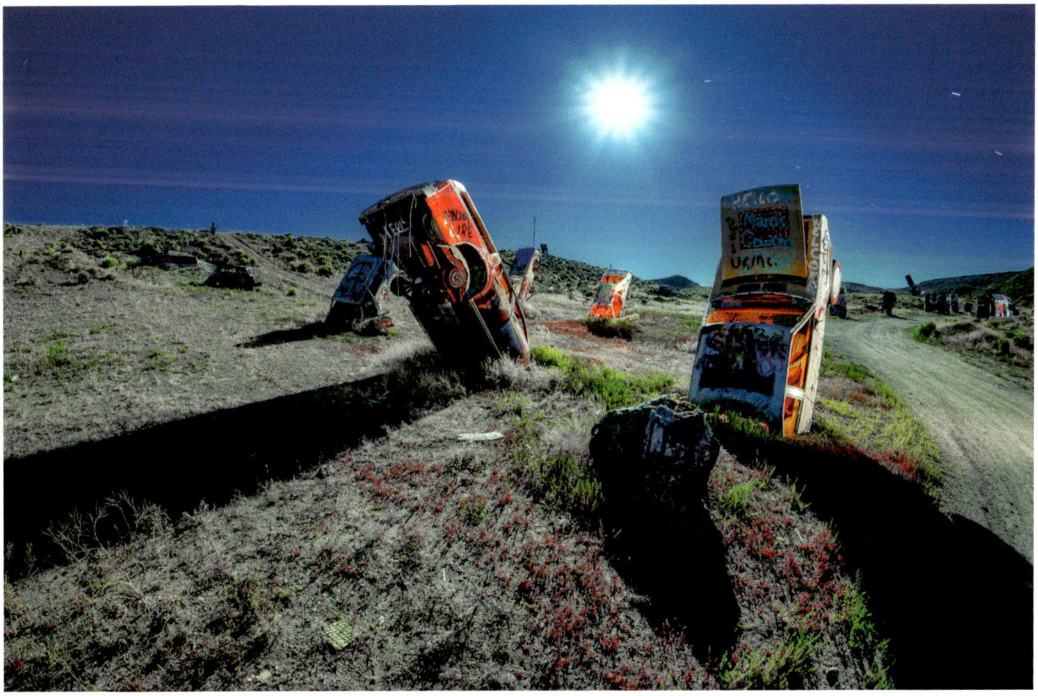

The Desert Night Casts Long Shadows · Car Forest, Nevada. Fisheye view of long shadows from the moon low in the horizon · Nikon D610/Rokinon 12mm f/2.8 fisheye lens. 211 seconds f/8 ISO 200. July 2019 · Full moon, ProtoMachines LED2 with warm white and red light.

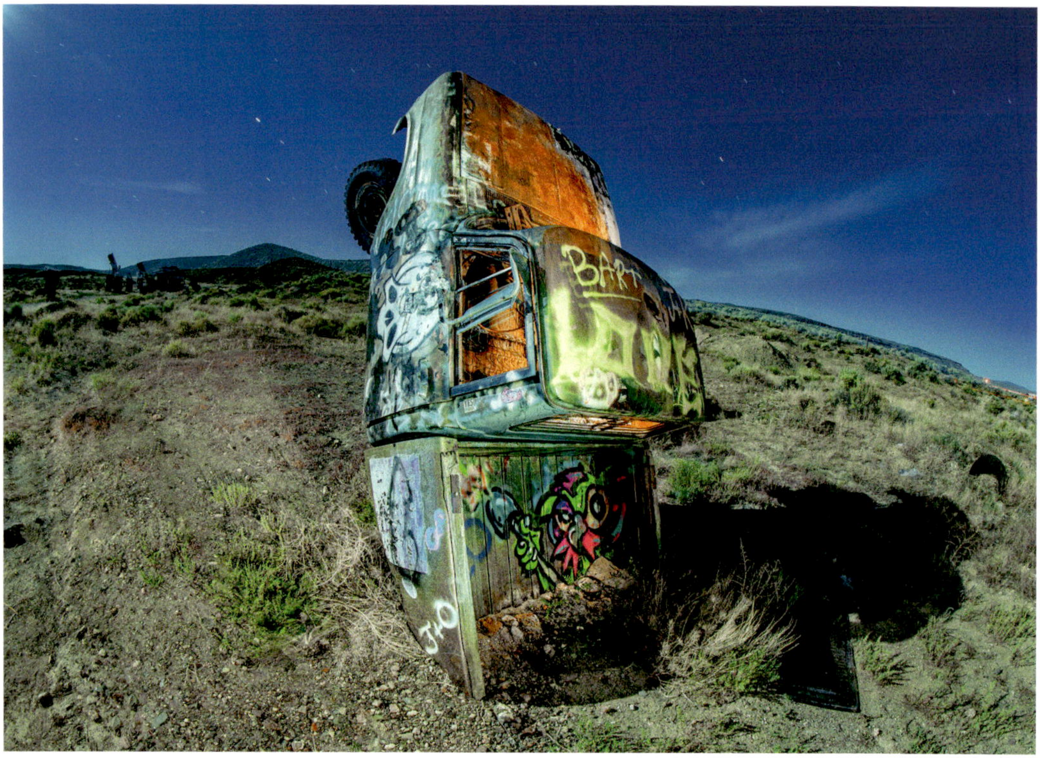

Bart the Truck · Car Forest, Nevada. Fisheye view of long shadows from the moon low in the horizon · Nikon D610/Rokinon 12mm f/2.8 fisheye lens. 136 seconds f/8 ISO 200. July 2019 · Full moon, ProtoMachines LED2 with warm white and red light.

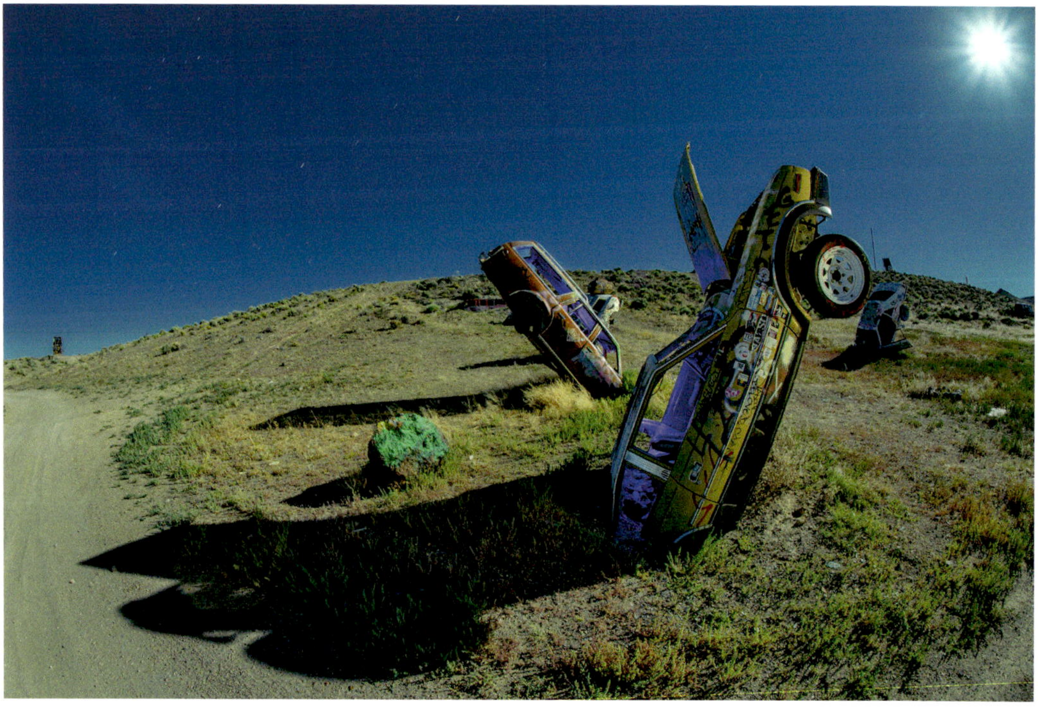

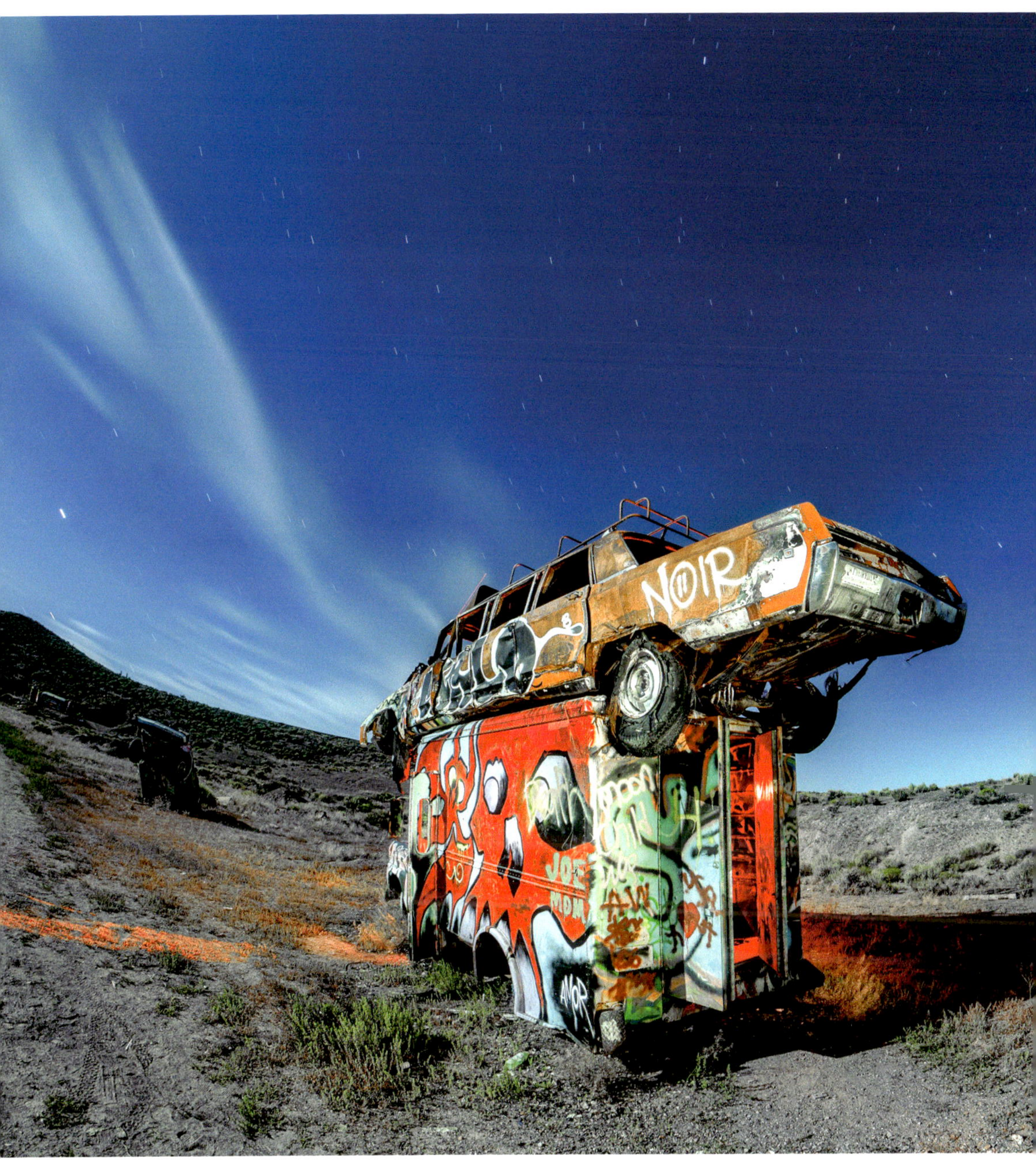

Limos With Your Rainbow Pops · Car Forest, Nevada · Nikon D610/Rokinon 12mm f/2.8 fisheye lens. 168 seconds f/8 ISO 200. July 2019 · Full moon, ProtoMachines LED2 with warm white and red light.

◄ **Tinky Winky** · Car Forest, Nevada. I can almost picture Tele-Tubbies sauntering over the hill · Nikon D610/ Rokinon 12mm f/2.8 fisheye lens. 181 seconds f/8 ISO 200. July 2019 · Full moon, ProtoMachines LED2 with warm white and blue light.

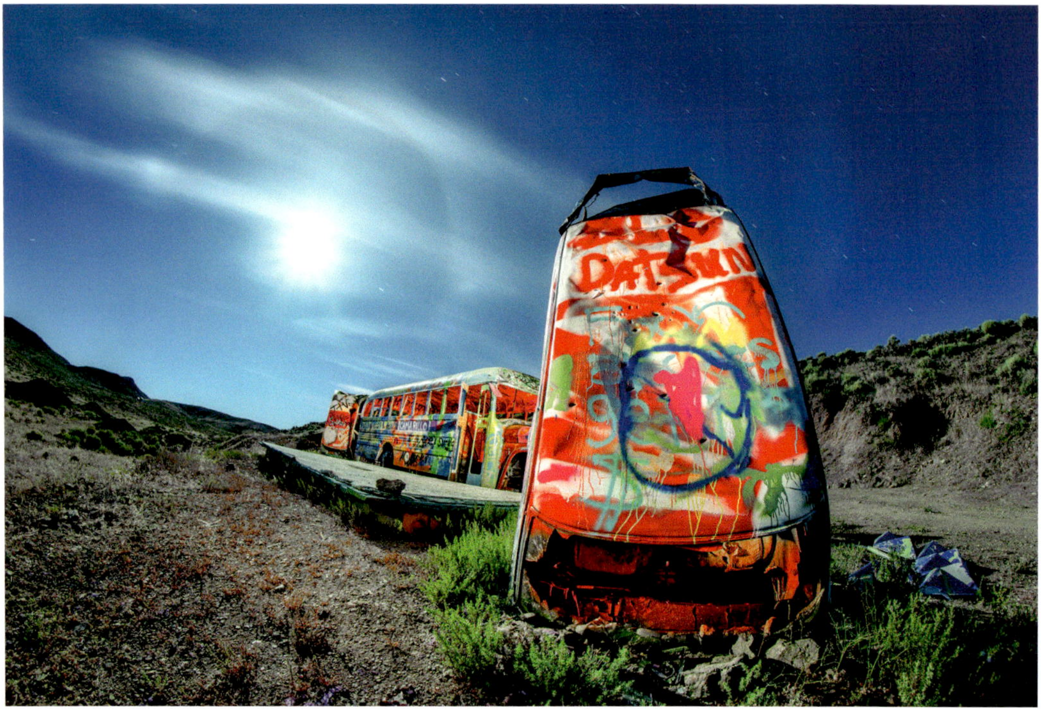

Creative Parking · Car Forest, Nevada · Nikon D610/Rokinon 12mm f/2.8 fisheye lens. 172 seconds f/8 ISO 200. July 2019 · Full moon, ProtoMachines LED2 with warm white and red light.

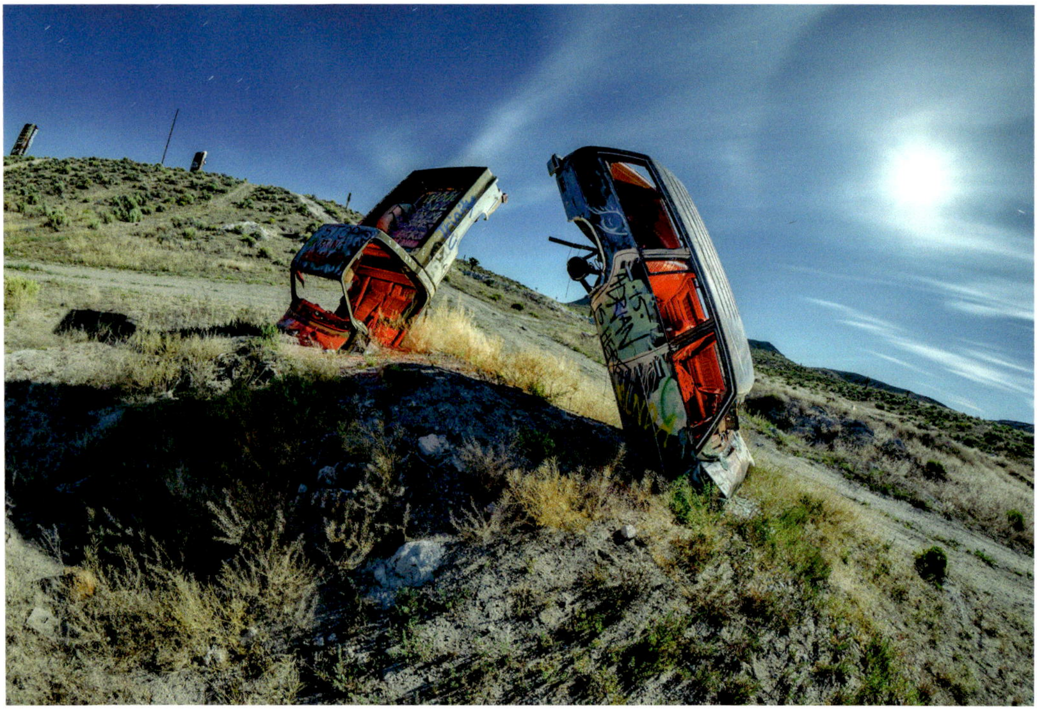

It's Raining Cars · Car Forest, Nevada · Nikon D610/Rokinon 12mm f/2.8 fisheye lens. 3 minutes f/8 ISO 200. July 2019 · Full moon, ProtoMachines LED2 with warm white and red light.

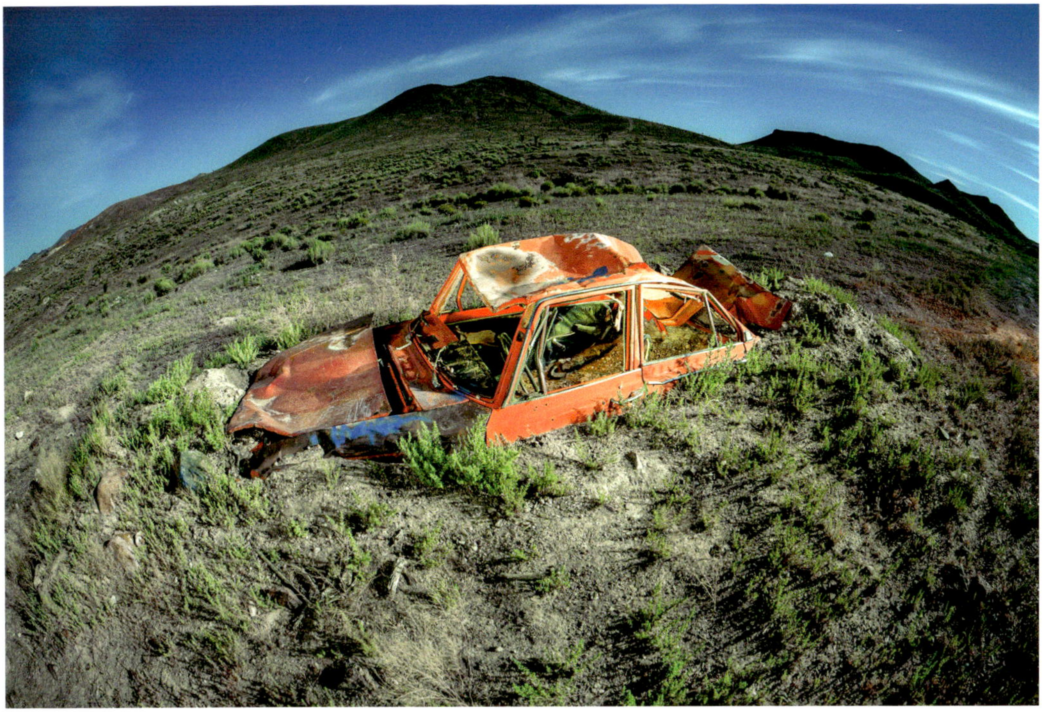

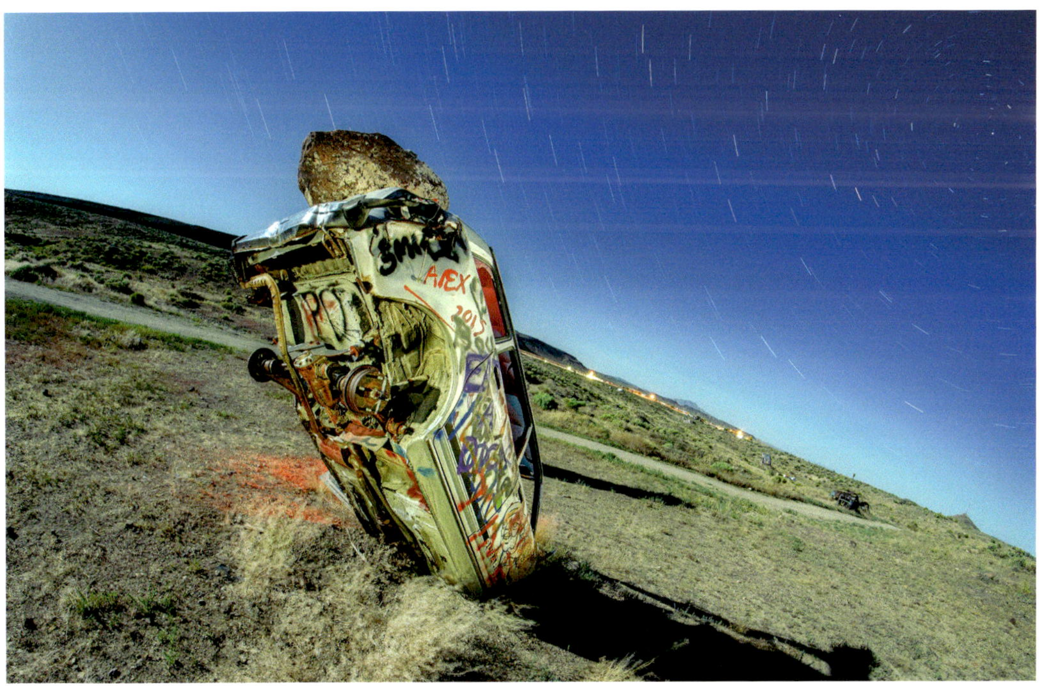

Low Rider · Car Forest, Nevada. Some of these photos almost name themselves · Nikon D610/Rokinon 12mm f/2.8 fisheye lens. 3 minutes f/8 ISO 200. July 2019 · Full moon, ProtoMachines LED2 with warm white and red light.

Toward Tomorrow Together · Car Forest, Nevada. The 21-minute exposure shows the perceived movement of the stars due to the rotation of the earth · Nikon D610/Rokinon 12mm f/2.8 fisheye lens. 21 minutes total "stacked." Each photo 3 minutes f/8 ISO 200. July 2019 · Full moon, ProtoMachines LED2 with warm white and teal light.

2

BEDROCK CITY, ARIZONA

I overheard the clerk talk a bit of business to a lady, who then called out as she was leaving, "Bye, Linda, I'll let you know!" Immediately guessing that "Linda" was the owner, I bolted from the Bedrock City store and ran out to the parking lot, remembering to slow down so I wouldn't startle anyone. Linda Speckels, the owner of Bedrock City, was gingerly climbing into a car to visit the doctor. I said I wanted to thank her quickly, introducing myself.

She said, "Oh, the night photographer!" and wanted me to leave my name and contact information at the desk. The lady behind the counter said that she would love to have a print of mine, adding that she keeps everything that people send to her.

I had spoken to Linda on the phone before, calling to obtain permission to photograph Bedrock City at night. I had sent her some of those photos. But now, she said she wanted to sell the property for two million dollars.

I had stopped here as a kid. I loved the kitschy recreation of *The Flintstones*, the first animated sitcom to air on primetime TV. I loved the odd feel of these faux-stone houses rising from the sparse Arizona vegetation, as if this were the only settlement left standing after aliens had decimated the earth. And who could resist the giant Brontosaurus slide?

Running Bedrock City hadn't always been easy. During the time the Speckels threw open the doors to Bedrock City, the oil embargo brought tourist traffic to a standstill. The family had to truck in all their water. The desert tried to take back this new "town" with its thistles and brush. The family battled this, the harsh realities of the desert on the town, graffiti, and more.

And one of the biggest challenges was the show's producer, Hanna-Barbera. Every time Hanna-Barbera had a new owner, the Speckels faced new licensing negotiations. The family-owned business tried to keep pace with all the changes both here and at their other Bedrock City location in South Dakota. The studio-mandated changes were too expensive for a place charging five-dollar admission fees. After Linda's husband, Francis, passed away in 1990, they just didn't bother.

Eventually, Warner Bros., Hanna-Barbera's latest owner, declined to renew Bedrock City's license for both the South Dakota and Arizona sites. The South Dakota site was suddenly shuttered. It was bulldozed in 2019.

Bedrock City was also in danger of being closed, and therefore, eventually razed. After all, what new owner would want to take over a property with decaying buildings and cartoon characters without the rights to any of it?

Linda's grandson, Brandon Dee, launched a crowdfunding campaign to raise the two million dollars necessary to purchase Bedrock City and stop it from falling into the hands of developers. He and I communicated frequently during this time. I contributed toward the crowdfunding campaign, stating that I believed Bedrock City was "an important part of our history and of roadside Americana." My quote was repeated in some newspapers that interviewed Brandon. Unfortunately, the crowdfunding campaign fell well short of its goal.

In 2019, the Speckels family sold it to Troy Morris and Ron Brown. The new owners announced that they would soon raze the property to create Raptor Ranch. It looked like Bedrock City would meet the same fate as the one in South Dakota.

I was distraught. By this time, Bedrock City had been left to the elements for a while and, owing largely to the desert elements, was in desperate need of repair. And now, it looked like it would also be destroyed soon. I wanted to say goodbye to the place.

I photographed it on a cloudy night under a full moon with my night photographer friends, George Loo, Mike Cooper, and Tim Little. The experience was bittersweet, as I was certain that this would be the last time I would see it

Later, I also called and emailed Raptor Ranch, pleading with them to incorporate Bedrock City into their birds of prey attraction. After several attempts, I received a reply in August 2020, stating that they had made the decision to incorporate Raptor Ranch into Bedrock City while noting that they would not be able to sell Bedrock merchandise due to licensing issues. I cannot exaggerate the sense of relief I felt.

The bulk of these night photos are from the time period in which Bedrock City lay abandoned, its fate hanging in the balance, and its buildings decaying. However, Raptor Park is now a functioning roadside attraction, with some of old Bedrock City still standing.

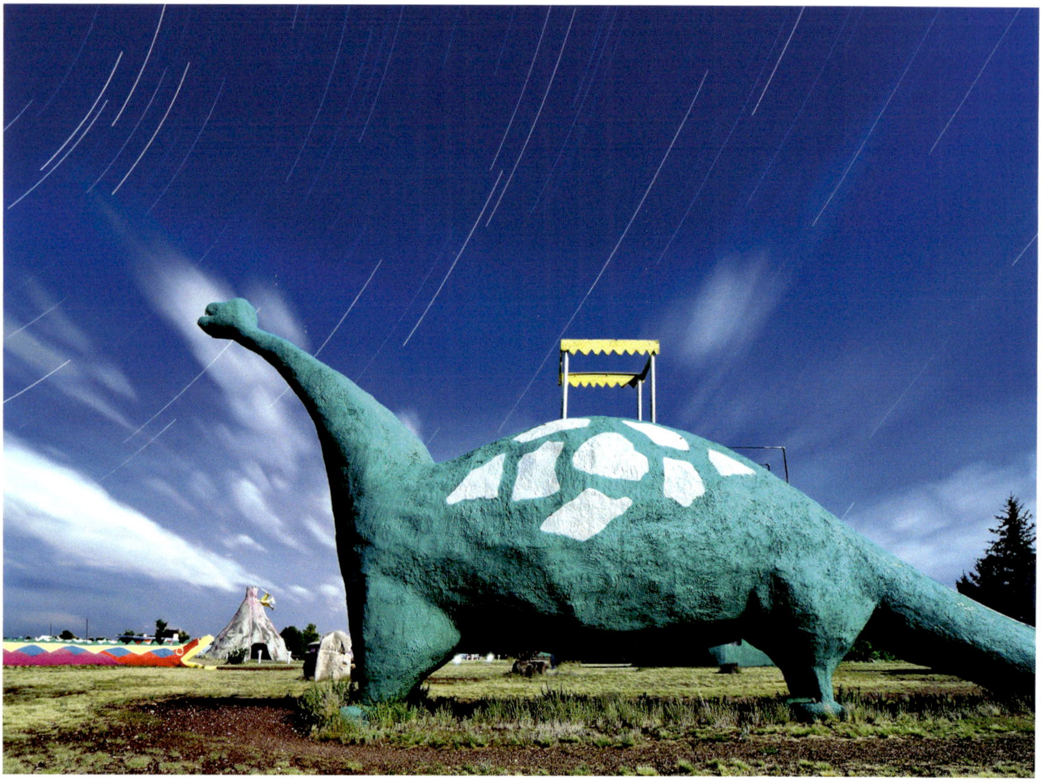

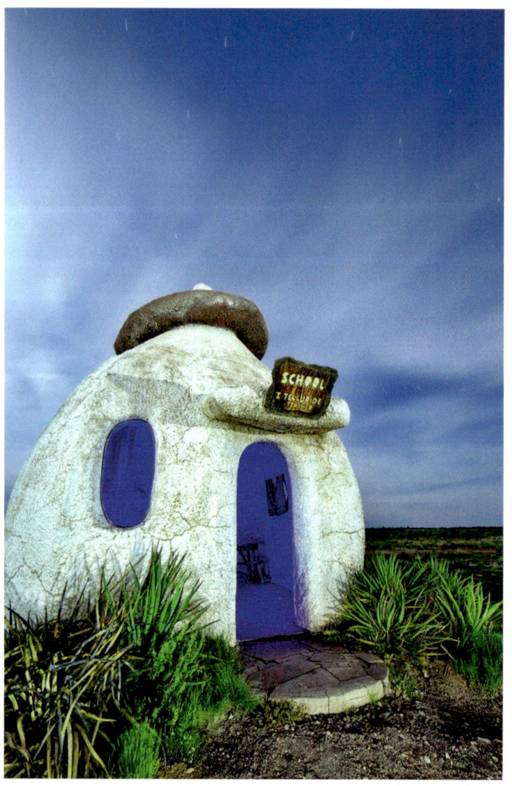

▲ **Forever Brontosaurus** · Bedrock City, Arizona. The 88-minute exposure shows the perceived movement of the stars due to the rotation of the earth. You can slide down the tail of the dinosaur just like Fred did! · Nikon D7000/Tokina 11-16mm f/2.8 lens. 88 minutes total "stacked." Each photo 3 minutes f/8 ISO 200. July 2015 · Full moon, ProtoMachines LED2 with warm white light.

◀ **Stone Age School** · Bedrock City, Arizona · Nikon D610/14-24mm f/2.8G ED lens. 252 seconds f/8 ISO 200. June 2015 · Full moon, ProtoMachines LED2 with warm white and blue light.

▶ **Through Sleet and Snow** · Bedrock City, Arizona · Nikon D610/14-24mm f/2.8G ED lens. 525 seconds f/8 ISO 200. June 2015 · Full moon, ProtoMachines LED2 with warm white and blue light.

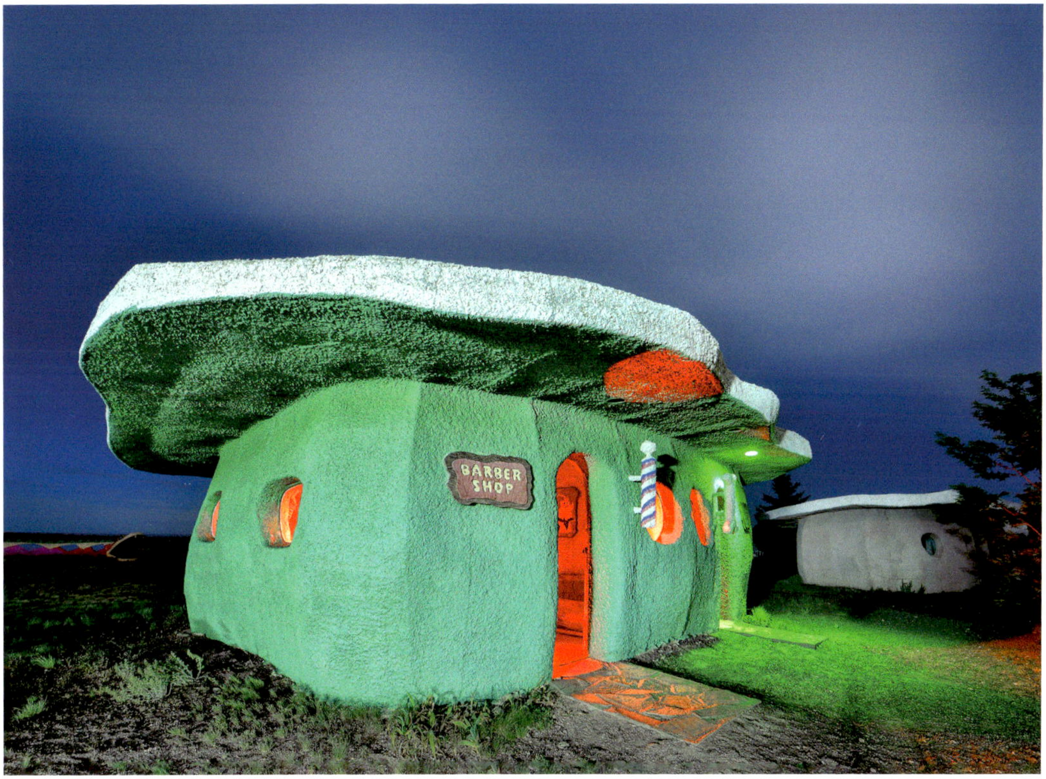

Did Stone Age People Cut Their Hair? · Bedrock City, Arizona · Nikon D610/14-24mm f/2.8G ED lens. 213 seconds f/8 ISO 200. June 2015 · Full moon, ProtoMachines LED2 with warm white and red light.

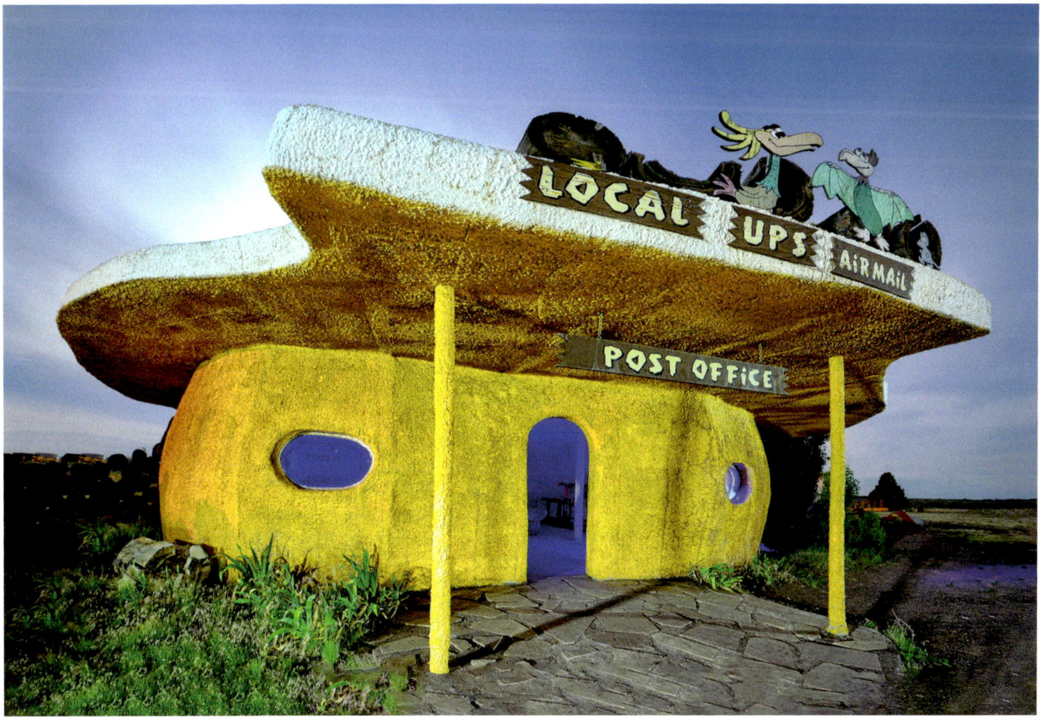

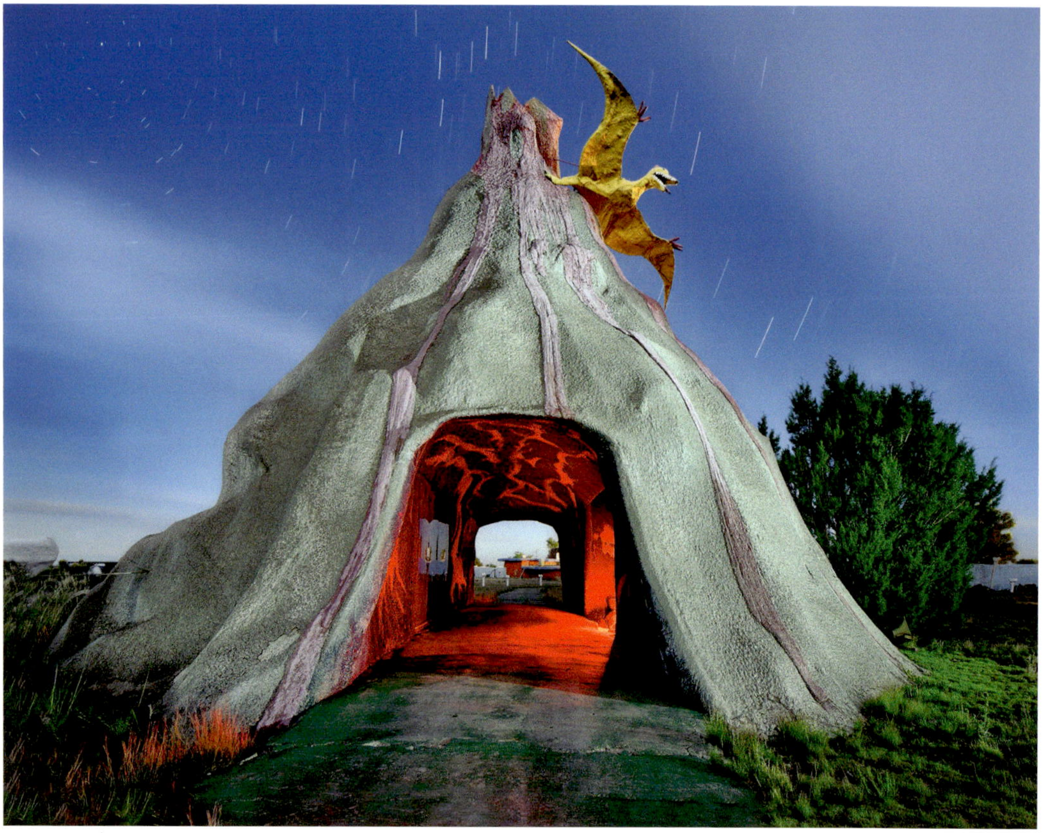

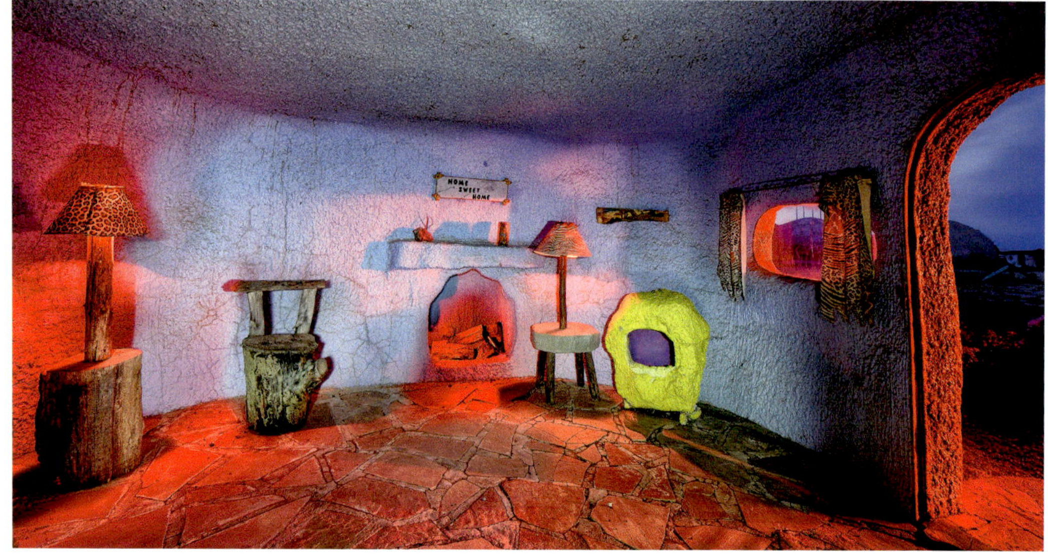

In the Ptime of Pteradactyls · Bedrock City, Arizona · Nikon D610/14-24mm f/2.8G ED lens. 397 seconds f/8 ISO 200. June 2015 · Full moon, ProtoMachines LED2 with warm white and red light.

Home Sweet Home · Bedrock City, Arizona. This is the living room of Barney and Betty Rubble's home · Nikon D610/14-24mm f/2.8G ED lens. 105 seconds f/8 ISO 200. June 2015 · ProtoMachines LED2 with warm white and red light. Lit in almost total darkness.

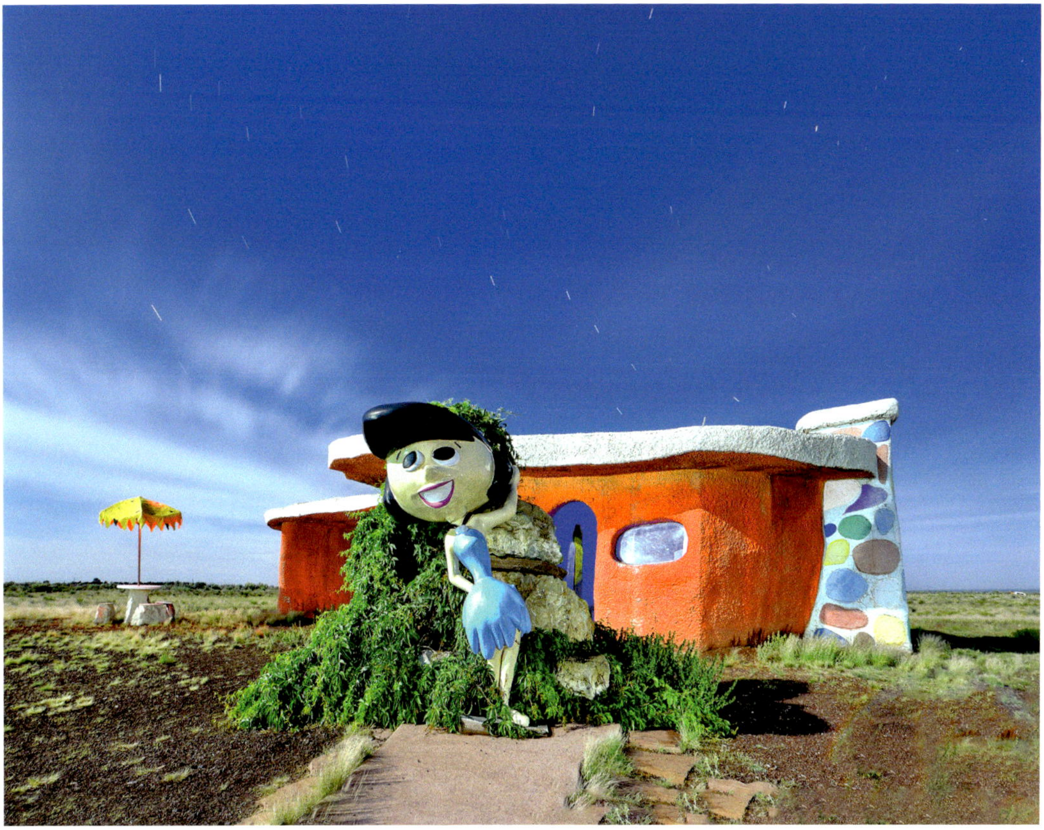

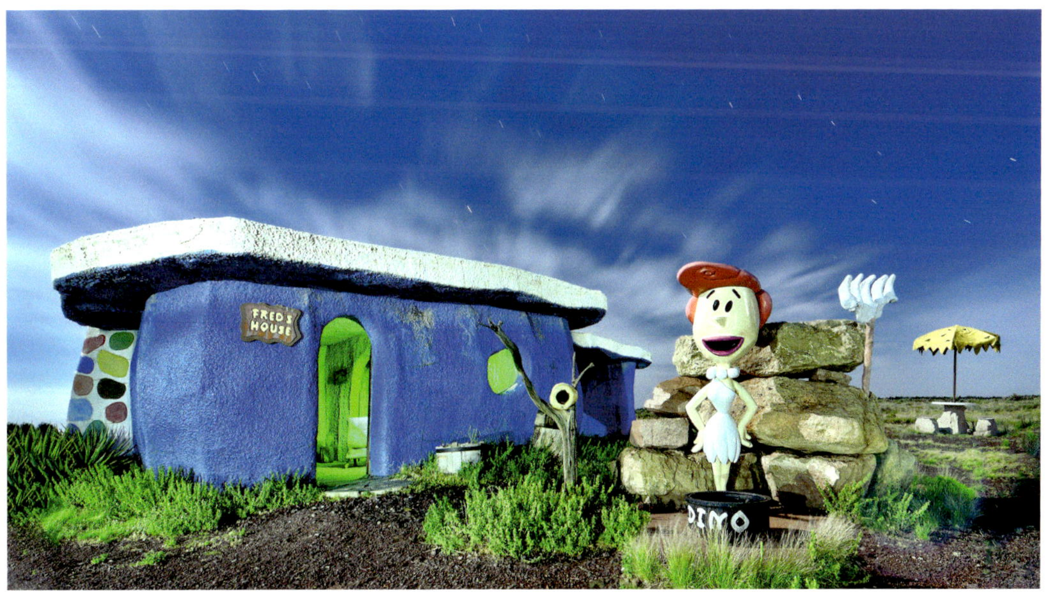

Betty · Bedrock City, Arizona. Home of Barney and Betty Rubble · Nikon D610/14-24mm f/2.8G ED lens. 356 seconds f/8 ISO 200. July 2015 · Full moon, ProtoMachines LED2 with warm white and blue light.

Wilmaaaaaaa!!!!! · Bedrock City, Arizona. Home of Fred and Wilma Flintstone · Nikon D610/14-24mm f/2.8G ED lens. 225 seconds f/8 ISO 200. July 2015 · Full moon, ProtoMachines LED2 with warm white and green light.

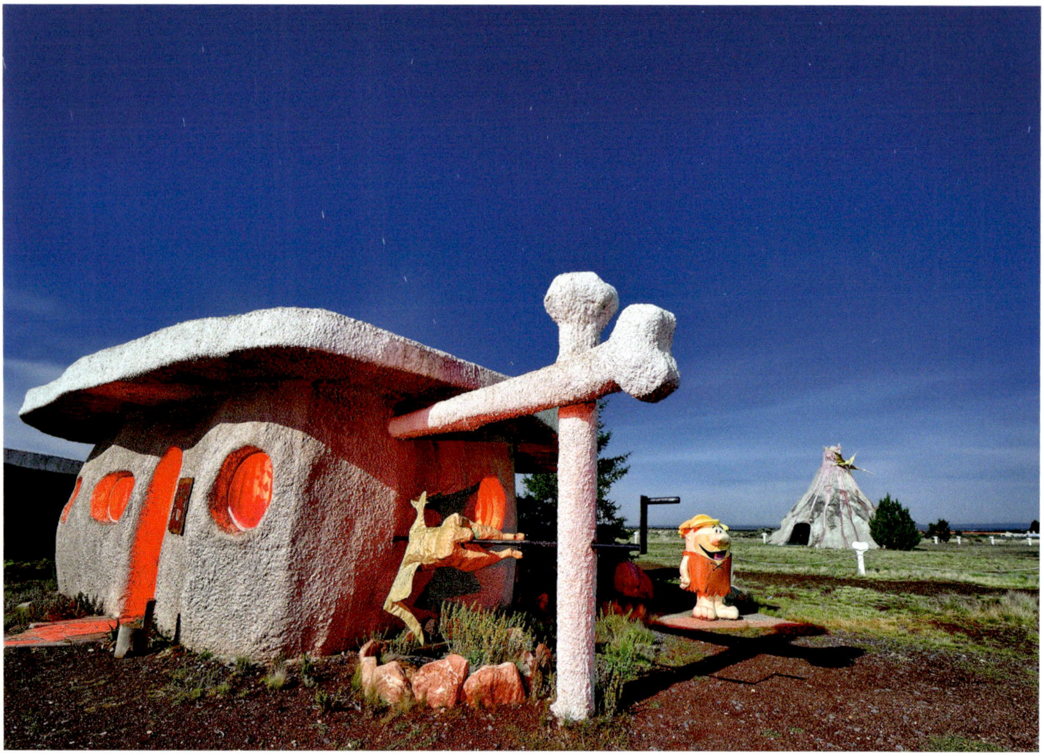

Save Time, Save Money, Everyday · Bedrock City, Arizona. Bedrock General Store · Nikon D610/14-24mm f/2.8G ED lens. 210 seconds f/8 ISO 200. July 2015 · Full moon, ProtoMachines LED2 with warm white and red light.

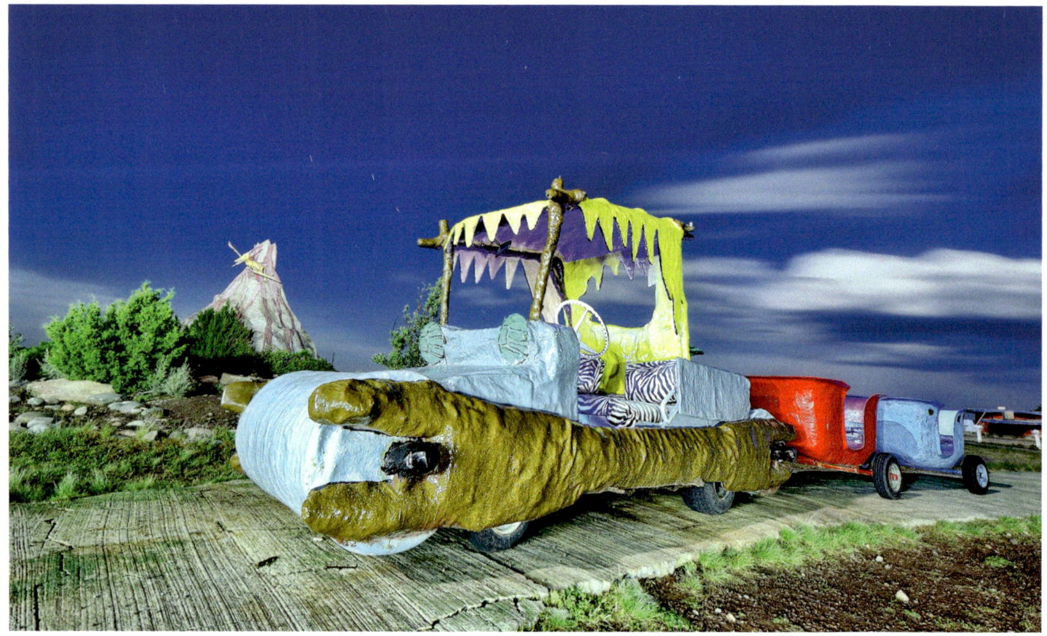

No Need for Foot Power · Bedrock City, Arizona. This train gave a tour of Bedrock City, going through the volcano. And you never had to push it with your feet · Nikon D610/14-24mm f/2.8G ED lens. 221 seconds f/8 ISO 200. July 2015 · Full moon, ProtoMachines LED2 with warm white light.

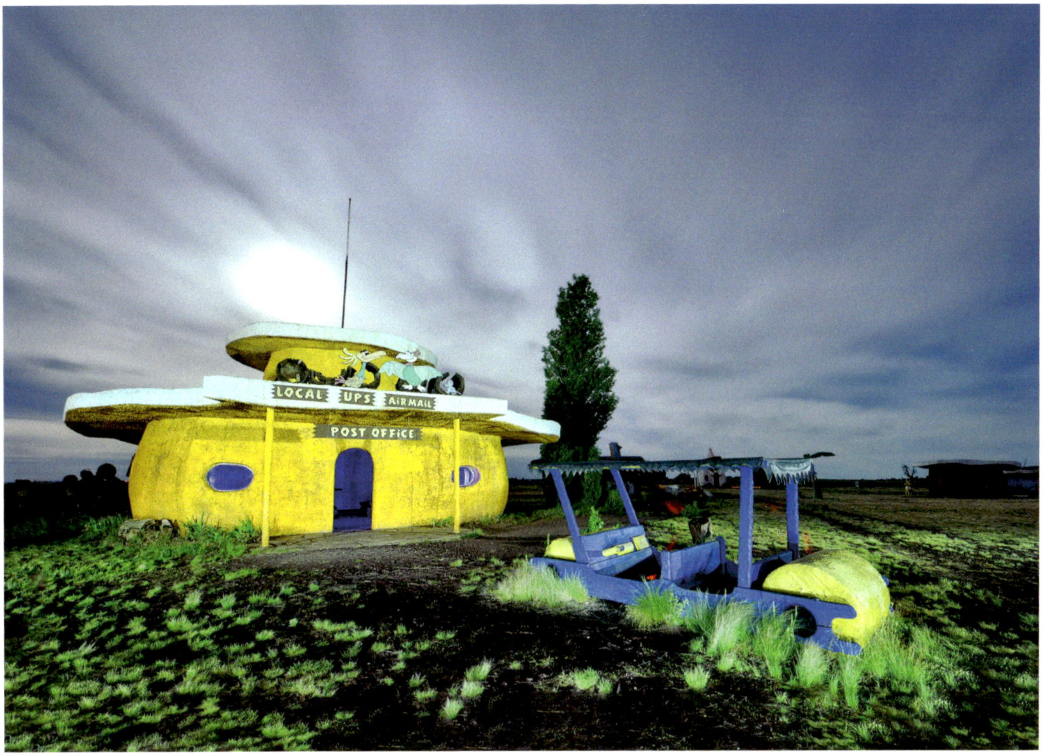

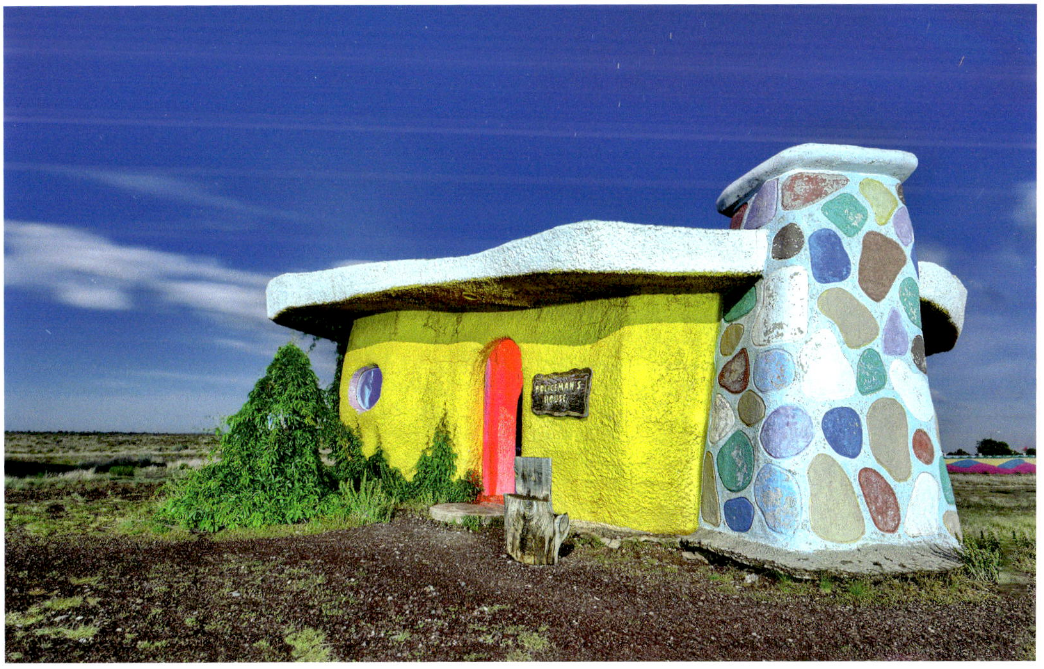

Long Life Vehicle · Bedrock City, Arizona. Special delivery · Nikon D610/14-24mm f/2.8G ED lens. 244 seconds f/8 ISO 200. June 2015 · Full moon, ProtoMachines LED2 with warm white and blue light.

To Protect and Serve · Bedrock City, Arizona. Policeman's house · Nikon D610/14-24mm f/2.8G ED lens. 210 seconds f/8 ISO 200. July 2015 · Full moon, ProtoMachines LED2 with warm white and blue light.

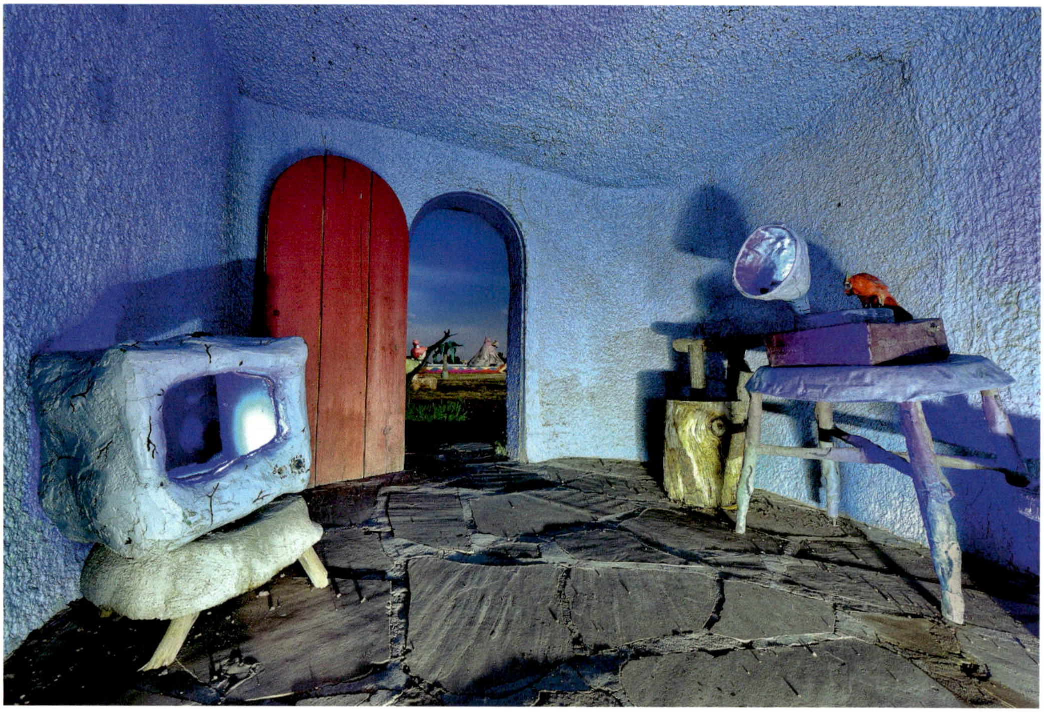

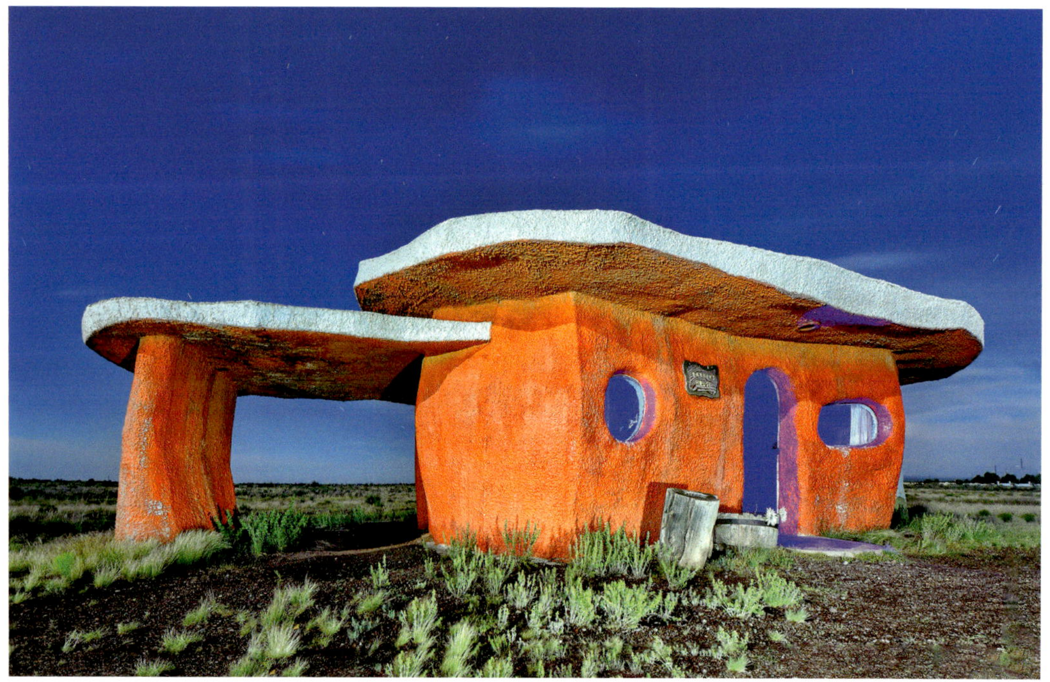

Stone Age Entertainment at the Rubbles · Bedrock City, Arizona. Policeman's house · Nikon D610/14-24mm f/2.8G ED lens. 153 seconds f/8 ISO 200. July 2015 · ProtoMachines LED2 with warm white and blue light. Lit in almost total darkness.

Where is Hoppy? · Bedrock City, Arizona. The Rubble home · Nikon D610/14-24mm f/2.8G ED lens. 215 seconds f/8 ISO 200. July 2015 · Full moon, ProtoMachines LED2 with warm white and blue light.

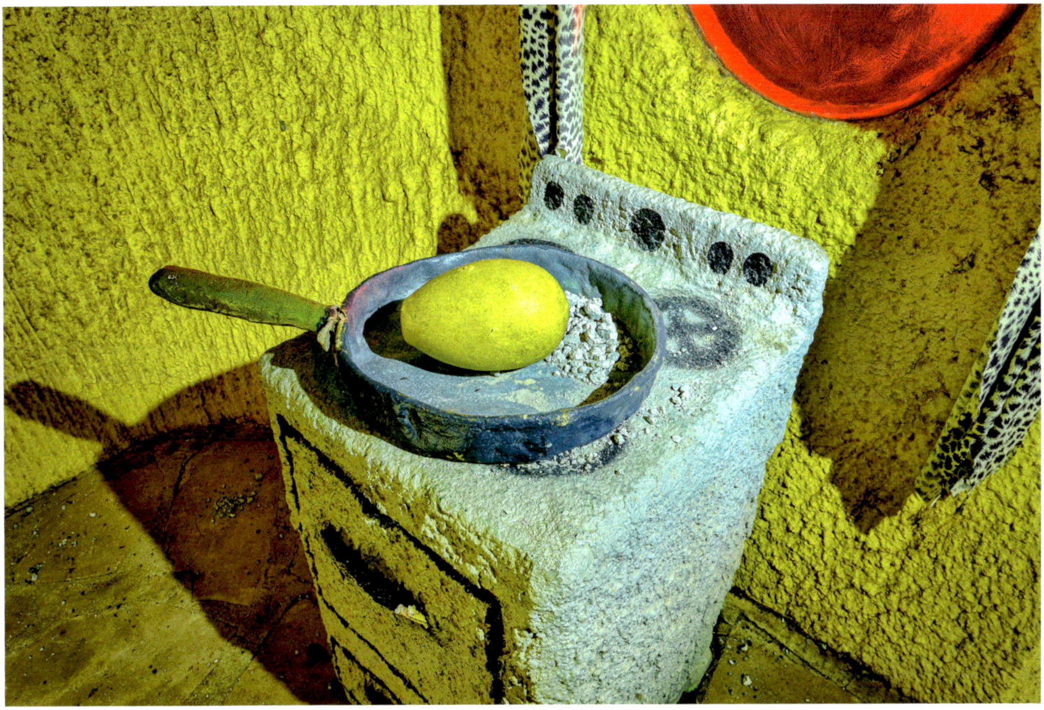

Where's the Baconsaurus? · Bedrock City, Arizona. Waiting to fry up something inside the Rubble home · Nikon D610/14-24mm f/2.8G ED lens. 95 seconds f/8 ISO 200. July 2015 · ProtoMachines LED2 with warm white light. Lit in almost total darkness.

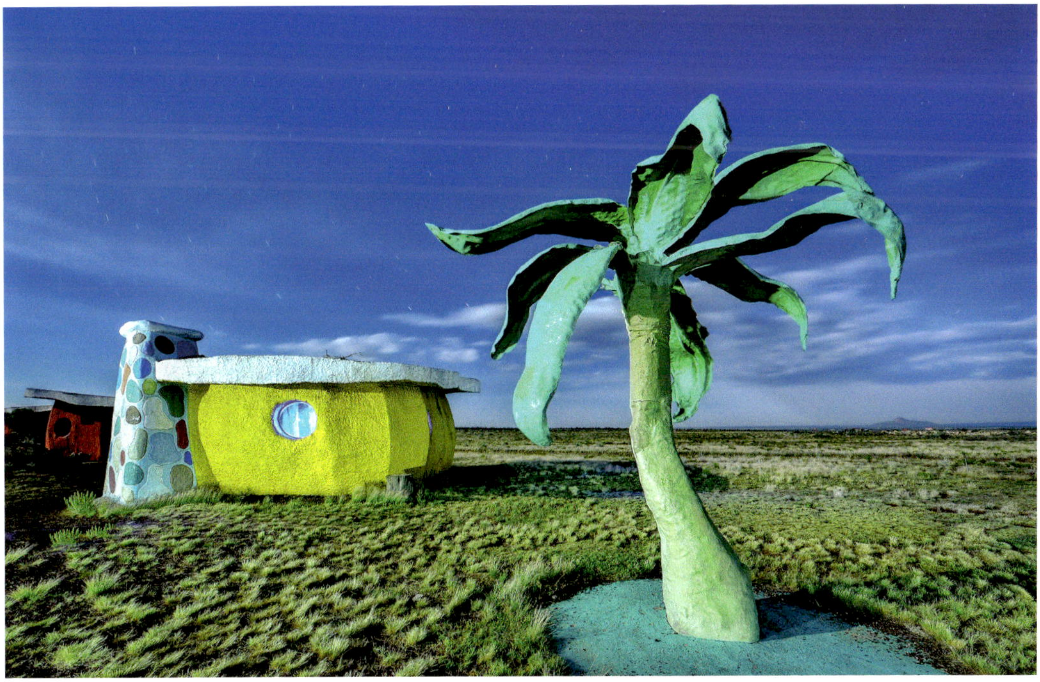

Keep Palm and Carry On · Bedrock City, Arizona · Nikon D610/14-24mm f/2.8G ED lens. 155 seconds f/8 ISO 200. July 2015 · Full moon, ProtoMachines LED2 with warm white light.

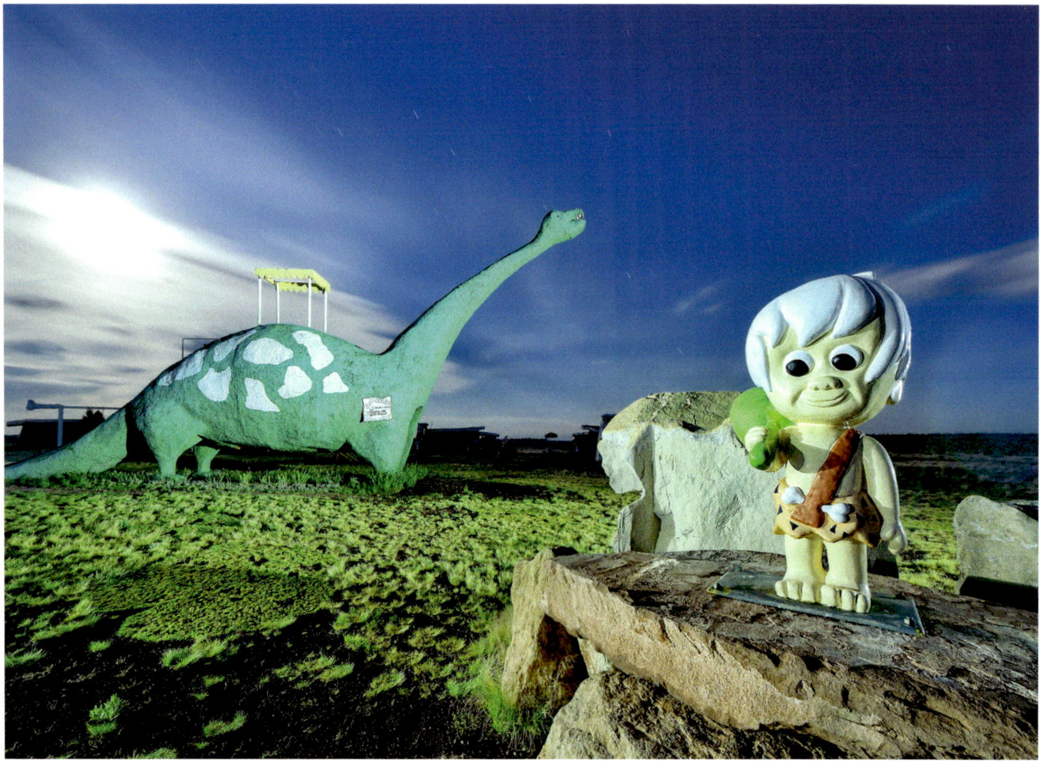

Bam Bam, Bam Bam Bam! · Bedrock City, Arizona. The creators of *The Flintstones* modeled Bam Bam after one of my co-workers · Nikon D610/14-24mm f/2.8G ED lens. 202 seconds f/8 ISO 200. July 2015 · Full moon, ProtoMachines LED2 with warm white light.

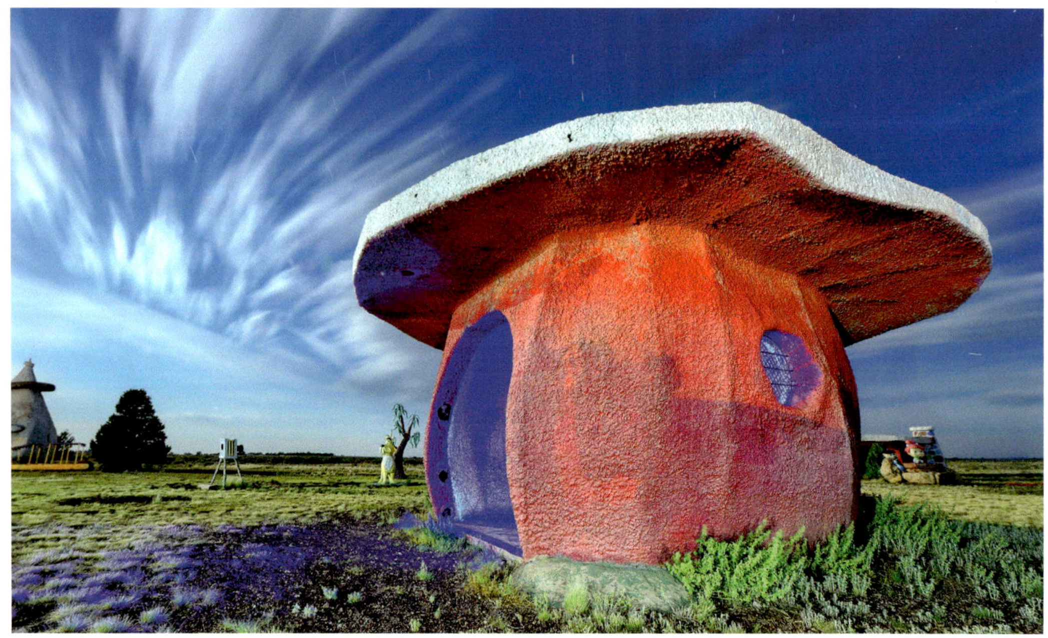

Have a Yabba Doo Time · Bedrock City, Arizona · Nikon D610/14-24mm f/2.8G ED lens. 399 seconds f/8 ISO 200. July 2015 · Full moon, ProtoMachines LED2 with warm white and blue light.

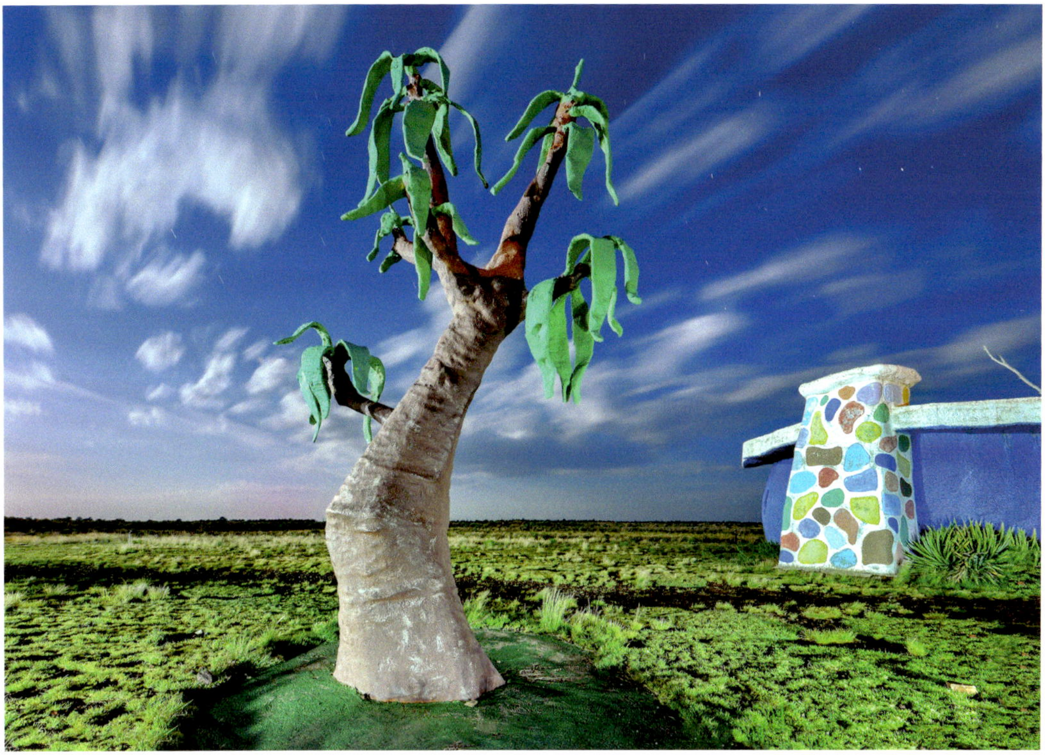

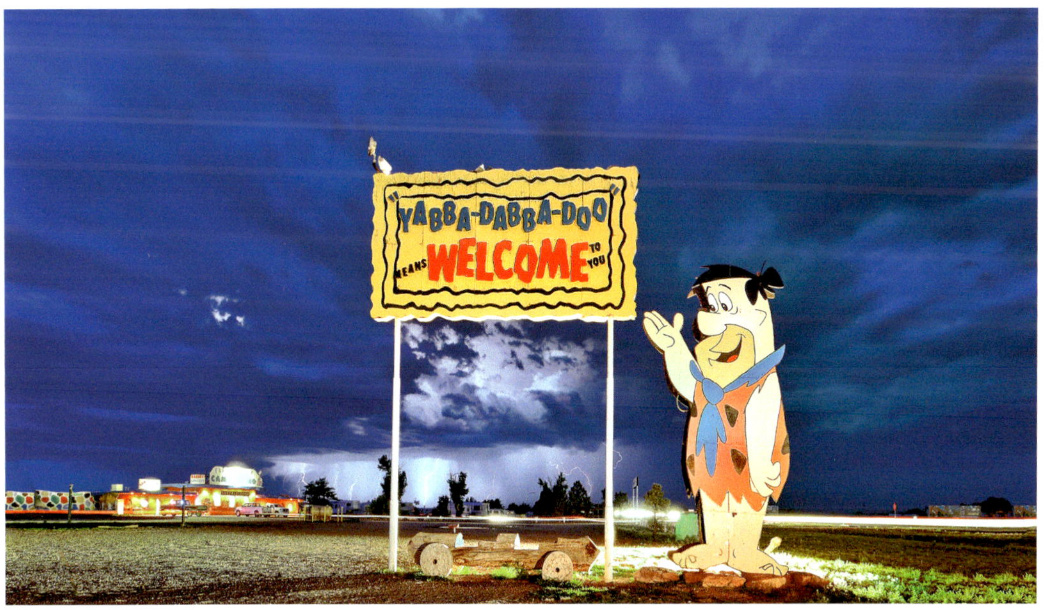

Shake Your Palm Palms · Bedrock City, Arizona · Nikon D610/14-24mm f/2.8G ED lens. 195 seconds f/8 ISO 200. July 2015 · Full moon, ProtoMachines LED2 with warm white light.

Yabba Dabba Doo Means Welcome To You · Bedrock City, Arizona as seen from Highway 64. This is a blend of ten photos, each 30 seconds, done to capture the lightning storm. The long streaks of light are from passing cars · Nikon D610/14-24mm f/2.8G ED lens. 5 minutes total "stacked." Each photo 30 seconds f/8 ISO 200. July 2015 · Full moon, ProtoMachines LED2 with warm white light.

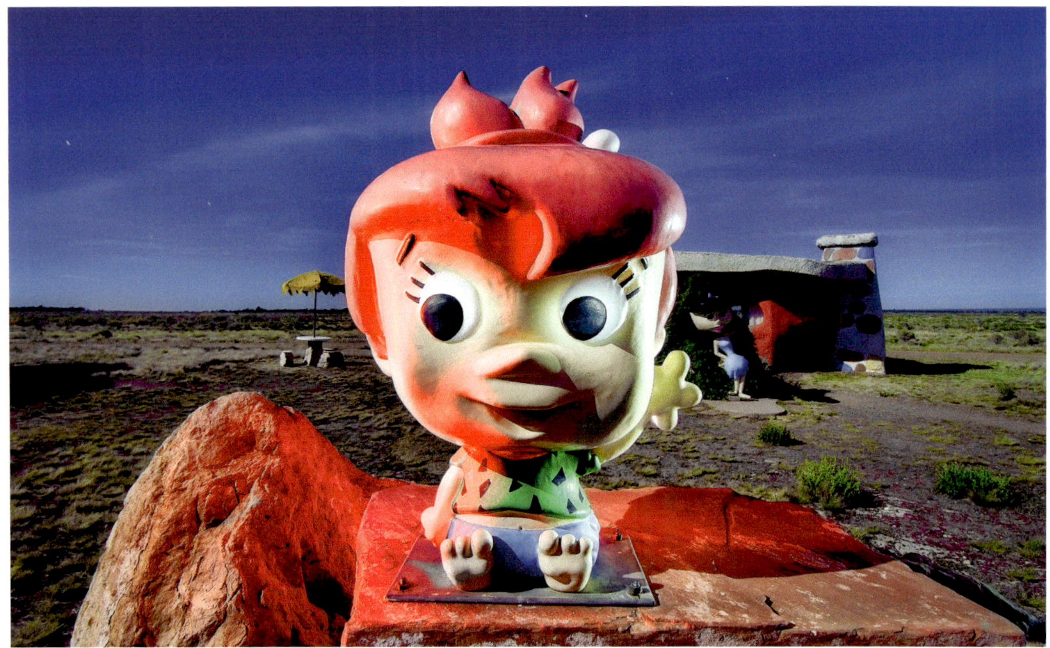

Pebbles · Bedrock City, Arizona. This 2017 visit was part of a larger Arizona trip that included Sedona and Tucson · Nikon D7000/Tokina 11-16mm f/2.8 lens. 70 seconds f/9 ISO 400. June 2017 · Full moon, ProtoMachines LED2 with warm white and red light.

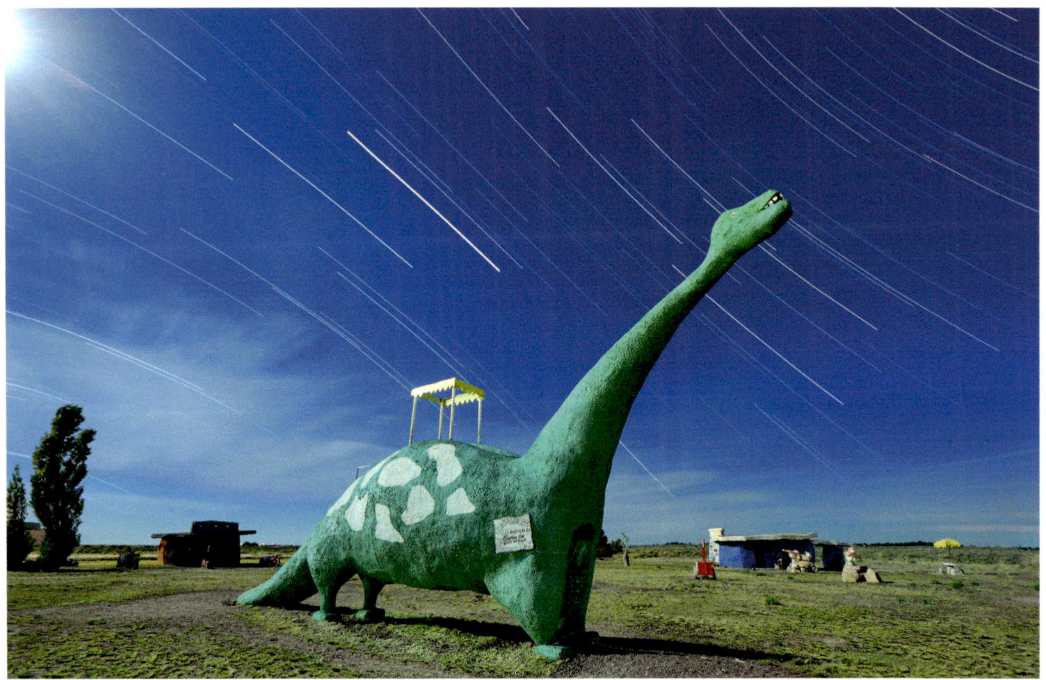

The Dinosaur and the Moon · Bedrock City, Arizona. This exposure shows the perceived movement of the stars due to the rotation of the earth, showing the stars that appear to rotate around both the South and North Celestial Poles · Nikon D610/14-24mm f/2.8G ED lens. 1 hour 30 minutes total "stacked." Each photo 3 minutes f/8 ISO 400. June 2017 · Full moon, ProtoMachines LED2 with warm white light.

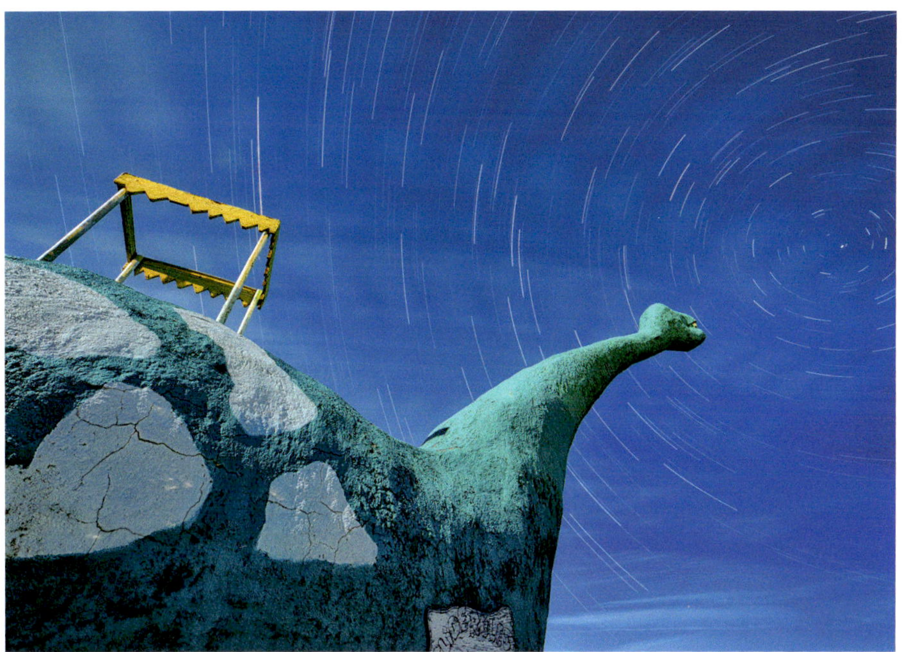

Gazing Into the Void · Bedrock City, Arizona. Looking up at the stars · Nikon D610/14-24mm f/2.8 lens. 45 minutes total "stacked." Each photo 3 minutes f/8 ISO 400. June 2017 · Full moon, ProtoMachines LED2 with warm white light.

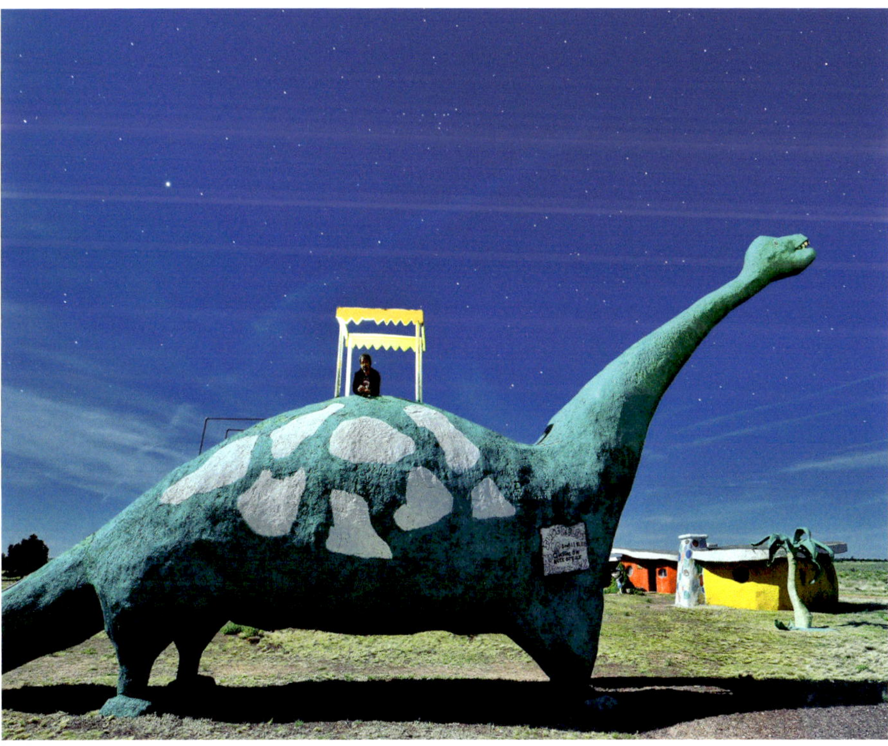

Jurassic Selfie · Bedrock City, Arizona. Selfie on top of the brontosaurus · Nikon D610/14-24mm f/2.8 lens. 30 seconds f/8 ISO 1250. June 2017 · Full moon.

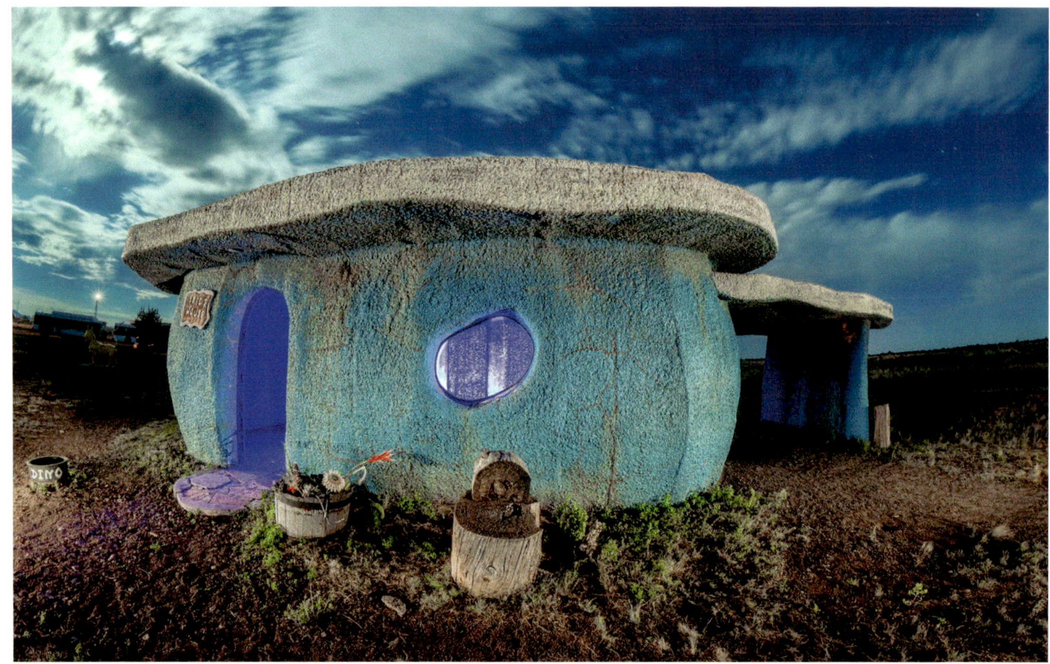

Looking for Dino · Bedrock City, Arizona. This 2019 visit was a rather bittersweet one since I thought for sure Bedrock City would be torn down in a matter of months. For some reason, I photographed all my 2019 photos using a fisheye lens · Nikon D610/Rokinon 12mm f/2.8 fisheye lens. 2 minutes f/8 ISO 640. July 2019 · Full moon, ProtoMachines LED2 with warm white and blue light.

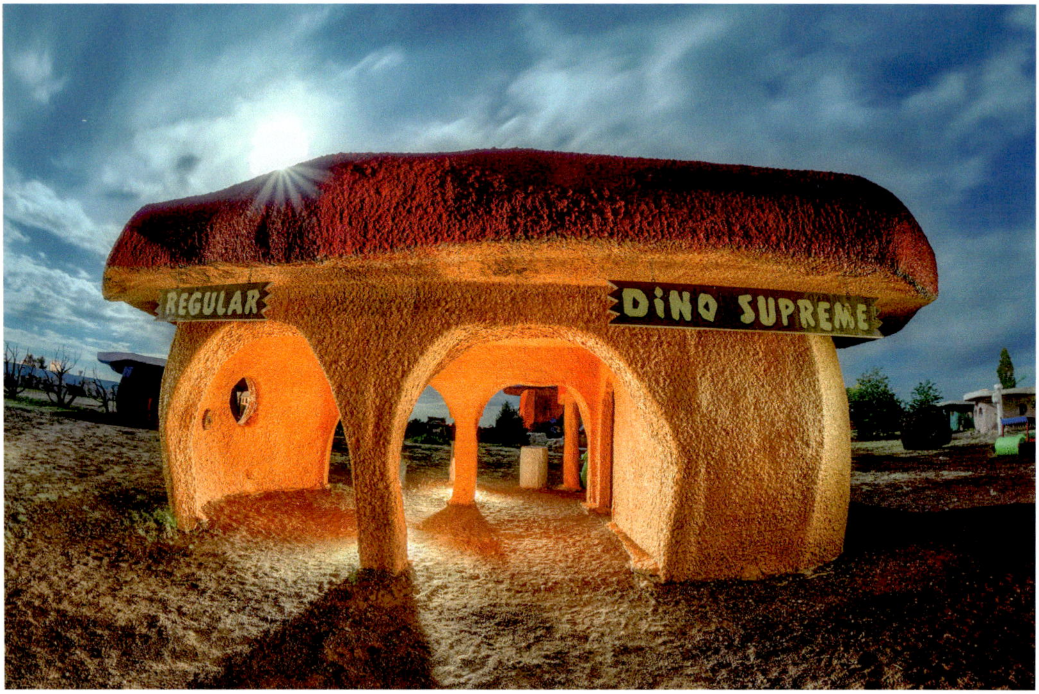

Dino Supreme · Bedrock City, Arizona · Nikon D610/Rokinon 12mm f/2.8 fisheye lens. 2 minutes f/8 ISO 640. July 2019 · Full moon, ProtoMachines LED2 with warm white light.

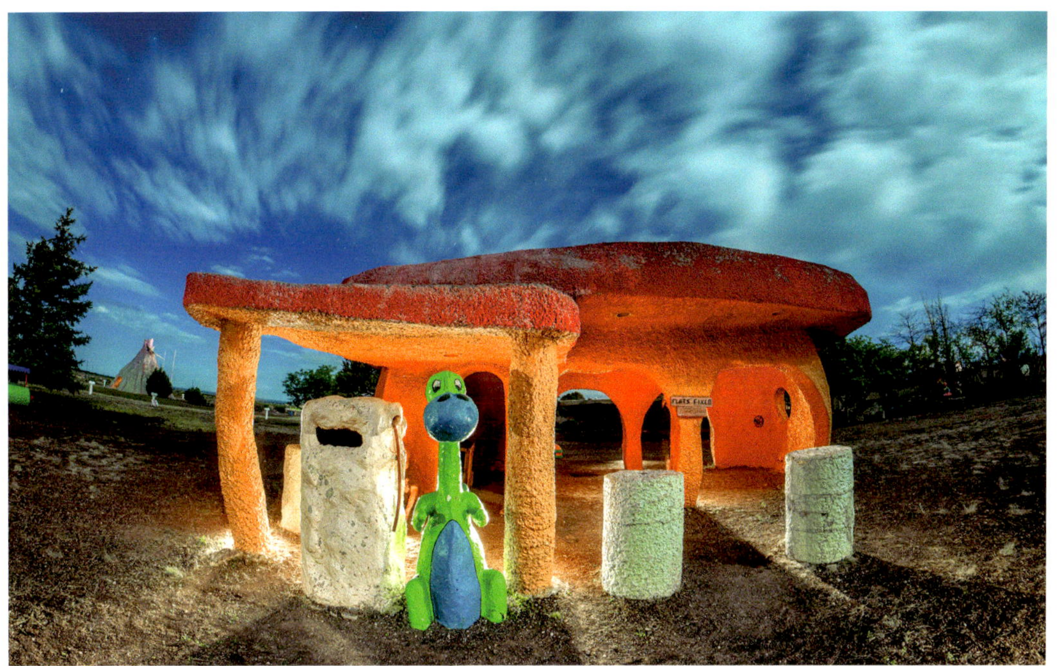

Fossil Fuel · Bedrock City, Arizona · Nikon D610/Rokinon 12mm f/2.8 fisheye lens. 2 minutes f/8 ISO 640. July 2019 · Full moon, ProtoMachines LED2 with warm white light.

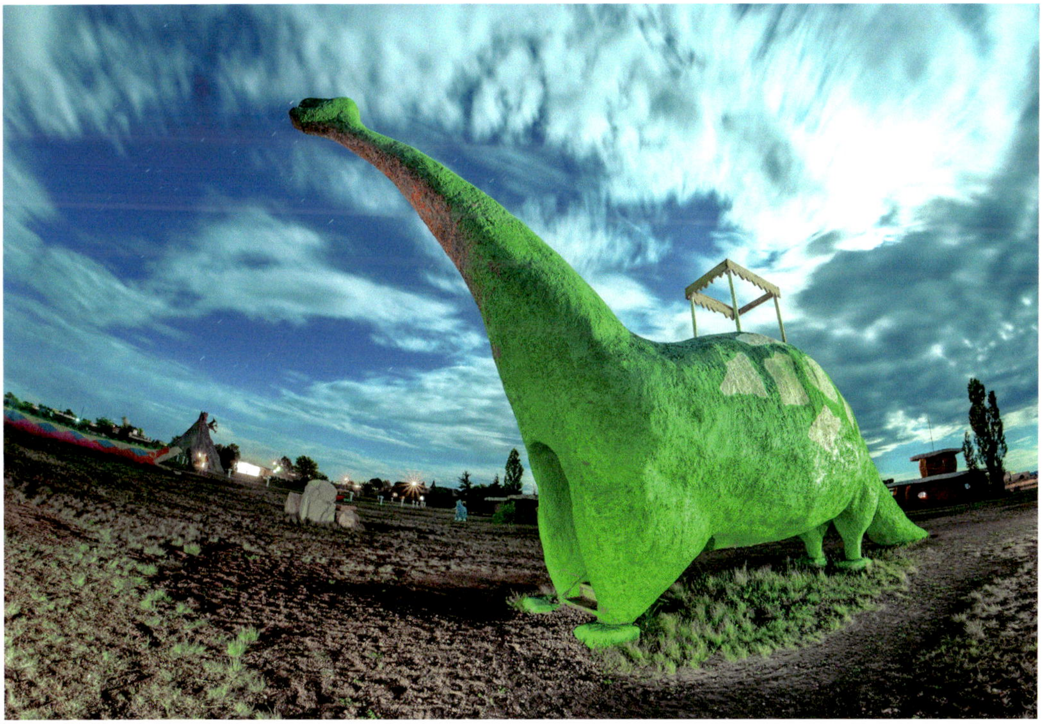

Beyond My Domain · Bedrock City, Arizona. The clouds were particularly interesting for the 2019 photo shoot · Nikon D610/Rokinon 12mm f/2.8 fisheye lens. 184 seconds f/8 ISO 500. July 2019 · Full moon, ProtoMachines LED2 with warm white and green light.

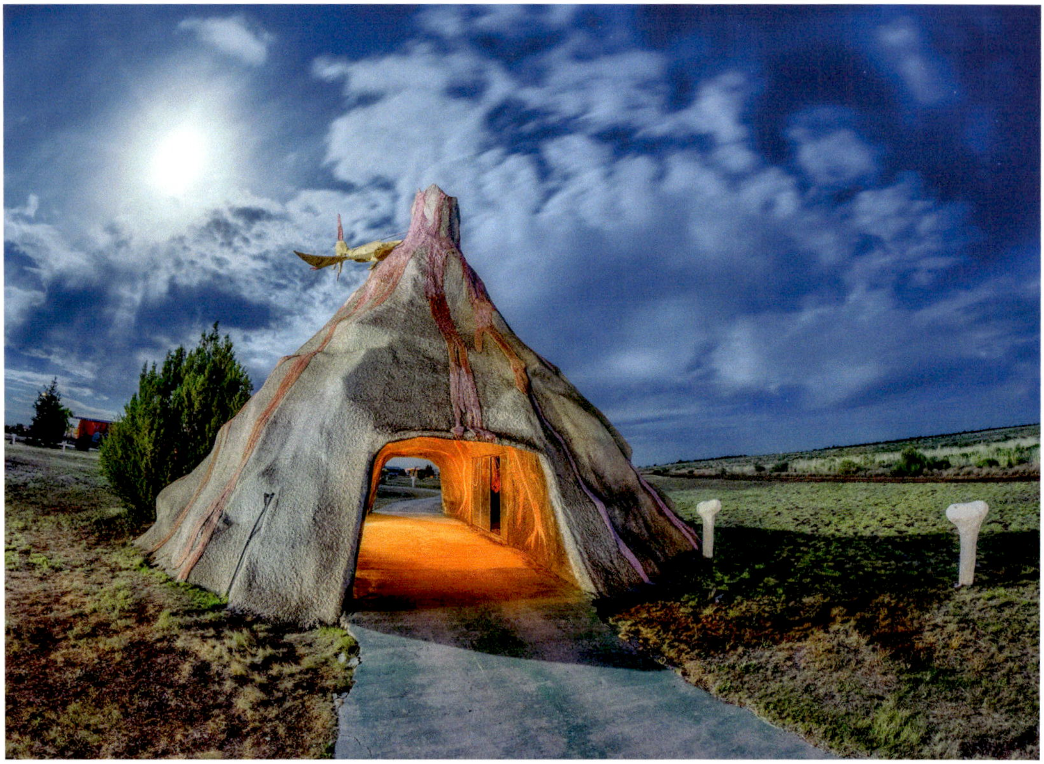

Mountain of Fire · Bedrock City, Arizona. The train would roll through Bedrock City and through the volcano ·
Nikon D610/Rokinon 12mm f/2.8 fisheye lens. 56 seconds f/8 ISO 800. July 2019 · Full moon, ProtoMachines
LED2 with warm white and red light.

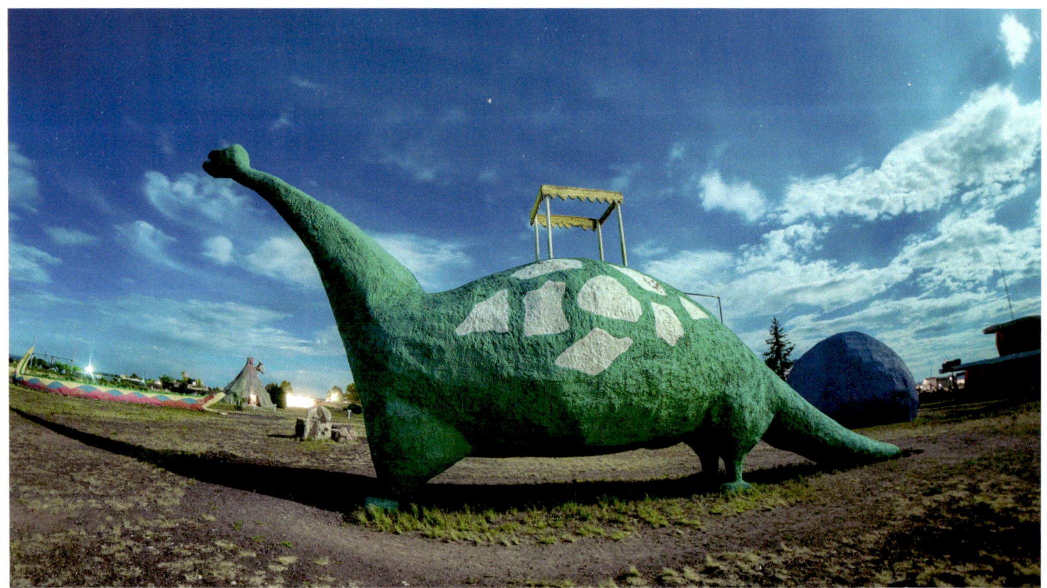

Large and in Charge · Bedrock City, Arizona. Every time I photographed here, I would always make certain to
slide down the Brontosaurus slide · Nikon D610/Rokinon 12mm f/2.8 fisheye lens. 20 seconds f/2.8 20 seconds.
July 2019 · Full moon, ProtoMachines LED2 with warm white light.

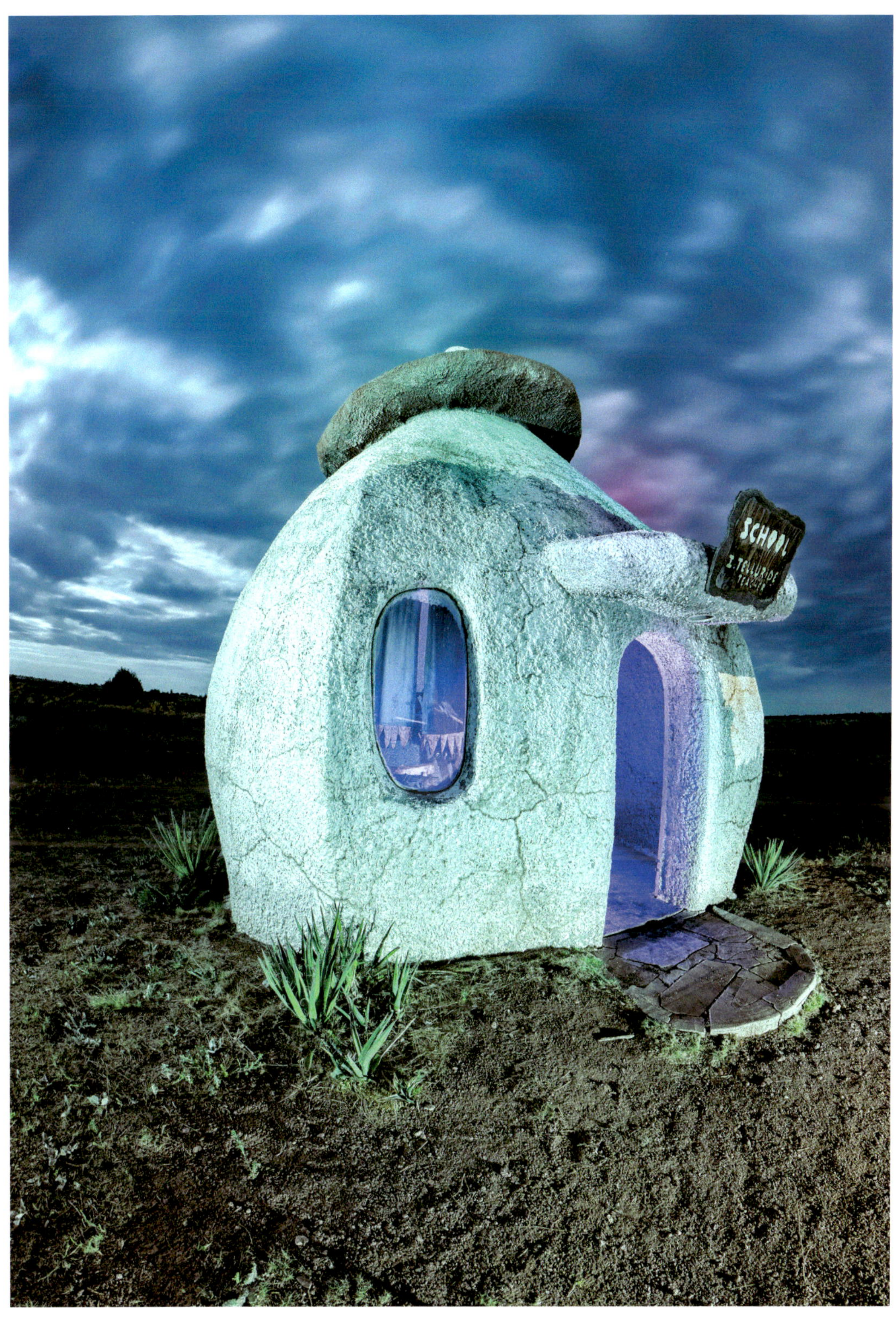

A School Right Out of History · Bedrock City, Arizona · Nikon D610/Rokinon 12mm f/2.8 fisheye lens. 144 seconds f/8 ISO 640. July 2019 · Full moon, ProtoMachines LED2 with warm white and blue light.

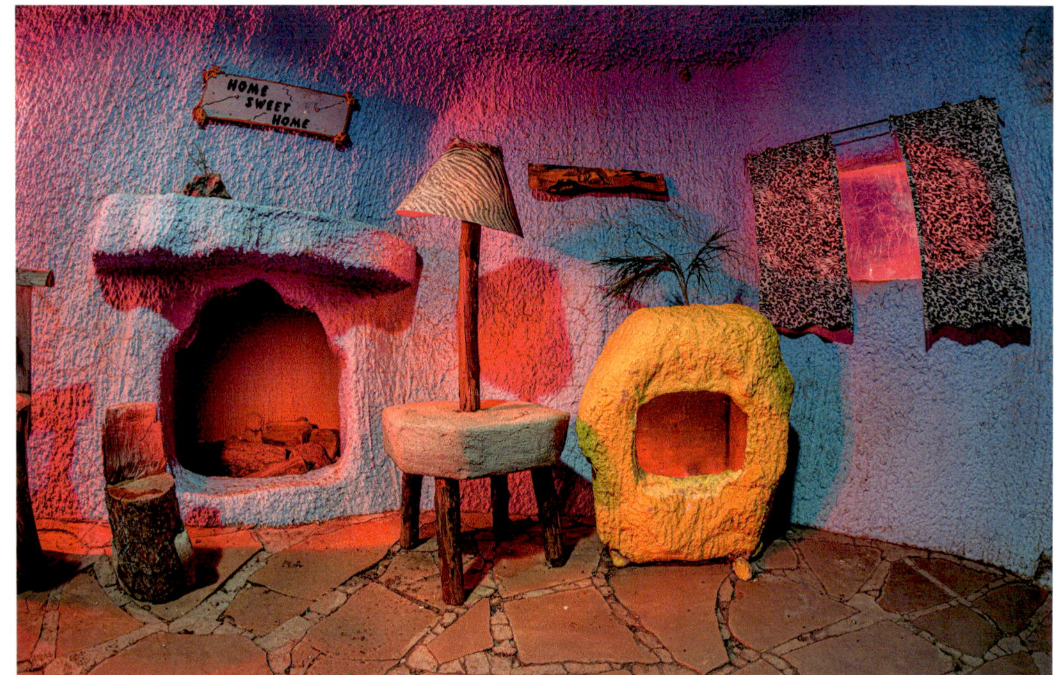

Rubble Room · Bedrock City, Arizona. Fisheye view of Barney and Betty Rubble's living room · Nikon D610/ Rokinon 12mm f/2.8 fisheye lens. 98 seconds f/8 ISO 200. July 2019 · ProtoMachines LED2 with warm white and red light. Lit in almost total darkness.

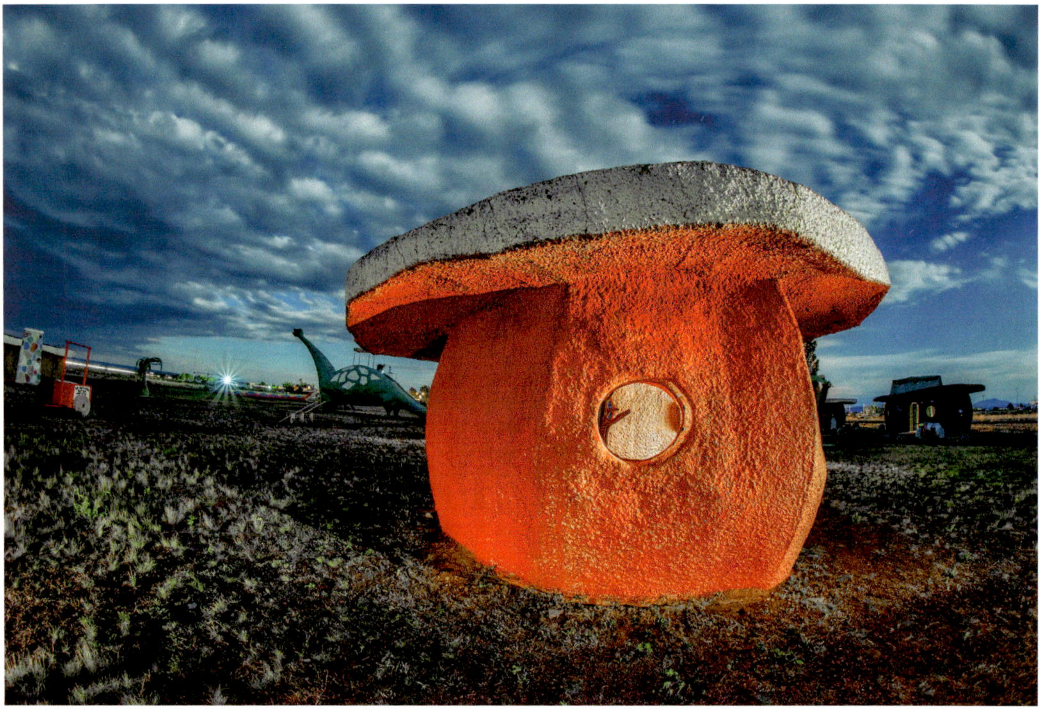

A Haunted House is not a Home · Bedrock City, Arizona · Nikon D610/Rokinon 12mm f/2.8 fisheye lens. 151 seconds f/8 ISO 800. July 2019 · Full moon, ProtoMachines LED2 with warm white light.

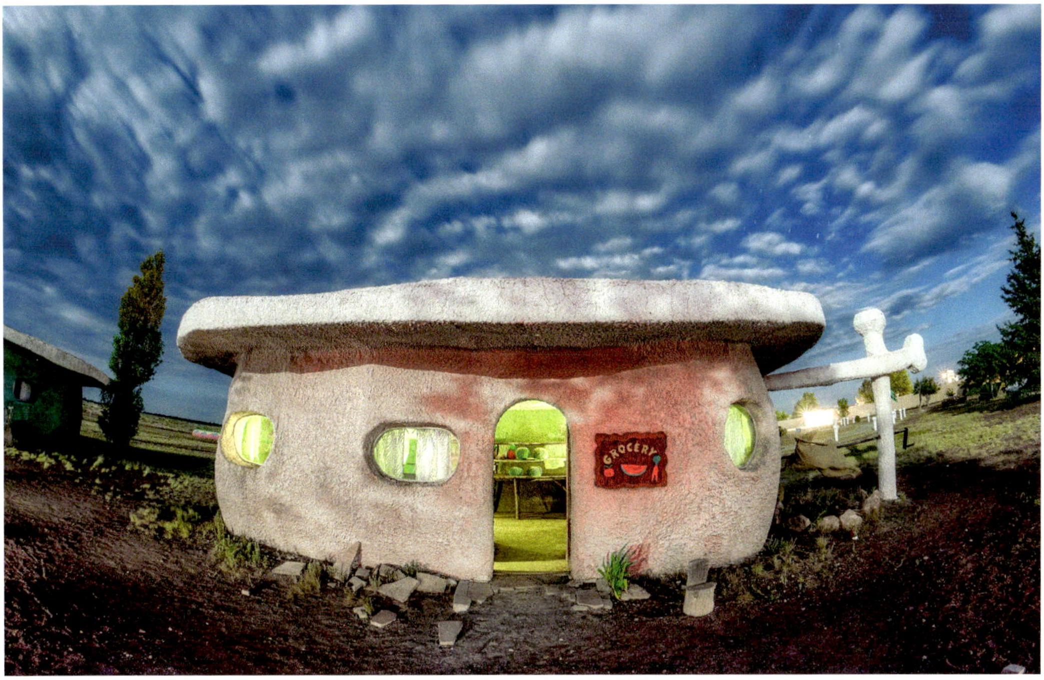

No Hurry at the Grocery · Bedrock City, Arizona · Nikon D610/Rokinon 12mm f/2.8 fisheye lens. 158 seconds f/8 ISO 800. July 2019 · Full moon, ProtoMachines LED2 with warm white light.

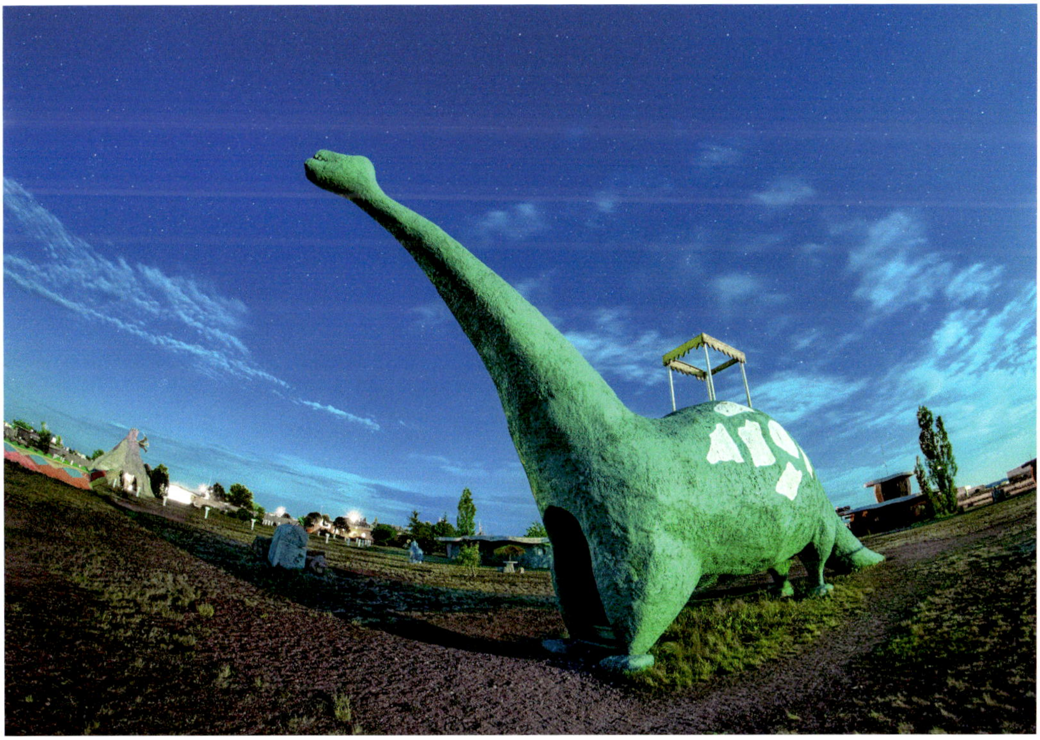

Prehistoric Skies · Bedrock City, Arizona · Nikon D610/Rokinon 12mm f/2.8 fisheye lens. 20 seconds f/4 20 seconds. July 2019 · Full moon, ProtoMachines LED2 with warm white light.

3

GALLETA MEADOWS, CALIFORNIA

In June 2007, Dennis Avery, heir to the fortune from the Avery Dennison Corp., pulled his car over and stared up at the enormous life-sized dinosaurs, elephants, and camels he had seen off Interstate 215. These were part of an immense sculpture garden and workshop in Perris, California, called Perris Jurassic Park. The gifted sculptor? Ricardo Breceda.

Dennis had a home in Borrego Springs. The tiny unincorporated town was basically the "donut hole" in the donut that is Anza-Borrego Desert State Park, the 660,000-acre Park completely surrounding it. He owned a little over three square miles of scattered, non-contiguous open land around the town. Furthermore, he had been familiar with the prehistoric creatures that inhabited this land long ago, as he had been part of a 2006 scientific publication on the paleontology of the area. What could he create in this remarkable setting?

An idea began to emerge.

Dennis returned to Perris Jurassic Park some weeks later with a drawing of an elephant-like gomphothere. This creature lived millions of years ago in the Anza-Borrego region. He asked if Ricardo could make one. Ricardo said that all he would need was the drawing and he could do it.

In April 2008, Ricardo and his workers drove his proud half-ton creation to Borrego Springs. The procession, as well as the unusual four-tusked gomphothere and her offspring, drew quite a bit of attention from the townspeople. It also attracted press from the *Borrego Sun* and a San Diego television news crew.

These four-tusked animals were the beginning of Galleta Meadows and of a creative partnership that would last for years. Years later, I taught my first night photography workshop at the location of the gomphotheres.

Eventually, Dennis commissioned Ricardo to produce about 130 different sculptures. These included gigantic life-sized dinosaurs, elephantidae, borregos, horses, raptors, and much more.

The last sculpture created was an immense rattledragon. Dennis had been rather taken with a Chinese New Year's dragon that he had seen. He and Ricardo worked together to design a 350-foot serpent. It would have a tail like a rattlesnake since it lived in the desert. The rattledragon would be made of large arches that would be planted on each side of the road to make it appear like the enormous serpent was undulating, dipping in and out of the desert sands and underneath the road. Ricardo would have to make thousands of scales. The design, work, and detail far exceeded any of the previous sculptures. Indeed, installation alone would take three months on site to complete.

The crew finished the work in 2012, just in time to usher in the Year of the Dragon. Dennis passed away later that year during the summer. Breceda has not created any sculptures in Borrego Springs since then.

Galleta Meadows has attracted visitors from all over the globe. One time, as I was pulling up to the sculptures of the battling dinosaurs, I was surprised to find a yellow school bus there. They had driven along half a mile of bumpy dirt roads to get there. I met an enthusiastic teacher leading a field trip with students from an elementary school in San Diego. The sculptures had enough accuracy, detail, and scale that schoolchildren could learn from them.

The passing years have not been so kind to the sculptures. A few have been removed. Several are falling apart or have fallen over. But although abandoned to the elements, the genius of Ricardo and the legacy of altruism from Dennis live on, as they are still available for everyone to enjoy.

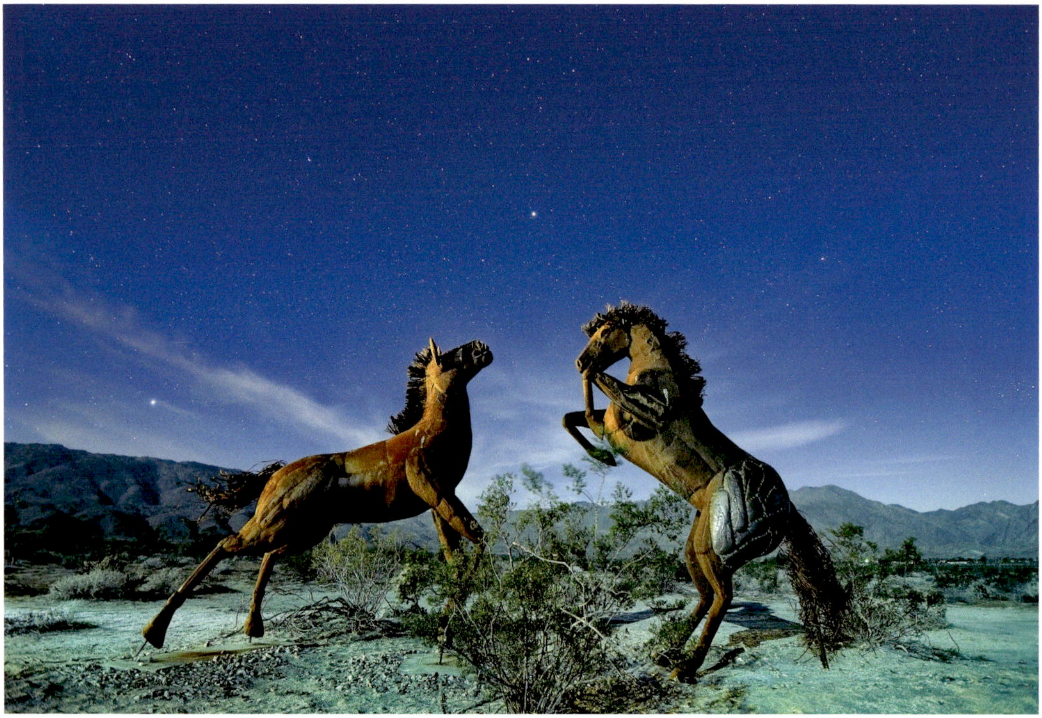

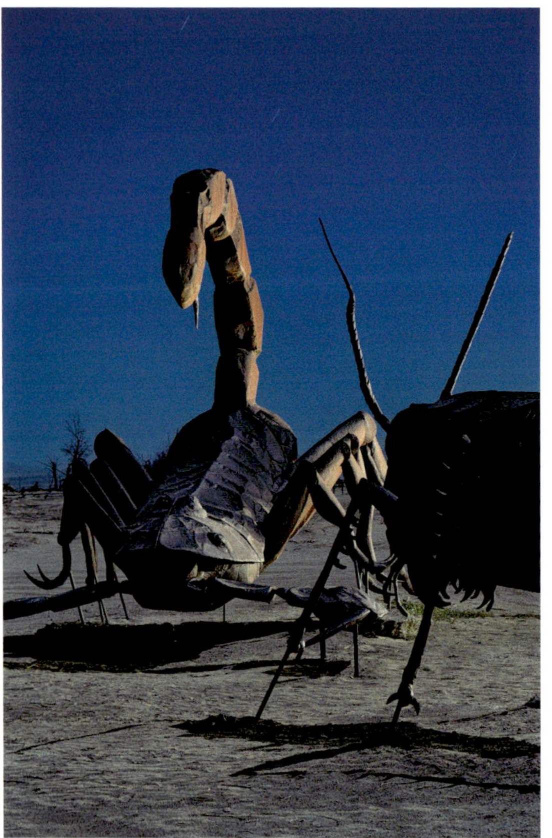

▲ **Break the Stalls, Live Like Horses** · Borrego Springs, California. Metal sculptures by Ricardo Breceda · Nikon D7000/Tokina 11-16mm f/2.8 lens. 20 seconds f/3.5 ISO 640. March 2014 · Full moon, Streamlight with natural white light.

◄ **Shadow of the Cricket** · Borrego Springs, California. The scorpion and the cricket face off under the light of the moon · Pentax K-1/28-105mm f/3.5-5.6 lens. 90 seconds f/8 ISO 200. October 2022 · Full moon, ProtoMachines LED2 with warm white light.

► **Land of the Lost** · Borrego Springs, California. When I first shared this on social media, a friend asked how I had managed to make such a tiny cricket look so large in the photo. But no, this is over six feet tall, not including the antennae · Nikon D7000/Tokina 11-16mm f/2.8 lens. 20 seconds f/3.2 ISO 2500. August 2013 · Streamlight LED flashlight with natural white light.

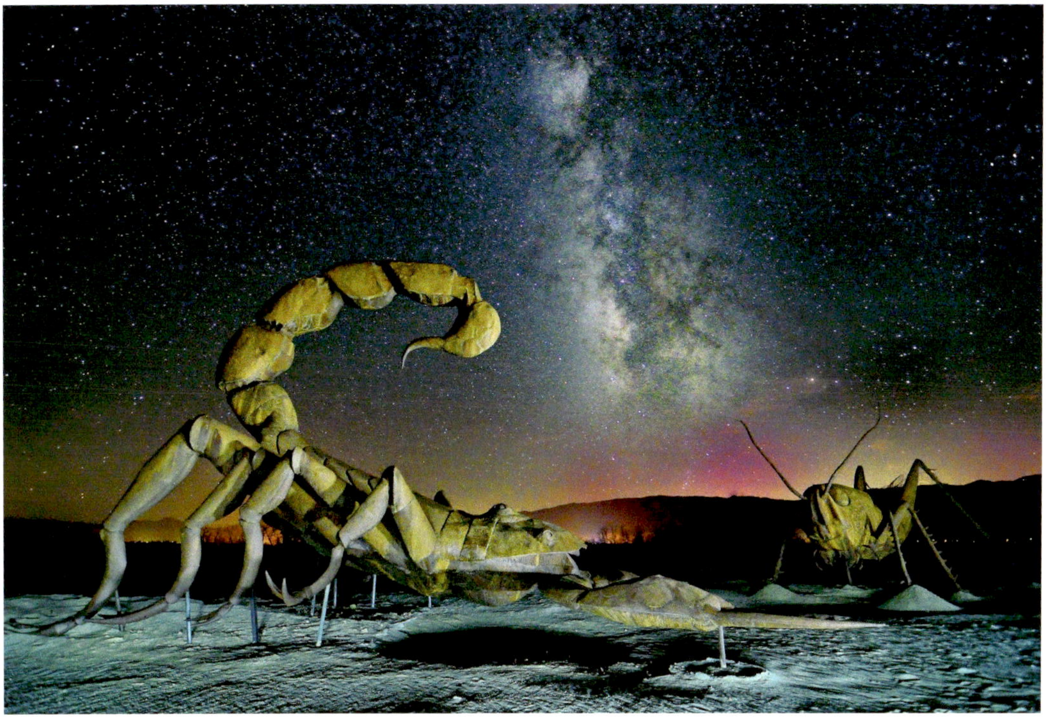

They Roamed The Earth · Borrego Springs, California. This was one of the earliest photos of the Milky Way for me, and to my surprise, was featured in several magazines as well as the Smithsonian and National Geographic websites · Nikon D7000/Tokina 11-16mm f/2.8 lens. 20 seconds f/3.2 ISO 2500. August 2013 · Streamlight with natural white light.

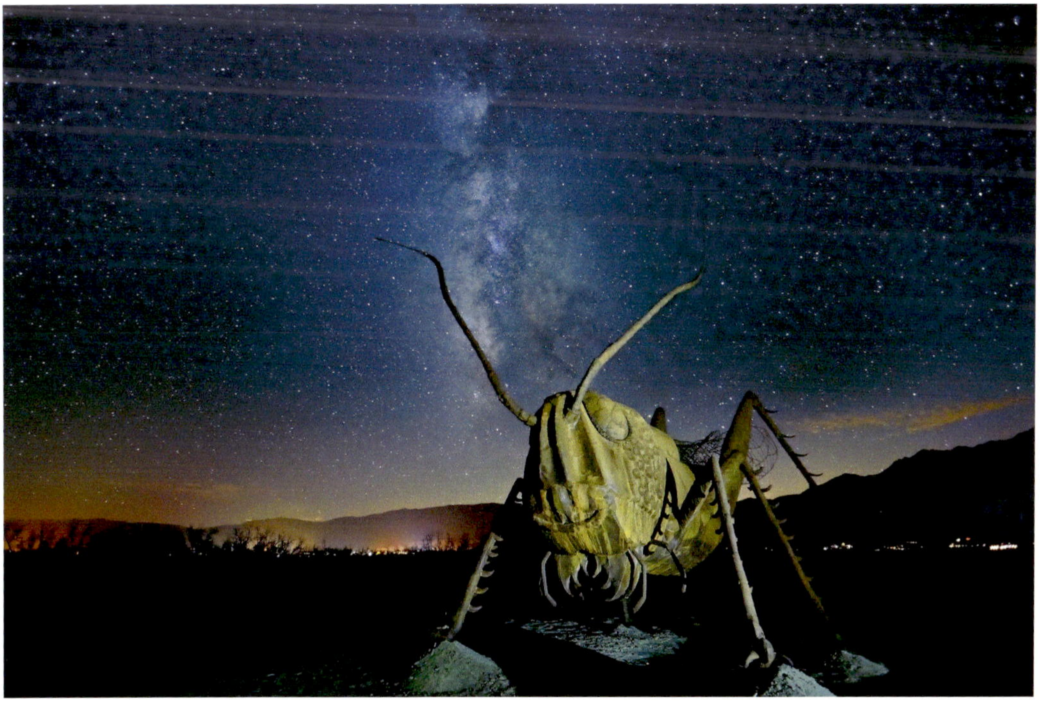

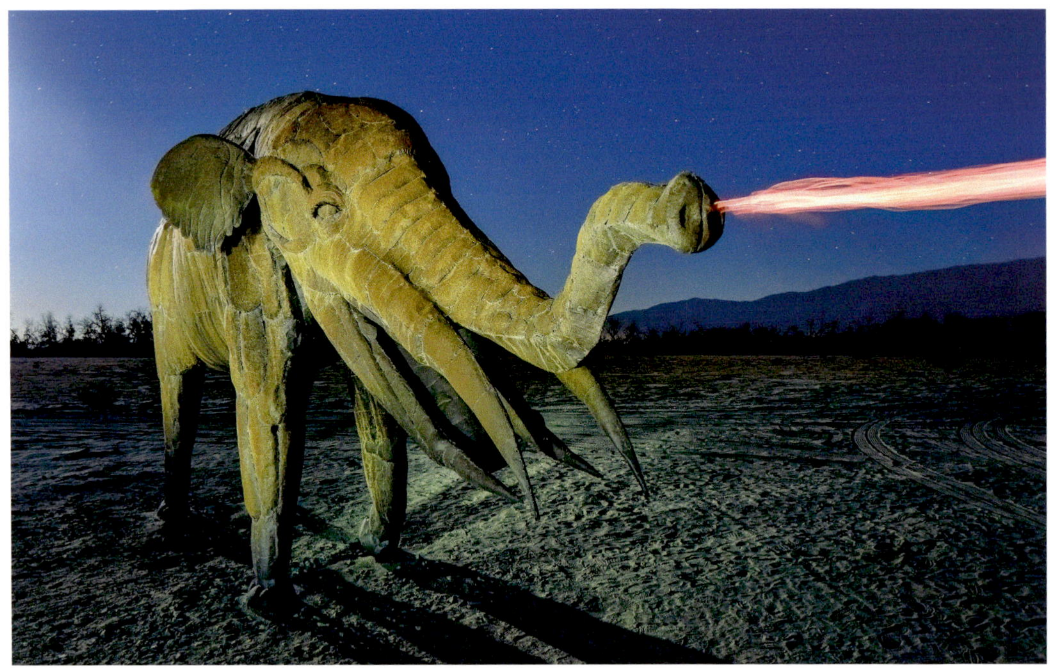

The Gomphothere Trumpet · Borrego Springs, California. I created the light from the trunk with thin electroluminescent wire that glows red · Nikon D7000/Tokina 11-16mm f/2.8 lens. 30 seconds f/6.3 ISO 640. March 2014 · Full moon, Streamlight LED flashlight with natural white light, red electroluminescent wire.

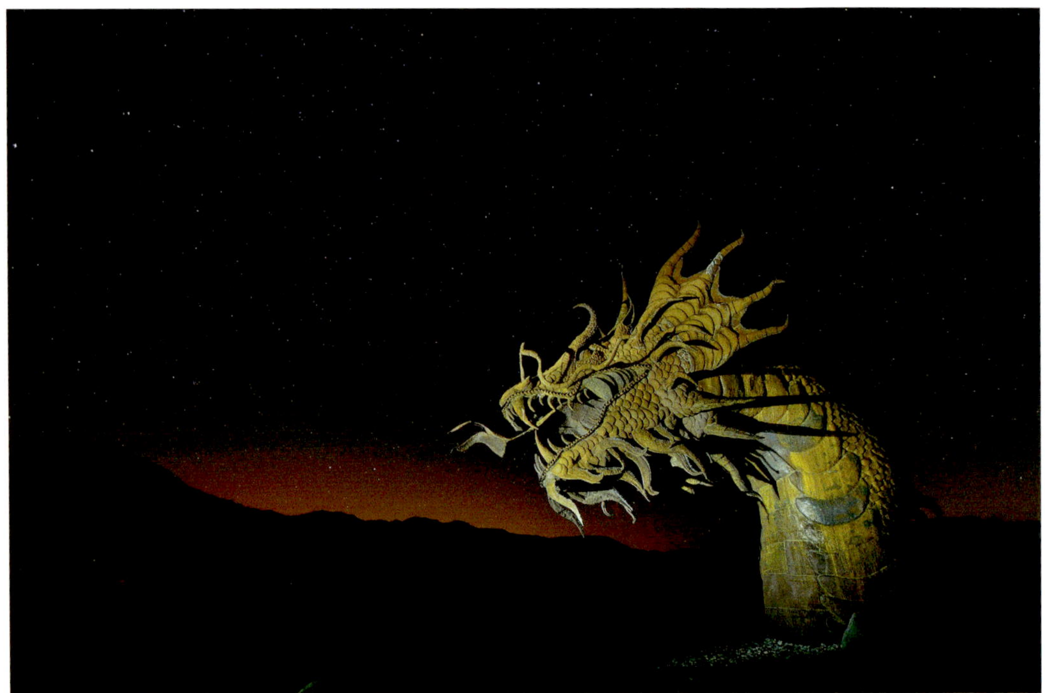

In Praise of Dragons · Borrego Springs, California. The head of the immense rattledragon, the last and by far the largest sculpture created by Ricardo Breceda on Dennis Avery's property in Borrego Springs · Nikon D7000/Tokina 11-16mm f/2.8 lens. 30 seconds f/2.8 ISO 640. April 2014 · Streamlight LED flashlight with natural white light.

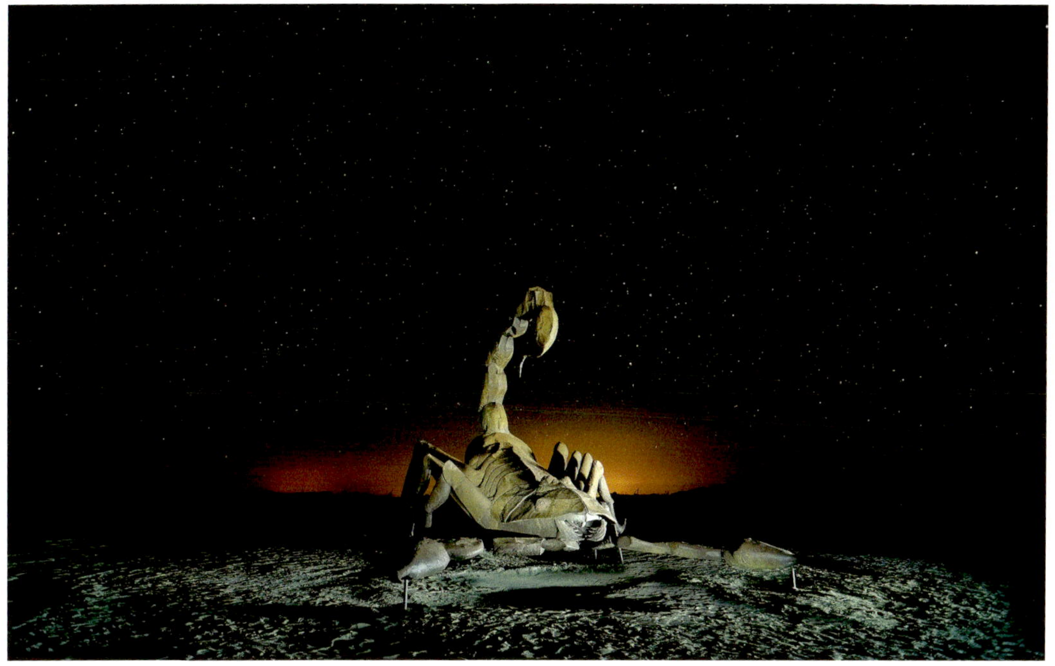

The Scorpion God · Borrego Springs, California · Nikon D7000/Tokina 11-16mm f/2.8 lens. 20 seconds f/2.8 ISO 800. April 2014 · Streamlight LED flashlight with natural white light.

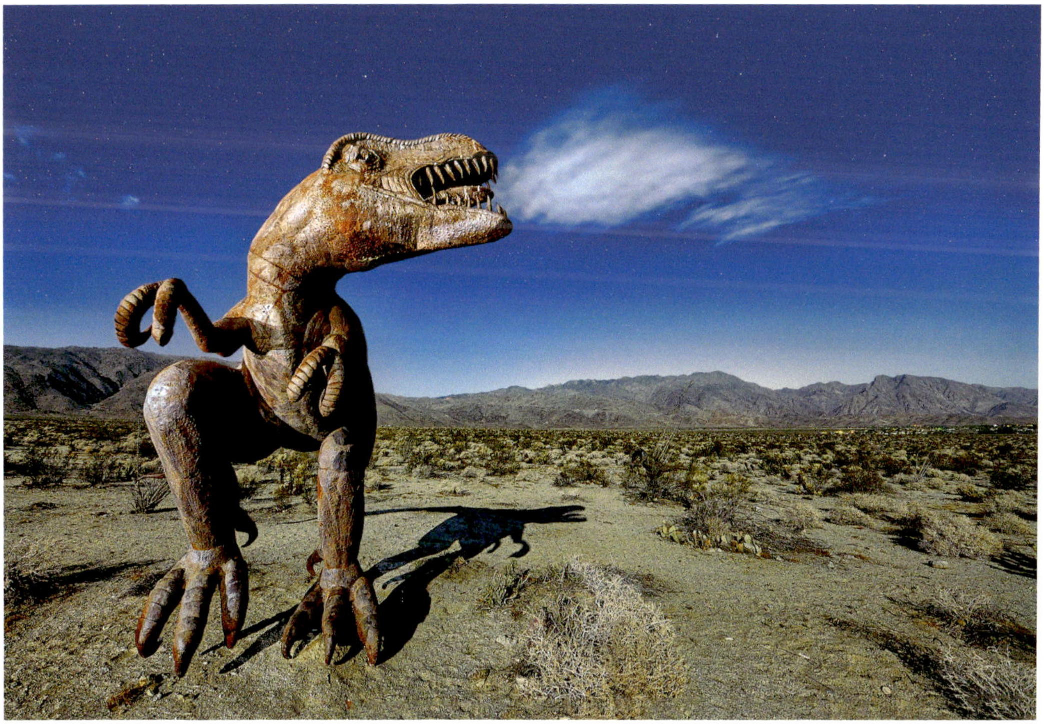

Atomic Breath · Borrego Springs, California. I photographed this Spinosaurus and the odd-looking cloud shortly after watching a Godzilla movie. Perhaps you can see its influence · Nikon D610/14-24mm f/2.8G ED lens, 20 seconds f/2.8 ISO 1000. June 2014 · Full moon, Streamlight LED flashlight with natural white light.

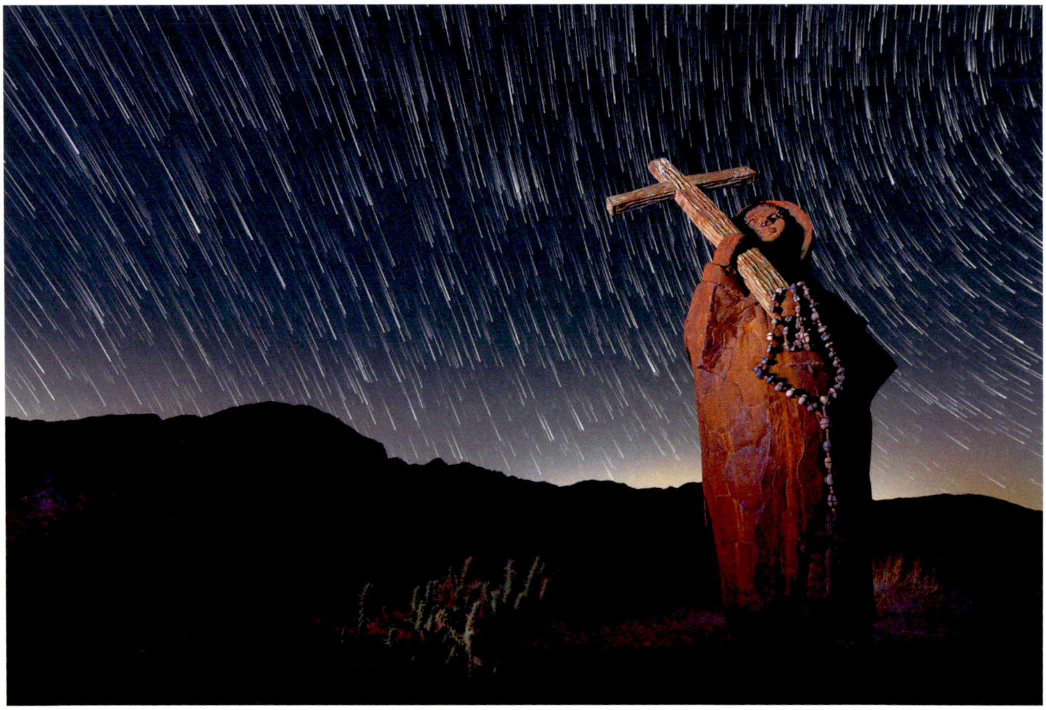

El Padre y La Lluvia de Estrellas · Borrego Springs, California. This sculpture represents Franciscan missionaries Francisco Hermenegildo Garcés and Pedro Font from the Anza expeditions · Nikon D610/14-24mm f/2.8G ED lens. 50 minutes total "stacked." Each photo 30 seconds f/3.5 ISO 2000. June 2014 · Streamlight LED flashlight with natural white light.

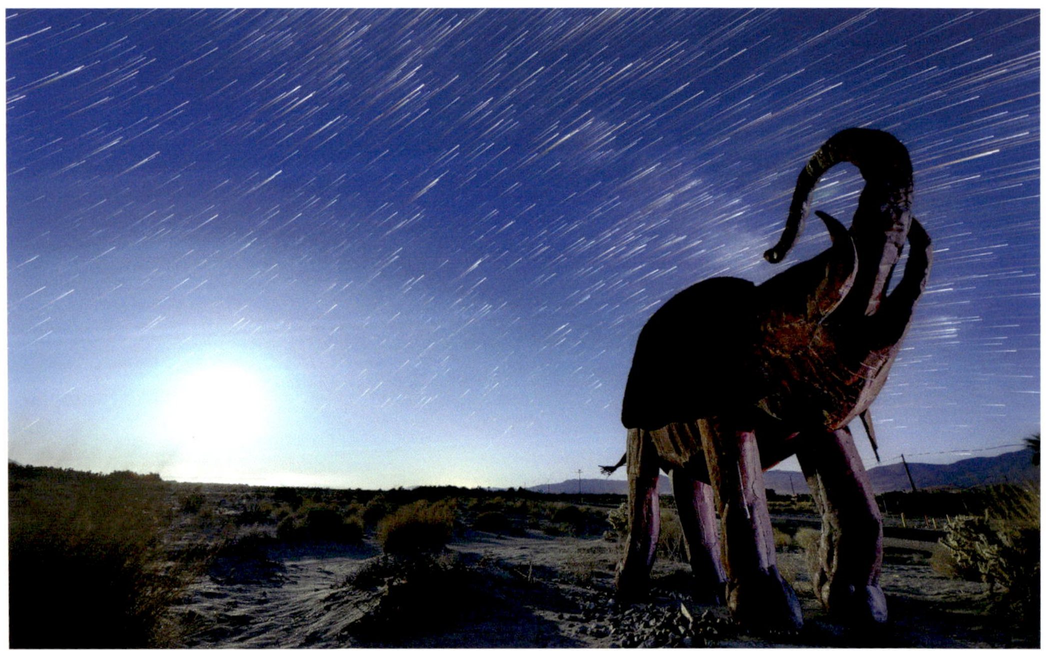

Solitude at Last · Borrego Springs, California · Nikon D610/14-24mm f/2.8G ED lens. 37 minutes total "stacked." Each photo 30 seconds f/3.5 ISO 2000 · Full moon, Streamlight LED flashlight with natural white light.

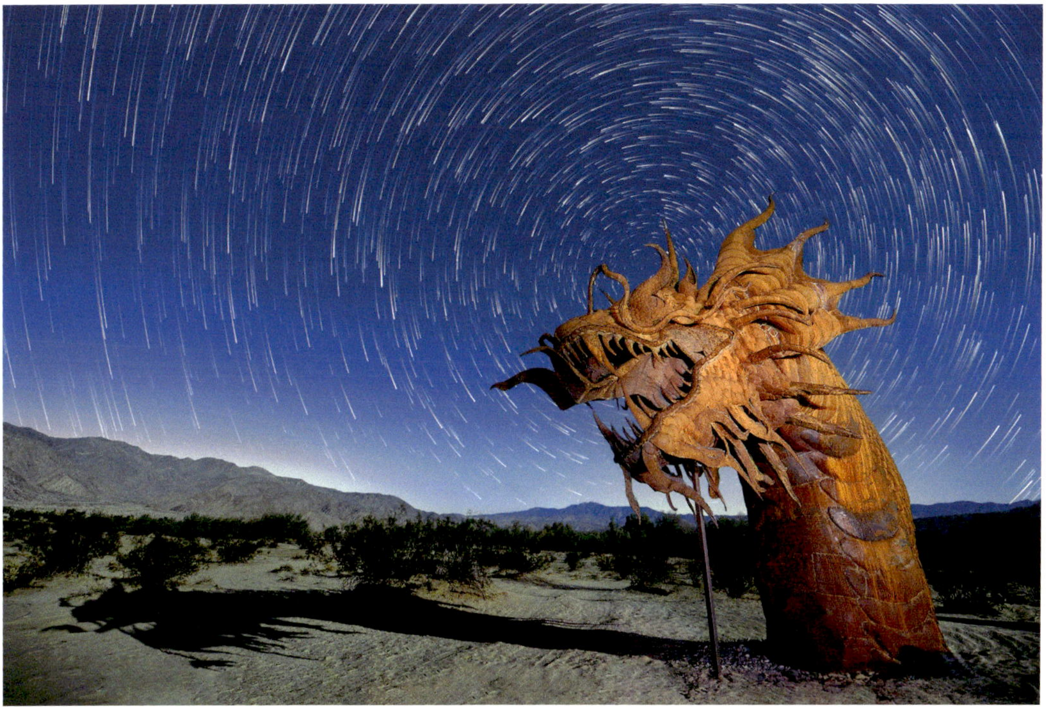

Where Dragons Cast Long Shadows · Borrego Springs, California. The 50-minute exposure shows the perceived movement of the stars due to the rotation of the earth · Nikon D610/14-24mm f/2.8G ED lens. 50 minutes total "stacked." Each photo 30 seconds f/3.5 ISO 1000. June 2014 · Full moon, Streamlight LED flashlight with natural white light.

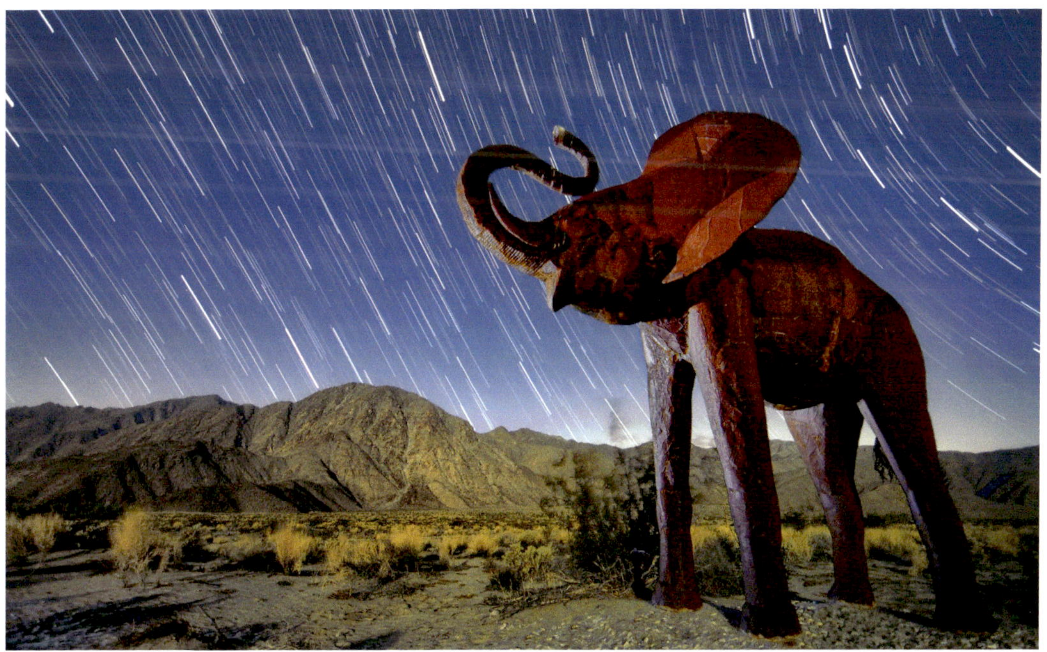

Airavata · Borrego Springs, California. The 25.5-minute exposure shows the perceived movement of the stars due to the rotation of the earth · Nikon D610/14-24mm f/2.8G ED lens. 25.5 minutes total "stacked." Each photo 30 seconds f/2.8 ISO 800. June 2014 · Full moon, Streamlight LED flashlight with natural white light.

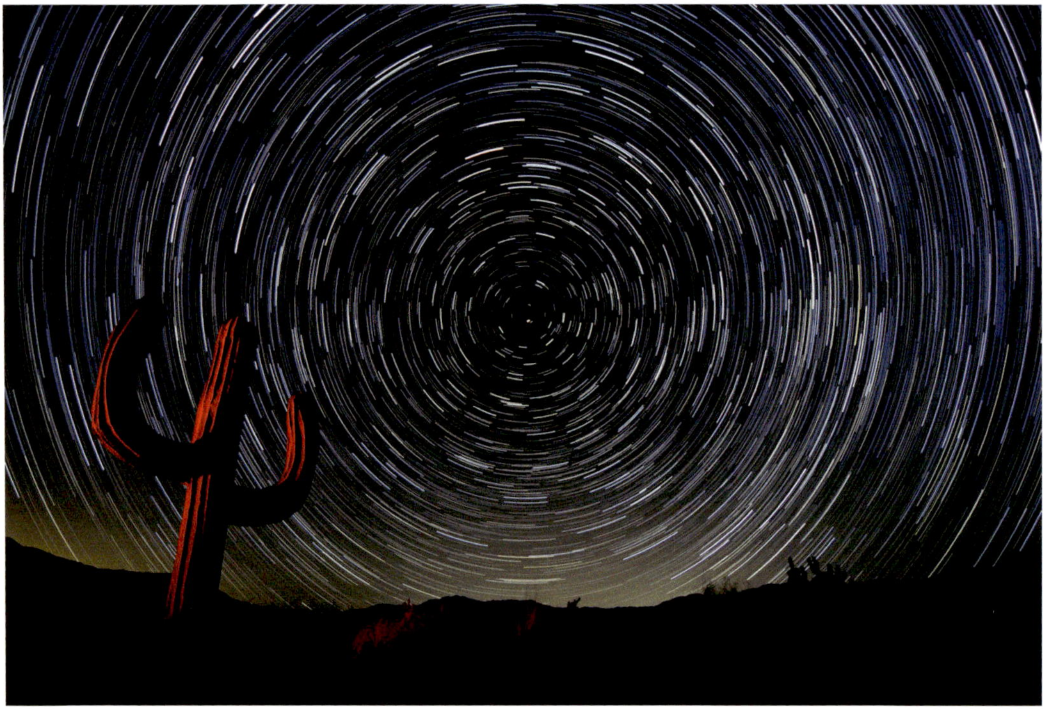

A Long Long Way From Home · Borrego Springs, California. This saguaro is a long way from home. It's also made of metal. Unfortunately, it toppled years ago. The 50-minute exposure shows the perceived movement of the stars due to the rotation of the earth · Nikon D610/14-24mm f/2.8G ED lens. 50 minutes total "stacked." Each photo 30 seconds f/3.5 ISO 800. June 2014.

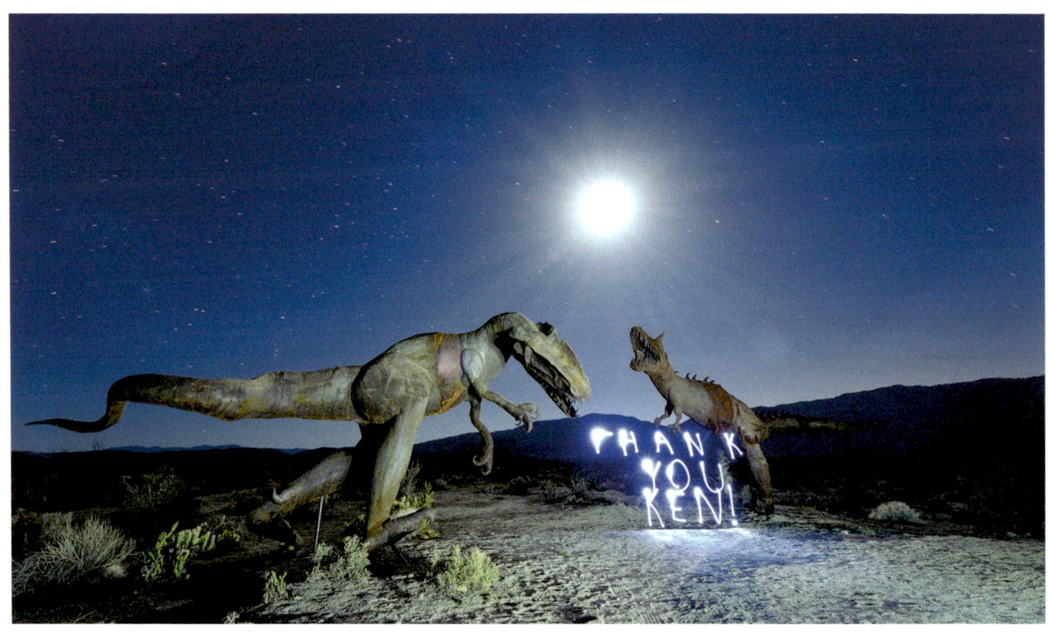

Thank You · Borrego Springs, California. Participants in my night photography workshop write a message with light · Nikon D610/14-24mm f/2.8G ED lens. 29 seconds s/5.6 ISO 800. July 2014 · Full moon, Streamlight LED flashlight with natural white light, LED flashlight for light writing.

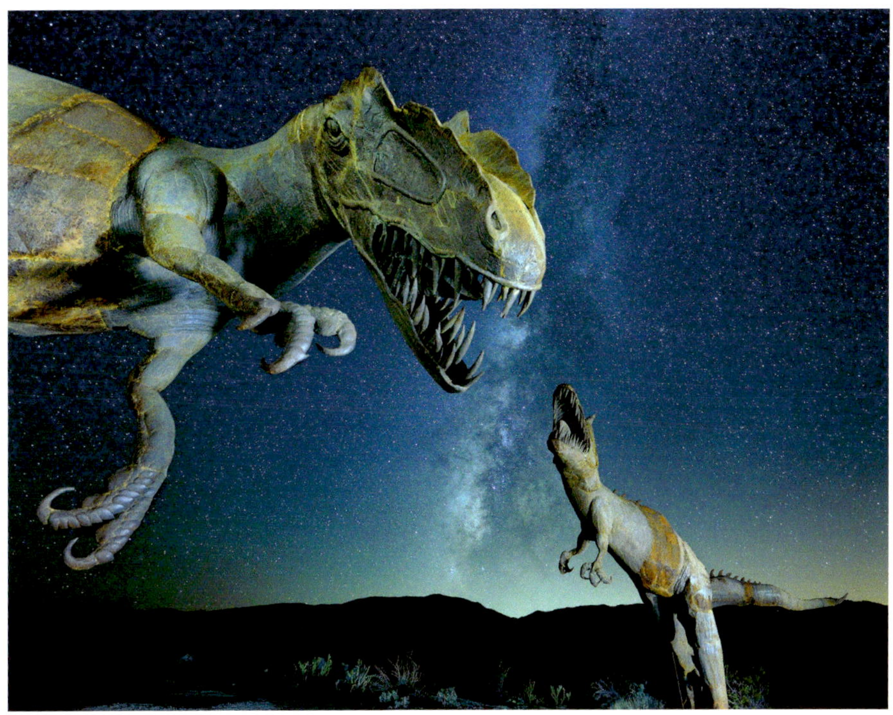

All Those Who Battle · Borrego Springs, California. Two dinosaurs engaged in an ancient battle that shakes the very stars above them · Nikon D610/14-24mm lens. Two photos are blended to reduce noise. Earth: 380 seconds, f/5.6, ISO 800. Sky: 20 seconds f/2.8 ISO 4000. July 2014 · Streamlight LED flashlight with natural white light.

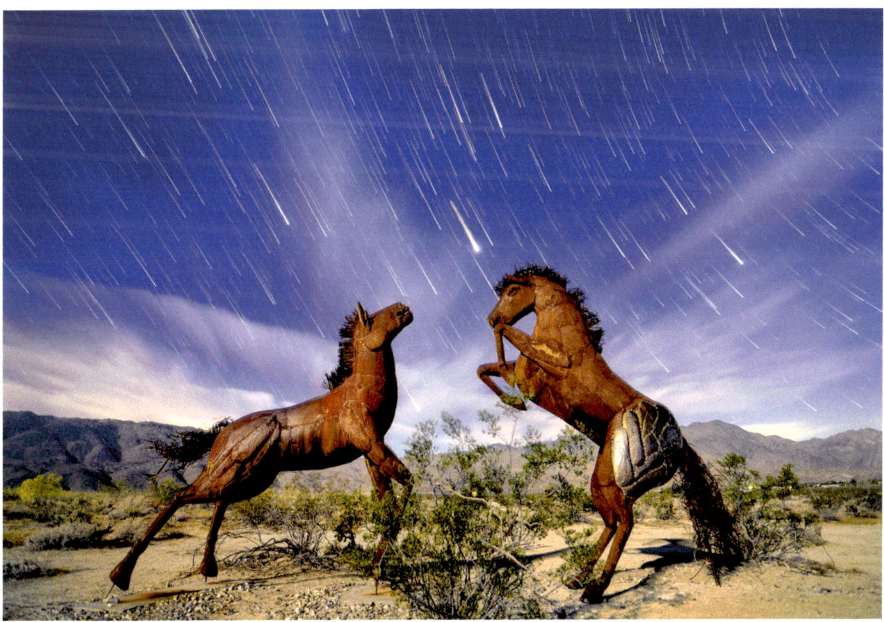

Dos Caballos · Wild horses couldn't drag me away from Borrego Springs, California · Nikon D7000/ Tokina 11-16mm f/2.8 lens. 27 minutes total "stacked." Each photo 30 seconds f/2.8 ISO 400. March 2014 · Full moon, Streamlight LED flashlight with natural white light.

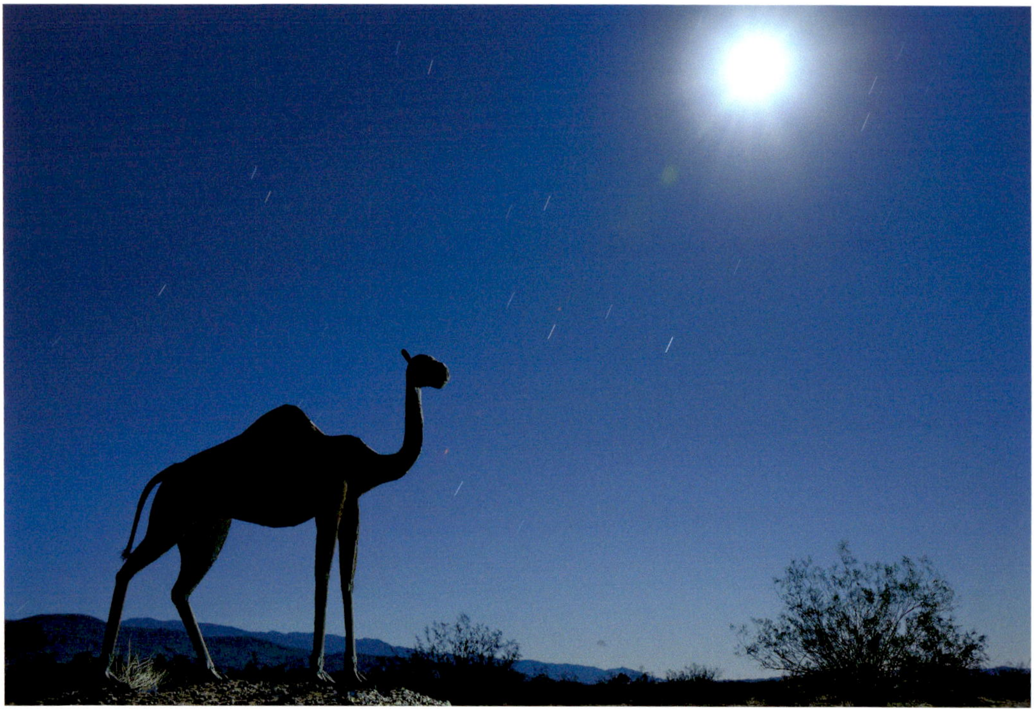

Balthasar of the Winter Light · Borrego Springs, California · Nikon D610/14-24mm f/2.8G ED lens. 276 seconds f/8 ISO 200. December 2015 · Full moon, ProtoMachines LED2 with warm white light.

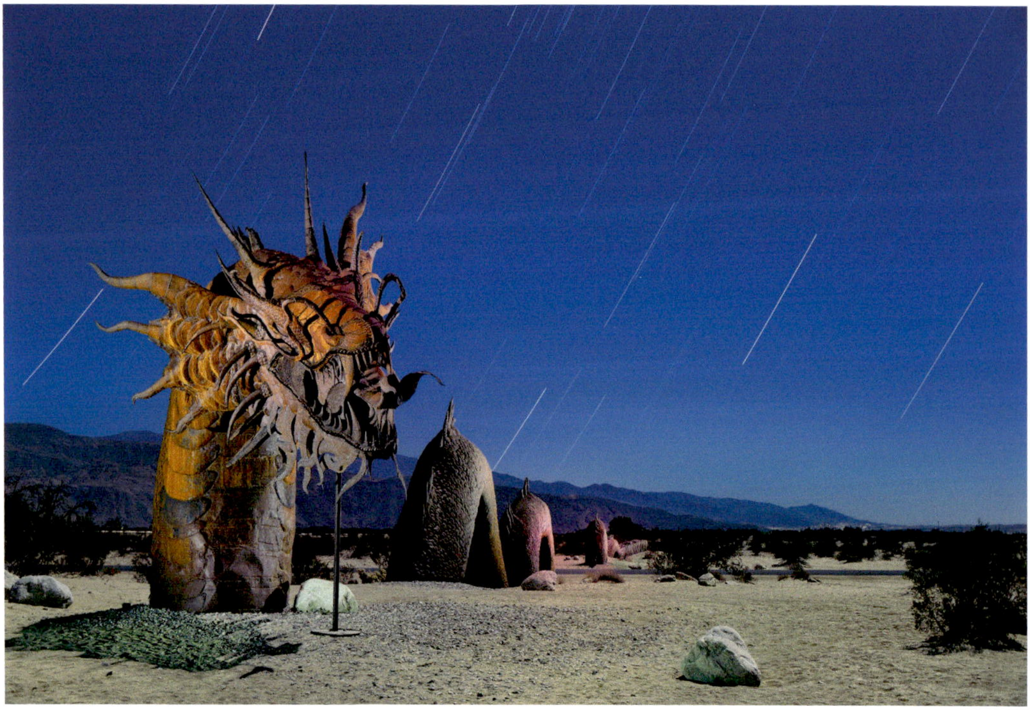

Drago Rosso · Borrego Springs, California · Nikon D610/28-300mm f/3.5-5.6. 28 minutes total "stacked." Each photo 2 minutes f/6.3 ISO 200. December 2015 · Full moon, ProtoMachines LED2 with warm white light.

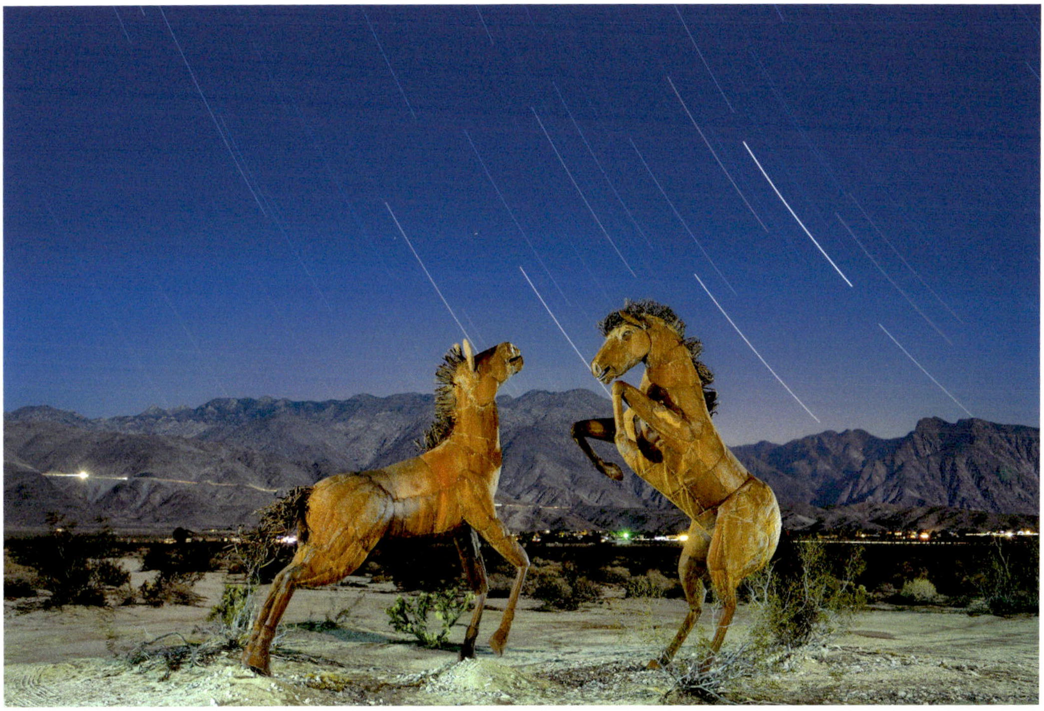

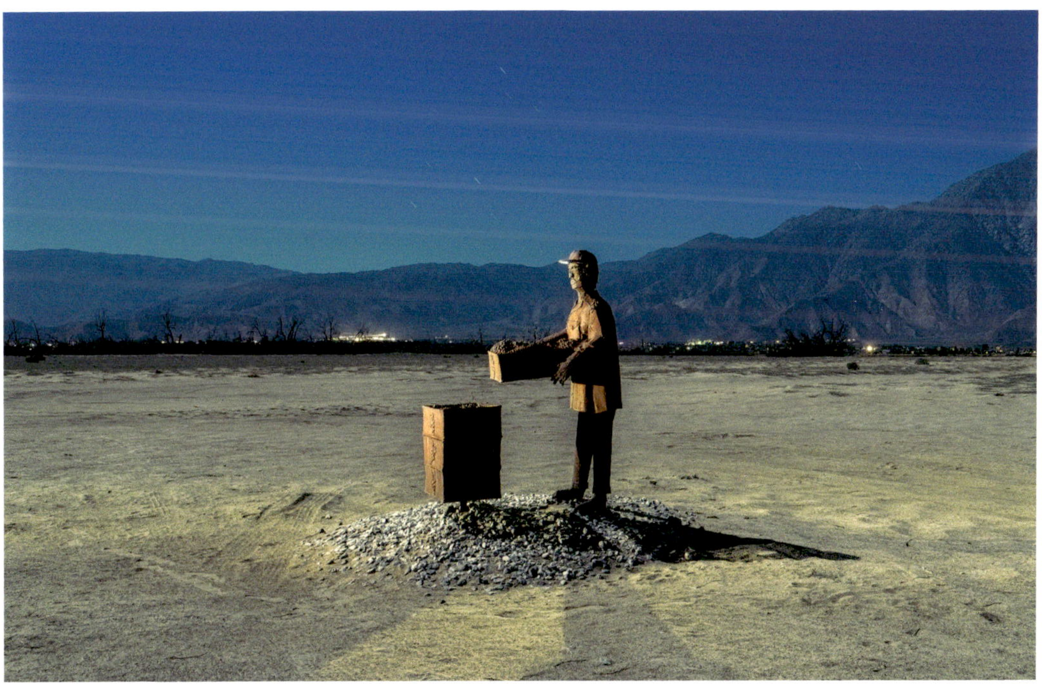

Balius and Xanthos · Borrego Springs, California · Nikon D610/28-300mm f/3.5-5.6. 45 minutes total "stacked." Each photo 3 minutes f/8 ISO 200. December 2015 · Full moon, ProtoMachines LED2 with warm white light.

Fruit of the Land · Borrego Springs, California. Part of a tribute to migrant farm workers who harvested grapes for the Di Giorgio Fruit Corporation in the Borrego Valley · Pentax K-1/28-105mm f/3.5-5.6 lens. 2 minutes f/8 ISO 200. October 2022 · Full moon, ProtoMachines LED2 with warm white light.

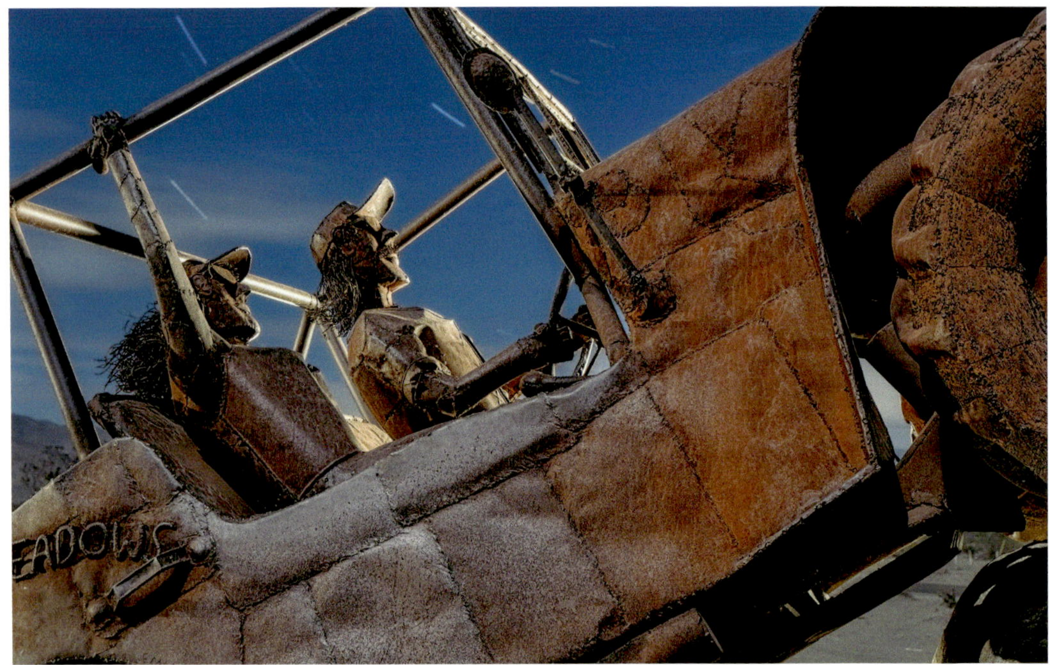

My Kingdom for a Jeep · Borrego Springs, California. A Jeep ride to infinity and beyond · Pentax K-1/28-105mm f/3.5-5.6 lens. 21 minutes total "stacked." Each photo 90 seconds f/8 ISO 200. October 2022 · Full moon, ProtoMachines LED2 with warm white light.

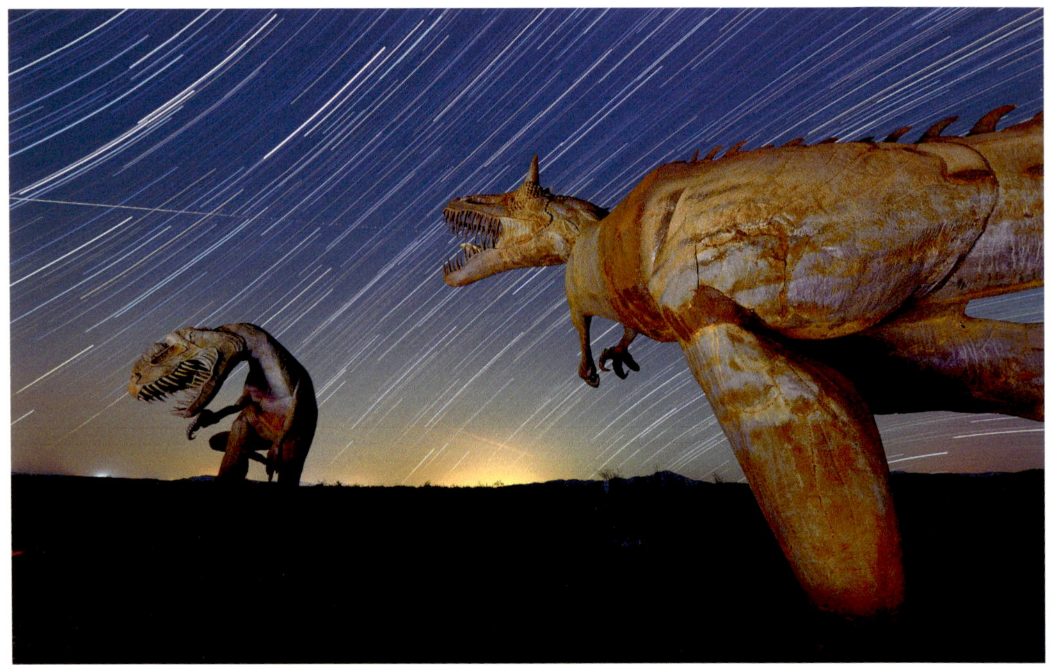

Spitting Stars · Borrego Springs, California. One of the dinosaurs seems to be spitting forth a star at its foe. If you guessed that the line that seems to be shooting forth from the mouth are lights from an airplane, you'd be correct · Nikon D610/14-24mm f/2.8G ED lens. 76 minutes total "stacked." Each photo 4 minutes f/4 ISO 640. March 2015 · Full moon, ProtoMachines LED2 with warm white light.

4

LAKE DOLORES WATERPARK, CALIFORNIA

This is where the ghosts are," the caretaker said. He pointed to a painting of a girl's face inside what had been a gift shop. "The girl inside the building keeps getting painted over, but when I come back the next day, that paint is gone." I peered closer. "They won't bother you, though," the caretaker assured me.

The caretaker continued driving around Lake Dolores Waterpark, a collection of badly damaged retro-futuristic abandoned structures and waterslides, now mostly frequented by urban explorers, taggers, skateboarders, and arsonists. He told of previous incarnations of the park that featured stand-up and 50-mile-per-hour waterslides, bumper boats, zip lines, high dives, trapeze-like swings, and more. "I came across people having a seance here," he said, pointing to an open area between the buildings.

The caretaker mentioned how the new owners were going to fix it up. They'd have camping, an RV park, dirt-biking and ATV trails, and eventually, a library, amphitheater, and more. I silently thought that if they did this, in a few years I might have a new abandoned site to photograph.

Earlier that hot dry day, I had parked in the back near an abandoned house with an RV. It turned out that the caretaker lived there along with a dog and two other people. Coincidentally, he had told me about two places he had lived before, places that I have frequently visited. "I lived in a tree in Boulder Creek for half a year," he mentioned. He also said that he lived in West Virginia for quite some time. Both were beautiful places that I had visited many times. Now he was giving me a personal tour of an abandoned waterpark in the Mojave Desert. The world can be a fascinating place at times.

The caretaker also spoke of people careening down 150-foot waterslides at speeds of 50 miles per hour before shooting out into the water like a human cannonball.

I've spoken to people who saw this either in person or in television advertisements in the 1970s and early 1980s. They all say, "A place like this could never exist now," usually mentioning an injury or two that they had heard about or seen.

Lake Dolores closed after a downturn in popularity. New owners purchased it and reopened it as Rock-A-Hoola Waterpark, which played 1950s and 1960s rock music and added numerous rides, including a river ride on inflatable tubes. However, the investors had amassed three million dollars in debt.

But that wasn't all. "After that, something terrible happened," the caretaker said. "At the end of one day, the pools for the slides were emptied. However, one of the park employees didn't know this. He slid down a water slide and crashed at the base. He was paralyzed and sued them for millions of dollars." The park closed that year after failing to attract large crowds.

A new investment group opened the park again, this time in 2002 as Discovery Waterpark. It welcomed visitors on weekends and intermittently, only to close in 2004. It's been closed ever since.

Lake Dolores has continued to attract visitors, however. Since 2004, it has been repeatedly vandalized and torn apart by people stealing its metal and wire. Skateboarder Rob Dyrdek and friends performed stunts there for an MTV reality show in 2008. In 2013, Boards of Canada publicly debuted an album by playing it there first. Skateboarder Tony Hawk filmed a Mini Cooper television commercial there a couple of years later. And in 2022, the immensely popular supergroup BTS filmed a mini concert there.

I returned at night, driving in through the "secret way" that the caretaker had told me I could use. The air was still dry, with some occasional hot breezes. The sky was hazy with smoke from catastrophic fires further north, including the Caldor and Dixie Fires.

During the long exposure photos, I sometimes used bold blue, red, and green colors on the interiors since the colors were already vivid and comical. I photographed everywhere, remembering that the caretaker had also said that he would make sure no one would bother me. He remained true to his word. I saw him circle the perimeter several times in his cart. No one ever bothered me—including the ghosts.

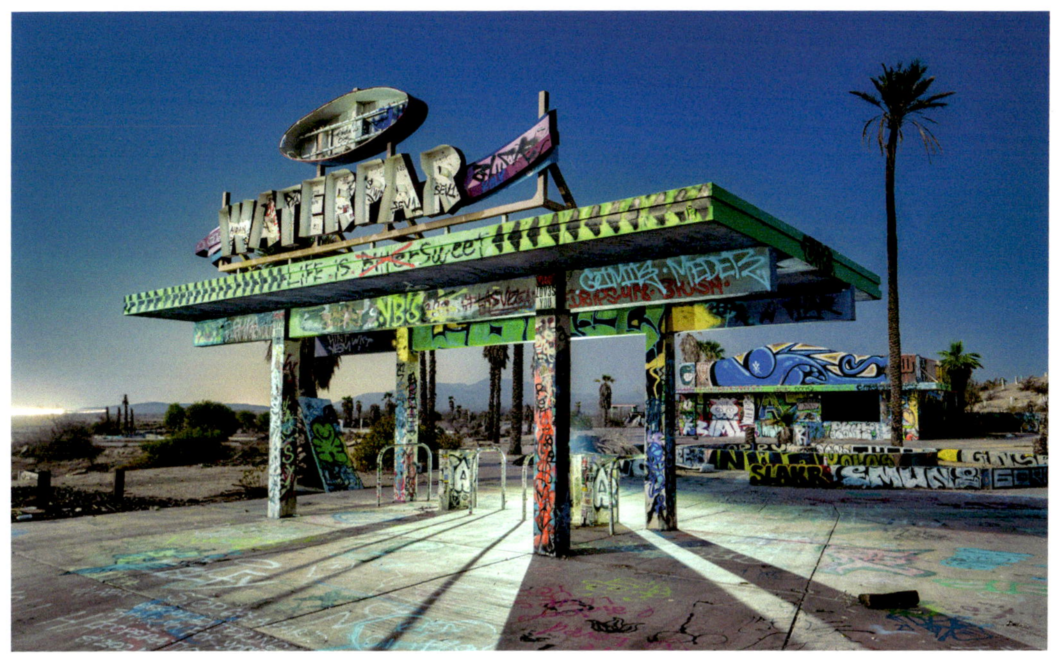

Water and Fire · Lake Dolores Waterpark, California. Fun with shadows. The sky was hazy with smoke from catastrophic fires further north, including the Caldor and Dixie Fires · Pentax K-1/15-30mm f/2.8 lens. 3 minutes f/8 ISO 200. August 2021 · Full moon, ProtoMachines LED2 with warm white light.

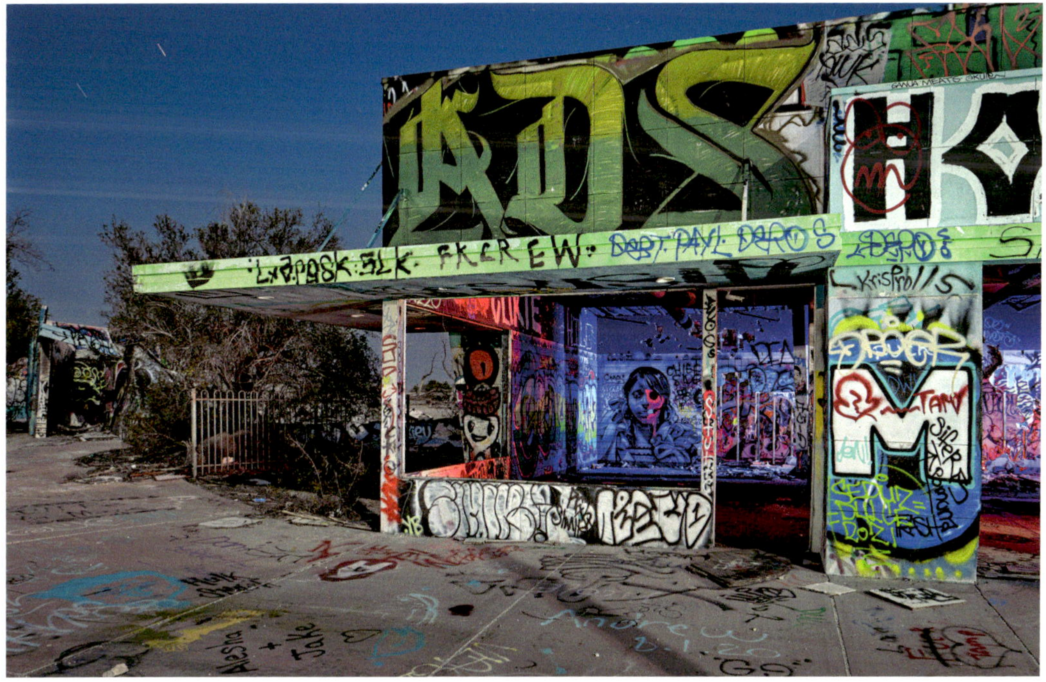

They're Heeeere! · Lake Dolores Waterpark, California. This former gift shop is allegedly haunted. According to the caretaker, the picture of the girl inside keeps getting painted over. However, when he returns the next day, the paint is gone · Pentax K-1/15-30mm f/2.8 lens. 3 minutes f/8 ISO 200. August 2021 · Full moon, ProtoMachines LED2 with warm white and blue light.

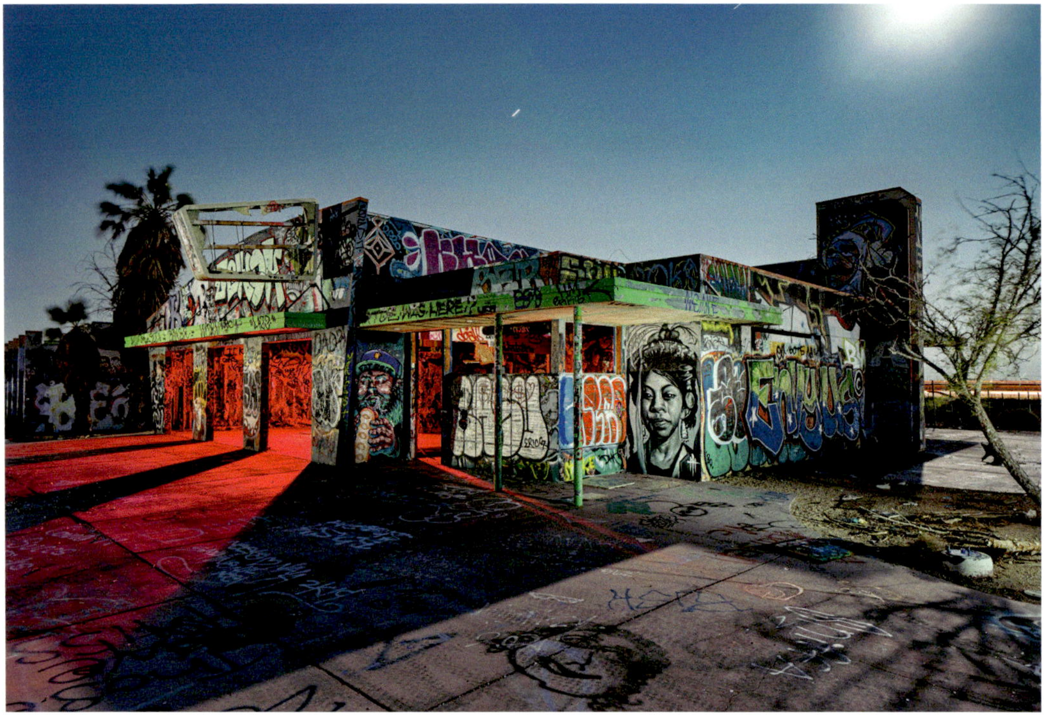

Captain and Professor · The former arcade at Lake Dolores Waterpark, California · Pentax K-1/15-30mm f/2.8 lens. 3 minutes f/8 ISO 200. August 2021 · Full moon, ProtoMachines LED2 with warm white and red light.

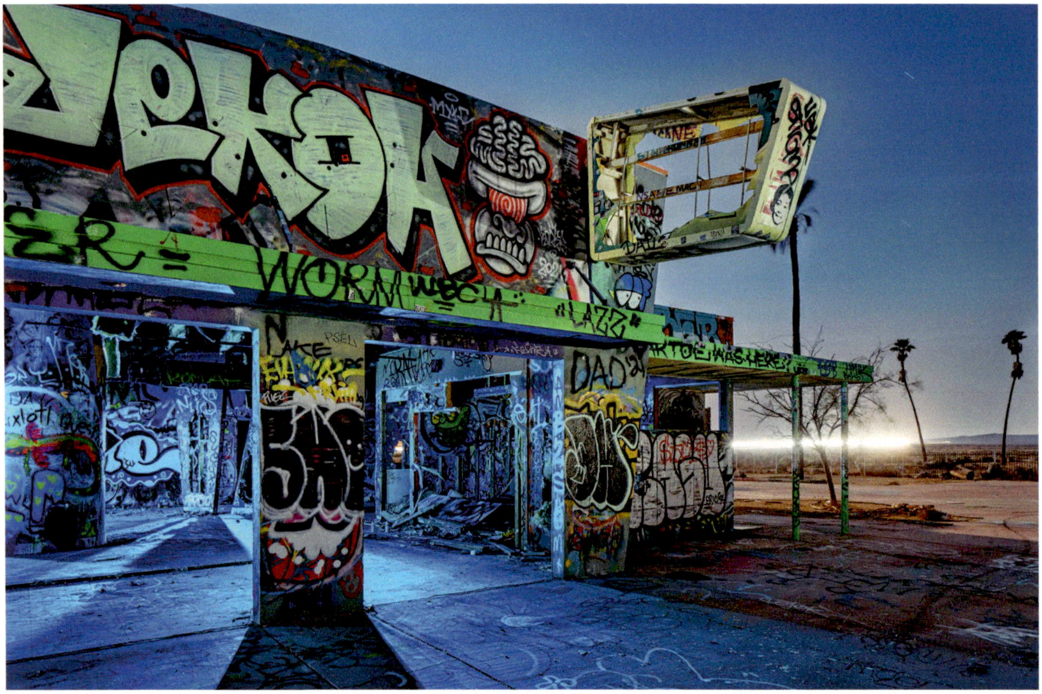

Blue Arcade · The former arcade at Lake Dolores Waterpark, California · Pentax K-1/15-30mm f/2.8 lens. 3 minutes f/8 ISO 200. August 2021 · Full moon, ProtoMachines LED2 with warm white and blue light.

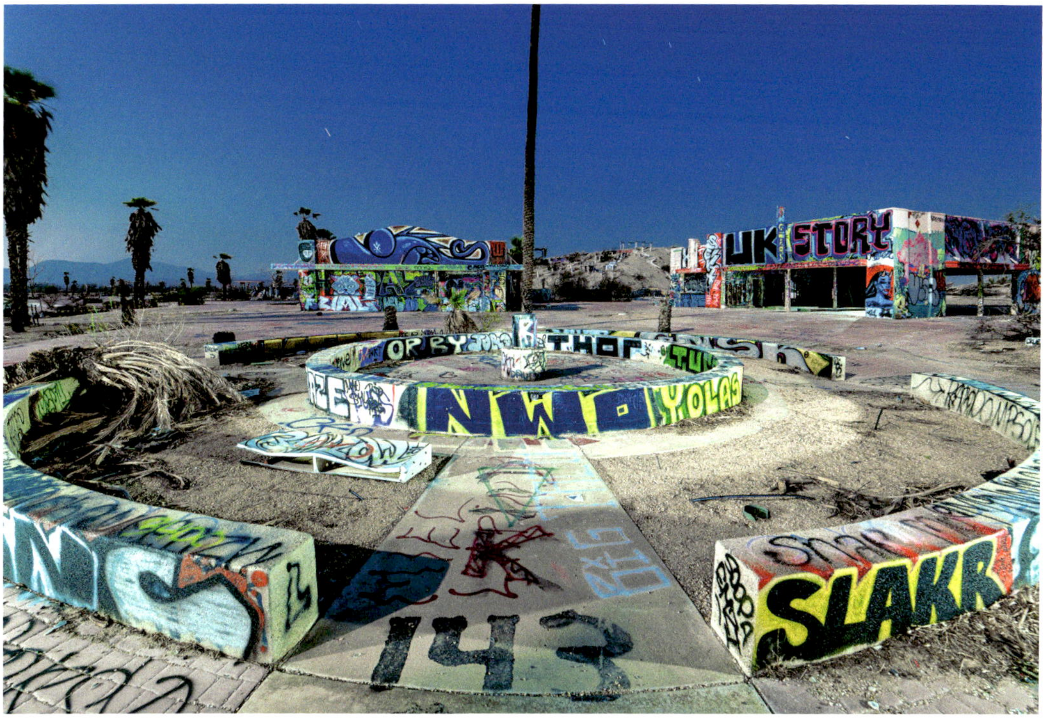

▲ **The Fountainhead** · The central fountain, Lake Dolores Waterpark, California. The former tube rental building is on the left and the locker room is to the right · Pentax K-1/15-30mm f/2.8 lens. 201 seconds f/8 ISO 200. August 2021 · Full moon, ProtoMachines LED2 with warm white light.

▶ **No TV Tonight** · Lake Dolores Waterpark, California · Pentax K-1/15-30mm f/2.8 lens. 3 minutes f/8 ISO 200. August 2021 · Full moon, ProtoMachines LED2 with warm white, yellow, blue, and red light.

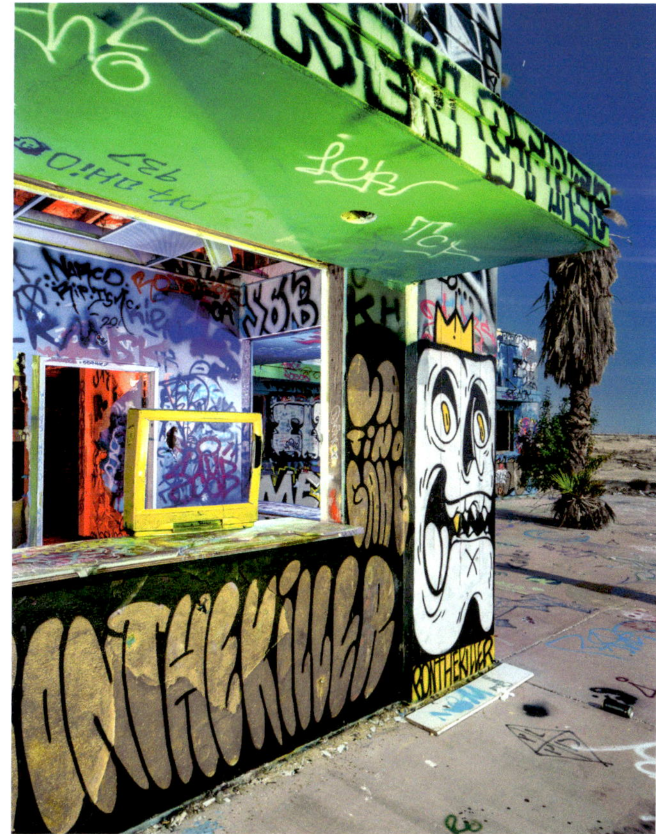

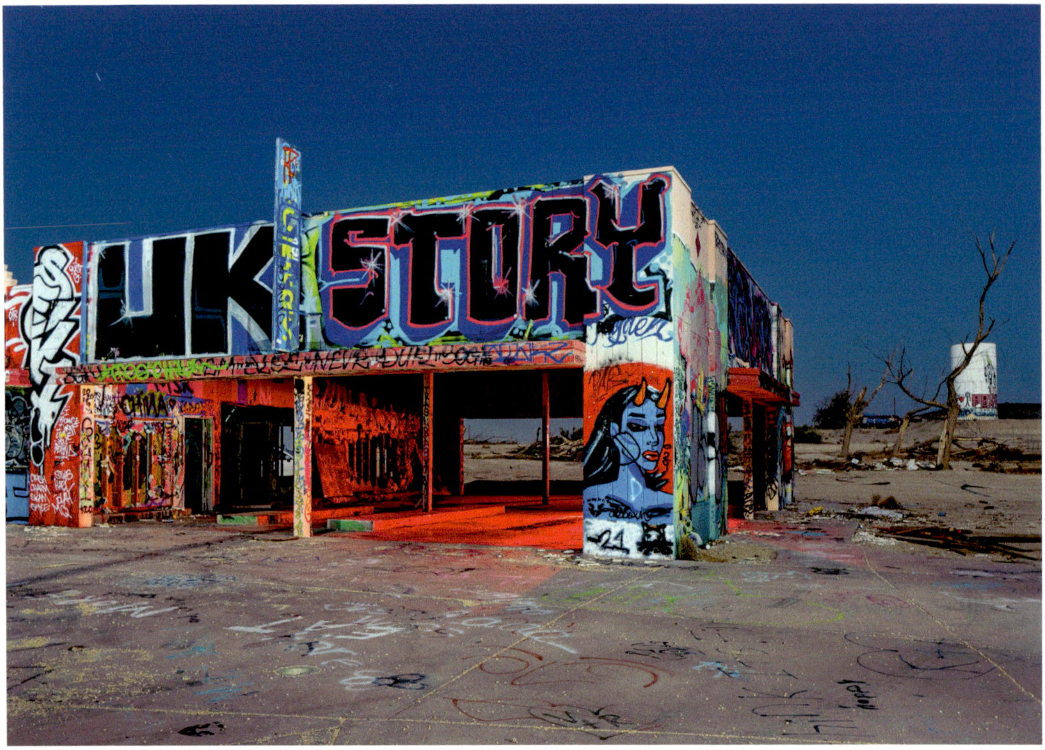

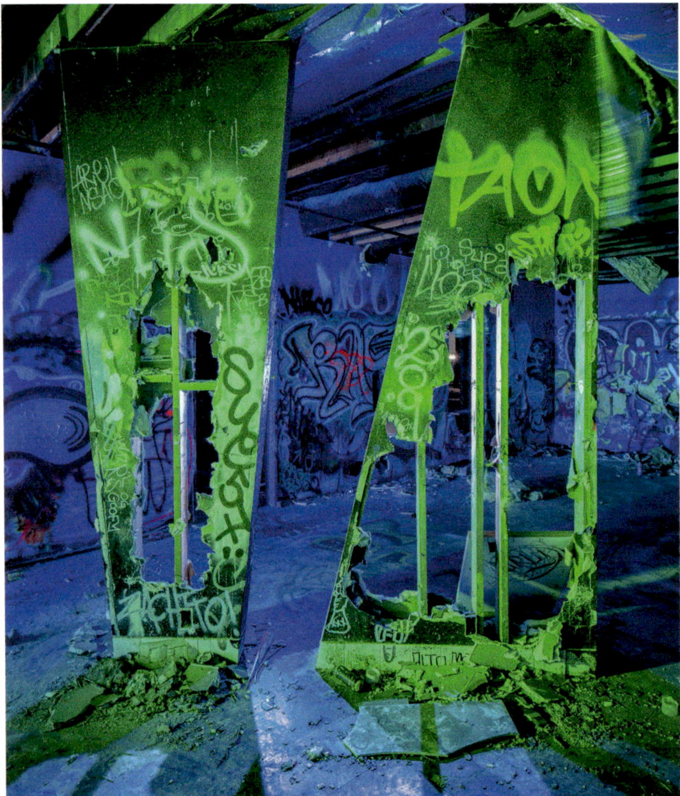

▲ **The Changing Room** · The former locker room, Lake Dolores Waterpark, California. In the distance is the white water tower, and to the left of that, the abandoned house where the caretaker was staying · Pentax K-1/15-30mm f/2.8 lens. 3 minutes f/8 ISO 200. August 2021 · Full moon, ProtoMachines LED2 with warm white and red light.

◄ **Pillars of Orion** · Inside the former arcade at Lake Dolores Waterpark, California · Pentax K-1/15-30mm f/2.8 lens. 115 seconds f/8 ISO 200. August 2021 · Full moon, ProtoMachines LED2 with green and blue light.

► **Breonna** · A painting of a beautiful woman on the side of the former arcade, Lake Dolores Waterpark, California · Pentax K-1/15-30mm f/2.8 lens. 3 minutes f/8 ISO 200. August 2021 · Full moon, ProtoMachines LED2 with warm white and blue light.

▼ **We're Low On Inner Tubes Right Now** · The former tube rental building, Lake Dolores Waterpark, California · Pentax K-1/15-30mm f/2.8 lens. 3 minutes f/8 ISO 200. August 2021 · Full moon, ProtoMachines LED2 with warm white and blue light.

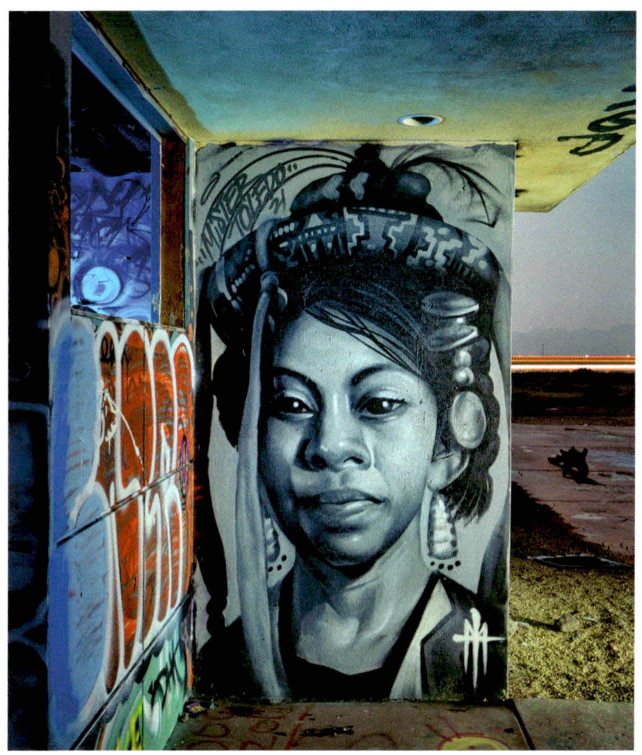

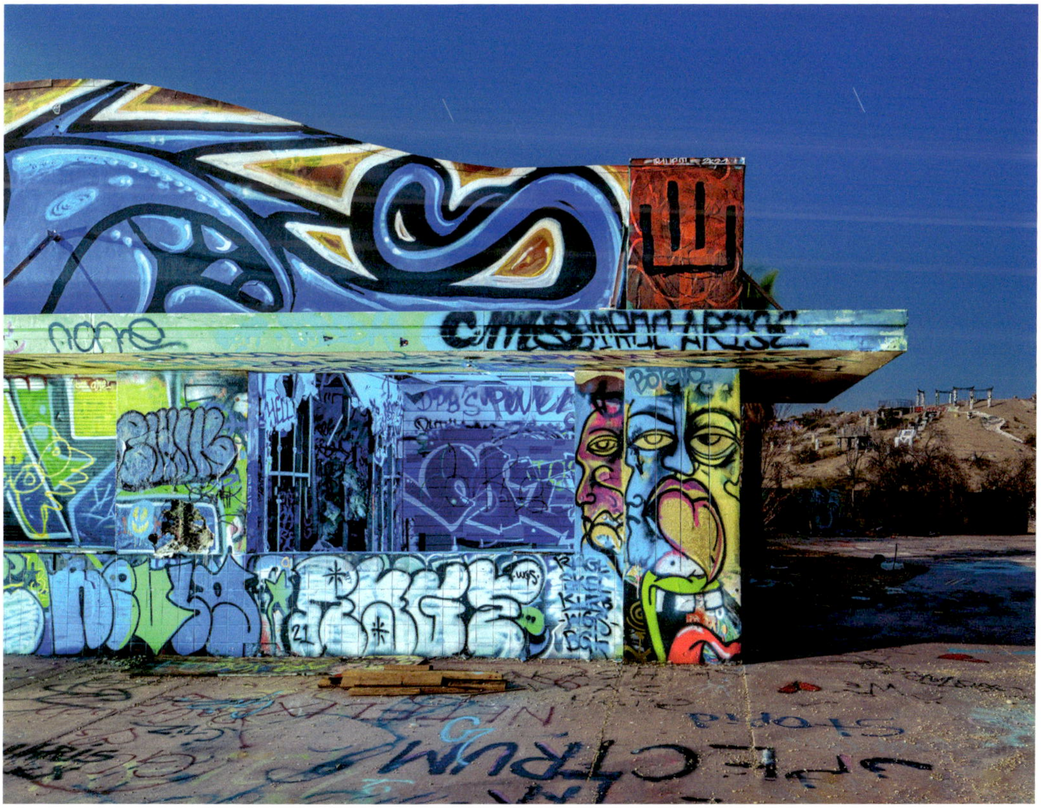

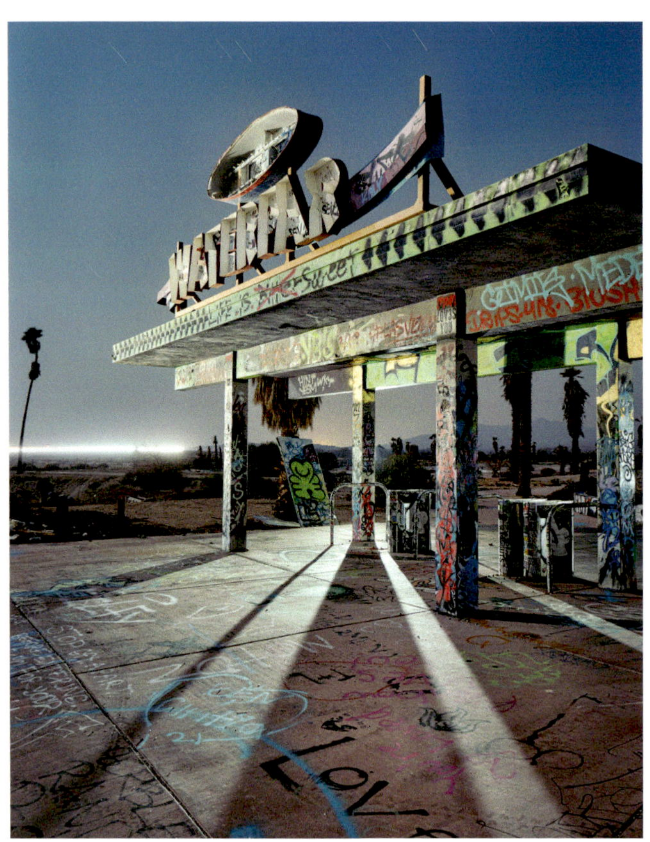

◀ **Smoke on the Water** · Shadowplay with the waterpark entrance, Lake Dolores Waterpark, California, with I-15 lighting up the horizon · Pentax K-1/15-30mm f/2.8 lens. 6 minutes total "stacked." Each photo 3 minutes f/8 ISO 200. August 2021 · Full moon, ProtoMachines LED2 with warm white light.

▼ **Rock-a-Loo-La** · The restroom is the oldest building at Lake Dolores Waterpark, California, perhaps due to being built like a brick, er, well, you know · Pentax K-1/15-30mm f/2.8 lens. 170 seconds f/8 ISO 200. August 2021 · Full moon, ProtoMachines LED2 with warm white and red light.

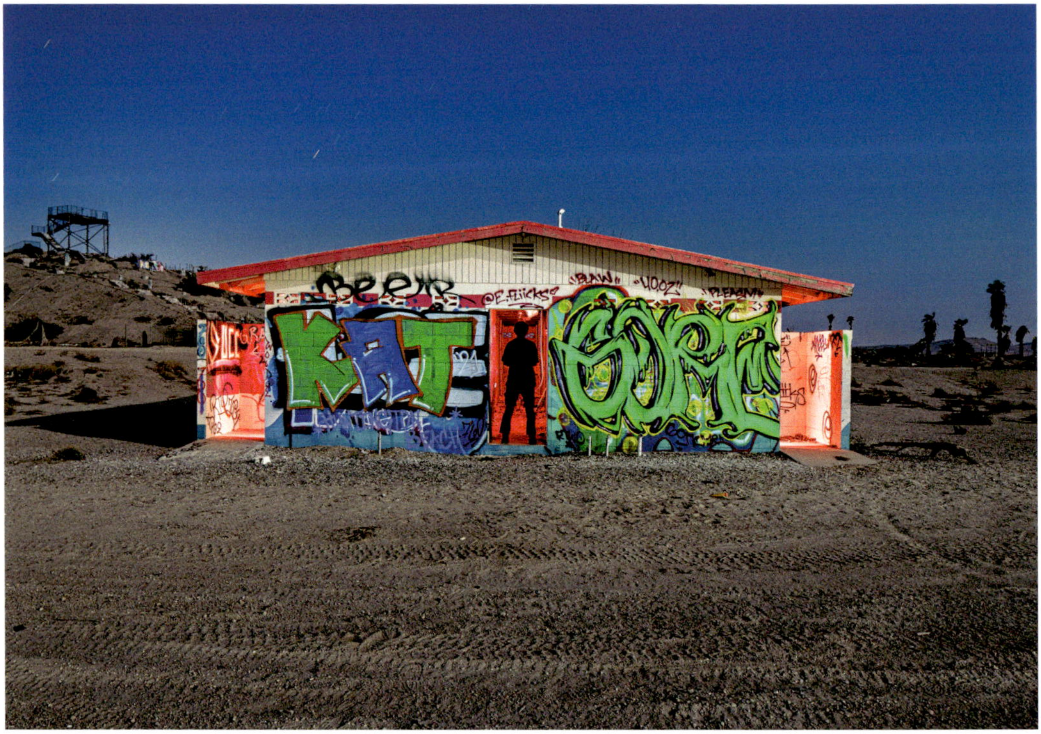

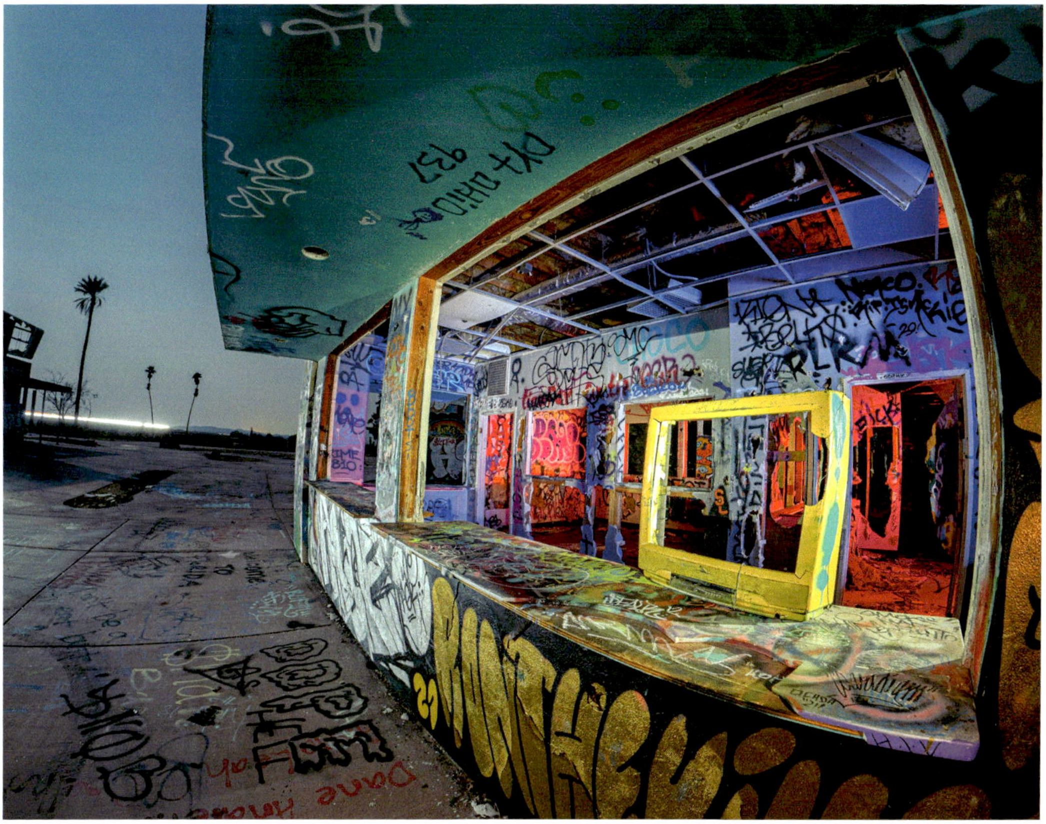

▲ **Morning Cartoons** · Lake Dolores Waterpark, California · Nikon D750/ Rokinon 12mm f/2.8 fisheye lens. 233 seconds f/8 ISO 200. August 2021 · Full moon, ProtoMachines LED2 with warm white, yellow, blue, and red light.

► **Regalos** · The former gift shop, Lake Dolores Waterpark, California · Pentax K-1/15-30mm f/2.8 lens. 3 minutes f/8 ISO 200. August 2021 · Full moon, ProtoMachines LED2 with warm white light.

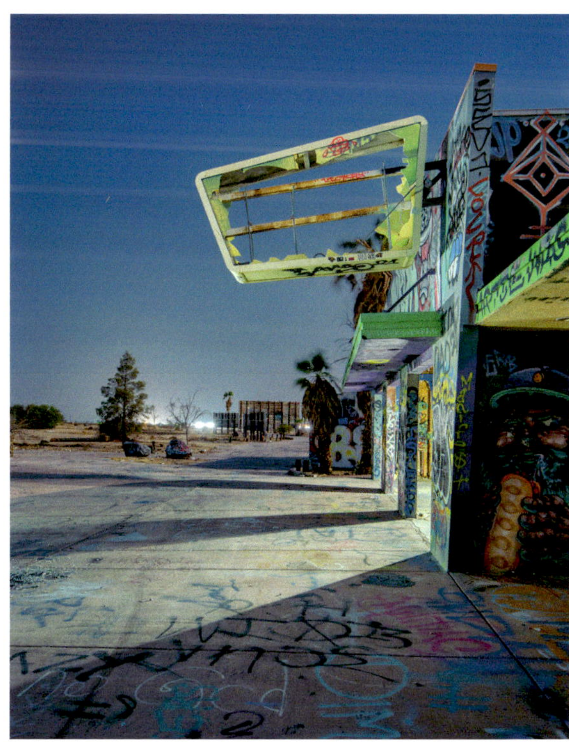

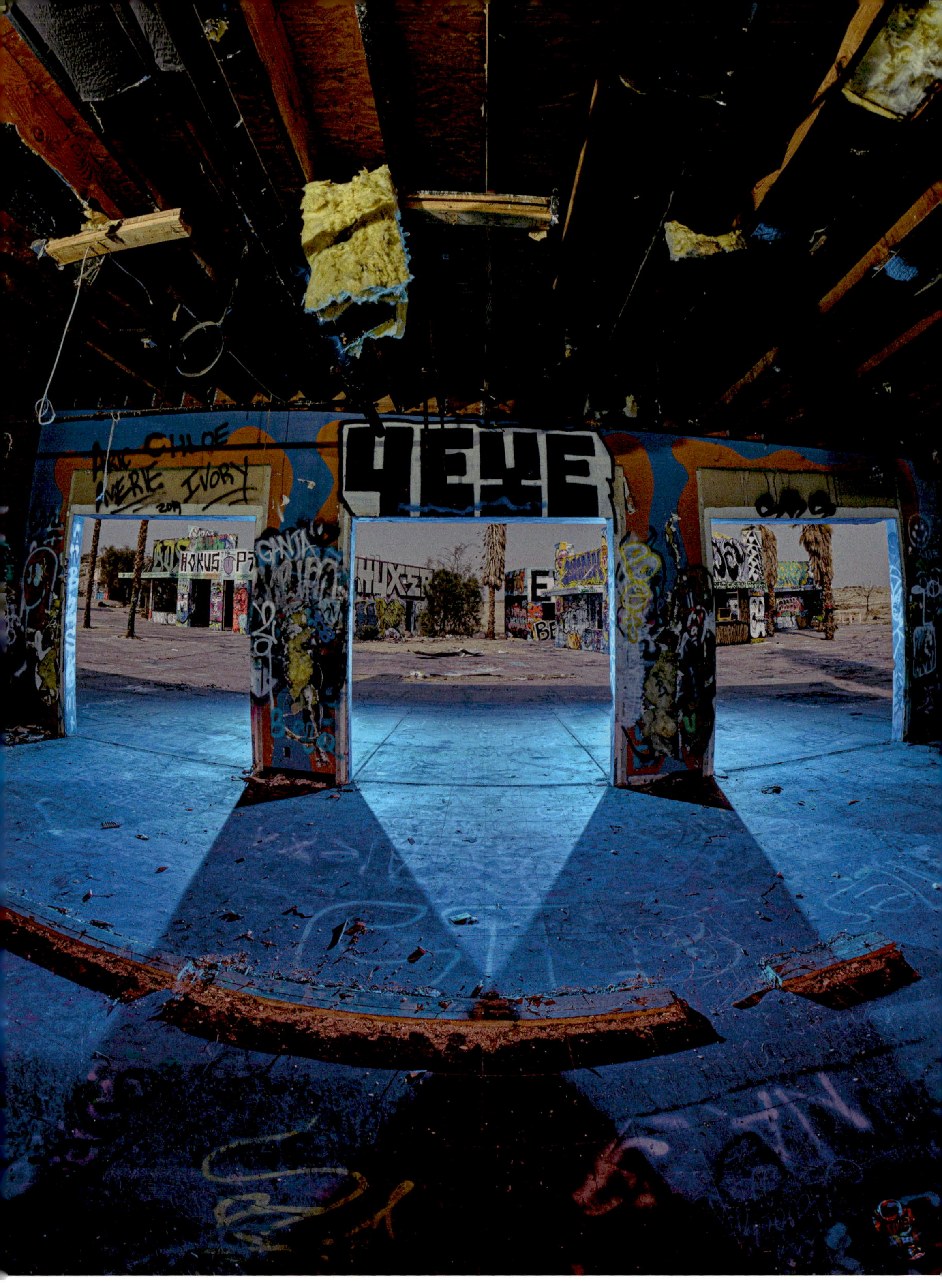

Quarter Sucker en Bleu · Inside the arcade, Lake Dolores Waterpark, California · Nikon D750/Rokinon 12mm f/2.8 fisheye lens. 190 seconds f/8 ISO 200. August 2021 · Full moon, ProtoMachines LED2 with warm white and blue light

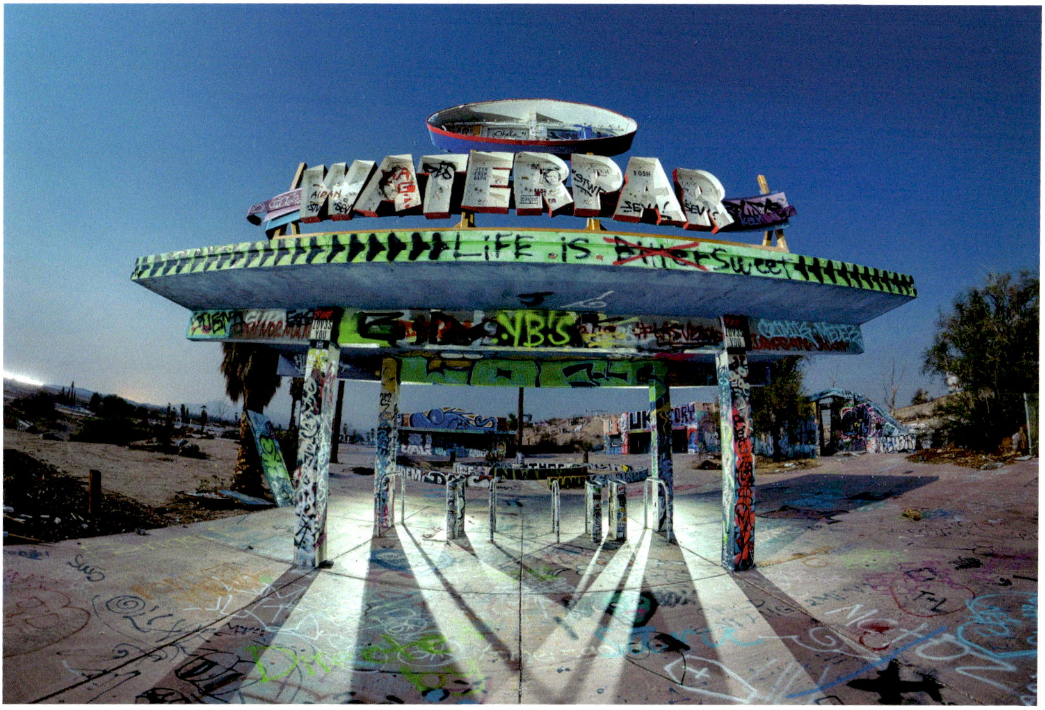

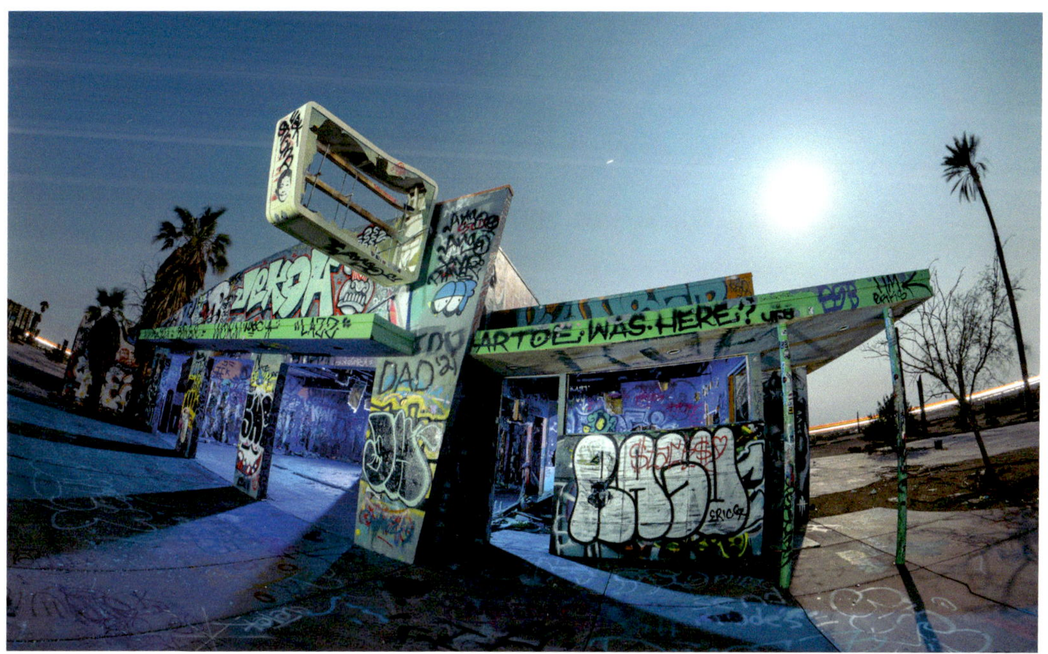

Waterpar · Fisheye view of the main sign and entrance for Lake Dolores Waterpark, California · Nikon D750/ Rokinon 12mm f/2.8 fisheye lens. 3 minutes f/8 ISO 200. August 2021 · Full moon, ProtoMachines LED2 with warm white light.

Blue Evening, Blue Day · The arcade, Lake Dolores Waterpark, California · Nikon D750/Rokinon 12mm f/2.8 fisheye lens. 210 seconds f/8 ISO 200. August 2021 · Full moon, ProtoMachines LED2 with warm white and blue light.

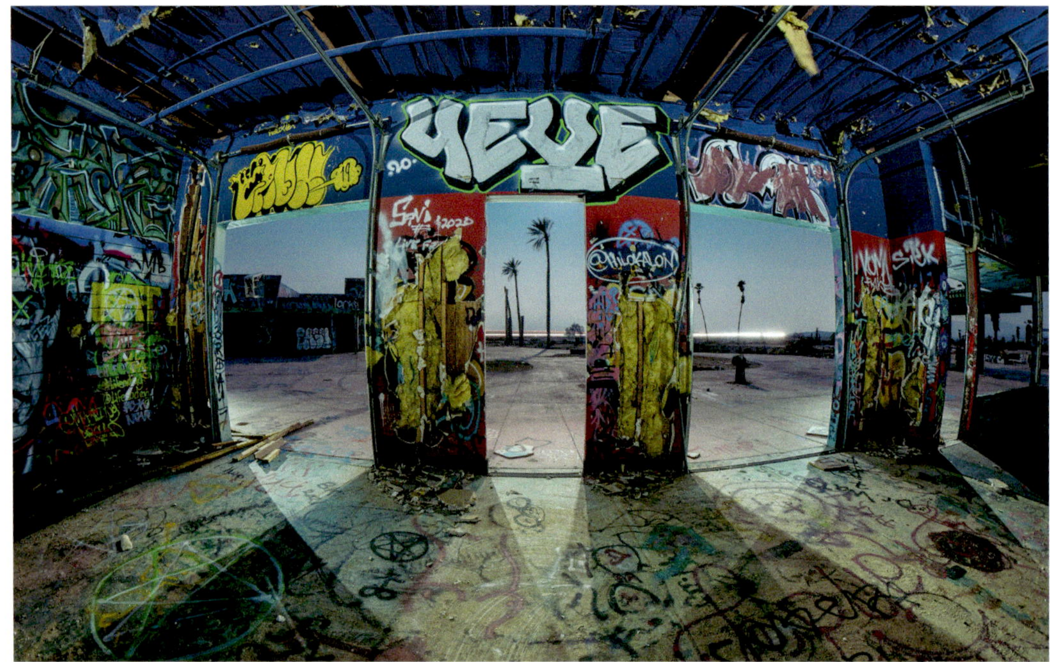

In the Glow of the Mojave Freeway · Lake Dolores Waterpark, California. As the caretaker said, the ghost inside the gift shop never bothered me · Nikon D750/Rokinon 12mm f/2.8 fisheye lens. 220 seconds f/8 ISO 200. August 2021 · Full moon, ProtoMachines LED2 with warm white light.

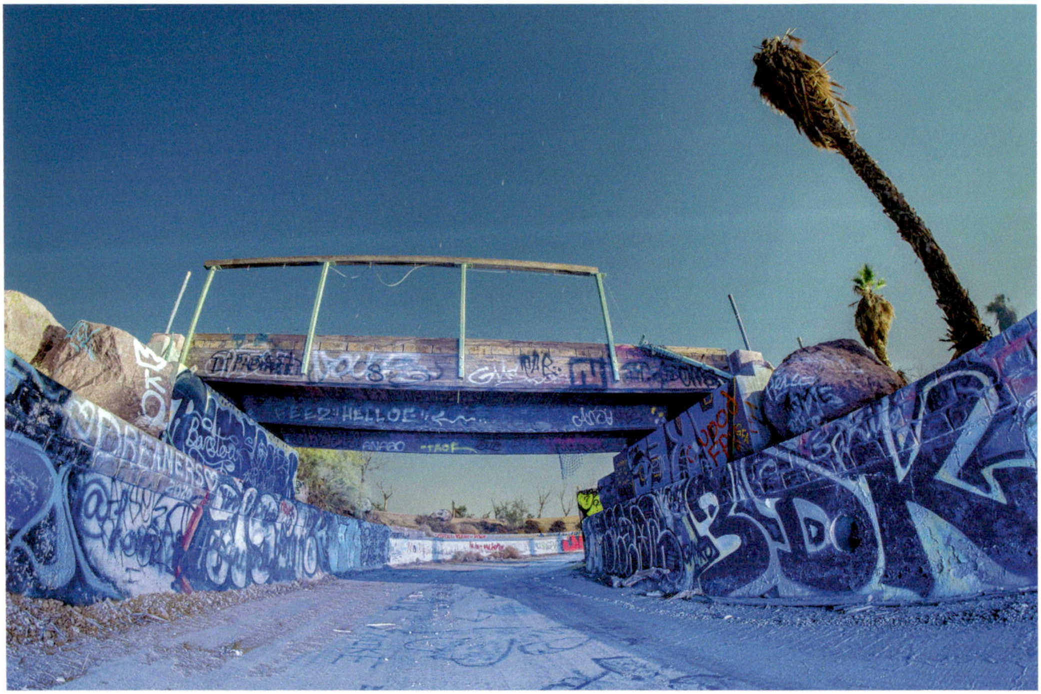

A Bridge over Troubled Water · In one of the water canals at Lake Dolores Waterpark, California · Nikon D750/ Rokinon 12mm f/2.8 fisheye lens. 194 seconds f/8 ISO 200. August 2021 · Full moon, ProtoMachines LED2 with warm white and blue light.

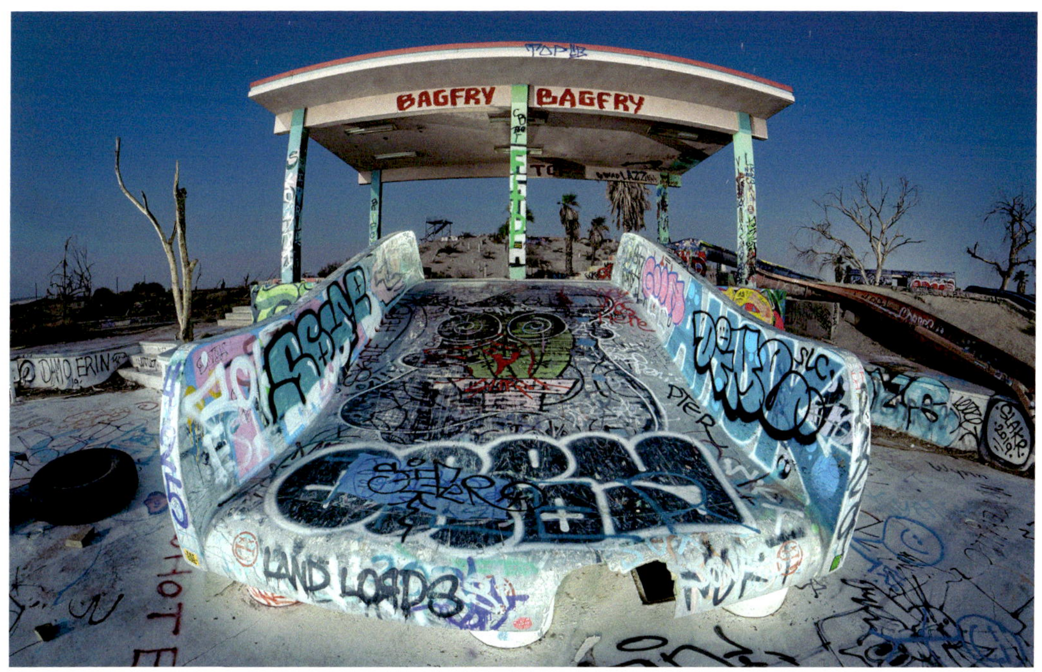

Let Slip The Dogs of Water · Waterslide, Lake Dolores Waterpark, California · Nikon D750/Rokinon 12mm f/2.8 fisheye lens. 227 seconds f/8 ISO 200. August 2021 · Full moon, ProtoMachines LED2 with warm white light.

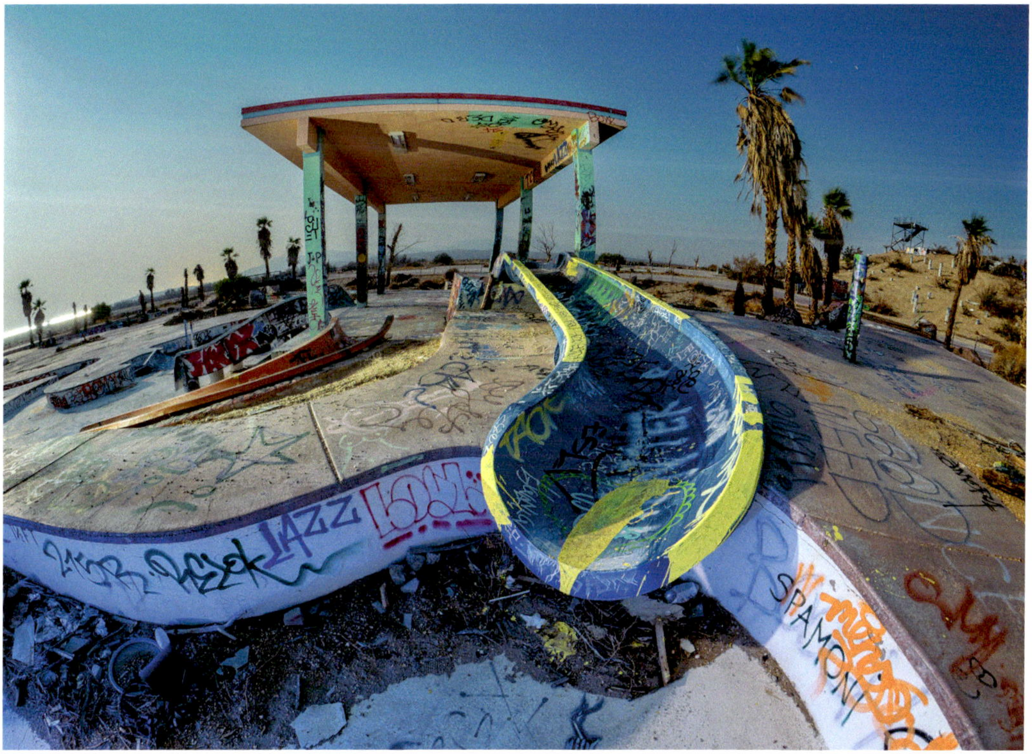

The Curve of Forgetting · Waterslide, Lake Dolores Waterpark, California · Nikon D750/Rokinon 12mm f/2.8 fisheye lens. 332 seconds f/8 ISO 200. August 2021 · Full moon, ProtoMachines LED2 with warm white and blue light.

5

SANTA'S VILLAGE, CALIFORNIA

The original Santa's Village, a storybook-style Christmas theme park nestled among the pine trees in the San Bernardino Mountains on the way to popular Lake Arrowhead, opened in 1955, just six weeks before the opening of Disneyland. At its apex, it was one of Southern California's biggest tourist attractions, drawing almost 180,000 visitors per year. Principal investor Glenn Holland was encouraged by this success and subsequently opened Santa's Village parks in Santa Cruz, California, and Dundee, Illinois. These were the first franchised theme parks in the United States.

Santa's Village offered a train ride through the forest, winterland workshops, a ride in horse-drawn pumpkin carriages, and sleighs pulled by reindeer. It even boasted a Bumblebee Monorail ride. This would later be used as a model for a larger-scale monorail at New York City's 1964 World's Fair.

It closed in 1998, largely the victim of a recession. Despite logging in the areas, a devastating wildfire known as "The Old Fire," as well as the usual vandals and thieves, most of the whimsical structures somehow remained standing.

In 2016, I stumbled across a video describing the abandoned Santa's Village. I immediately wanted to explore and photograph it, only to discover that there were plans to rebuild it. I emailed Bill Johnson. He was a mountain resident whose first job had been at the original Santa's Village. He was now a real estate developer, working seemingly around the clock to get it going again.

Bill replied, "Thanks for the interest in photographing the park. The park is under repair at the moment and it's kinda top secret. It's like Walt Disney not showing Main Street until its completion. We would be happy to have you photograph the park after its completion."

I had conflicting emotions. Of course, I was happy that it was being given new life. And I was overjoyed that Bill liked my night photography and wanted me to photograph it later. But I might miss the window of opportunity for photographing and documenting the abandoned areas.

Bill greeted me at the gate on an early evening some months later. I had complete access to the interior. It would still be many months until Santa's Village opened, so I was honored that I was even there. Bill wanted no money for this, so I offered to let him use some of my night photos instead. He had seen my photos online and was excited about the opportunity.

Almost to the second that night fell, a thick blanket of fog slipped in, and with that, everything also grew darker and darker. There would be no starry skies that evening.

However, I was here. I was determined to make lemonade out of lemons. I used my handheld light to light the very air around me while the camera shutter was open during the long exposure, adding an aura of mystique and eeriness. After an hour or so, Bill walked up to see how I was doing.

"It's going well, and I'm having a lot of fun, thanks. However, I don't think you are going to want to use any of these photos!"

"Oh, why not?"

"Well, uh, they're looking very eerie due to the fog. I don't know that slapping creepy-looking photos on your website is the way to lure in guests!"

Upon seeing the photos on the back of the camera, he burst out laughing. "Yes, I think you're probably right!"

As I thought, the original buildings were being repaired and restored. Still, though, they weren't completed. And Bill had left the old Bumblebee Monorail track and some of the original cars there. He would not be using these again due to new safety laws. Some of the original buildings, such as the Gingerbread House and winterland chalets, looked intact.

I said my goodbyes that evening. He was inside one of the new buildings, sawing logs that would be used for a railing. "I hope I didn't keep you up too long," I said. "No worries," he replied, "I'm going to be working on this for quite a while longer!"

Bill and his crew worked a total of thirty months to open SkyPark at Santa's Village. Far more than just a Santa's Village, you can pedal, zipline, hike, climb, and camp there now. There are live shows, wheelchair rentals, fishing, glamping, RV parks, and restaurants as well. As you might guess, the park is open all year.

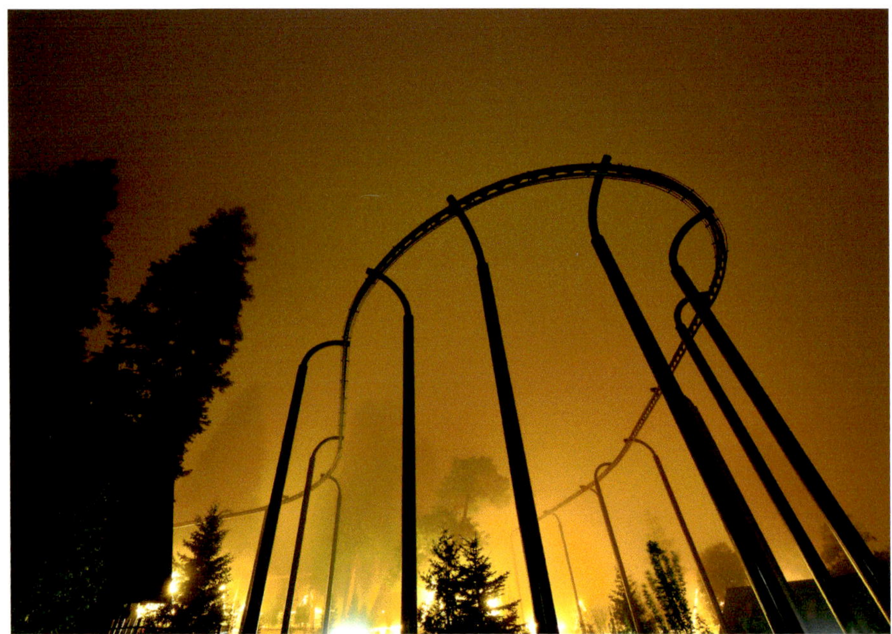

You Take the Skyway · The old Bumblebee Monorail Ride at Santa's Village, Skyforest, California. This would later be used as a model for a larger-scale monorail at New York City's 1964 World's Fair · Nikon D610/14-24mm f/2.8G ED lens. 296 seconds f/8 ISO 200. May 2016 · Full moon heavily diffused through fog, work lights from construction.

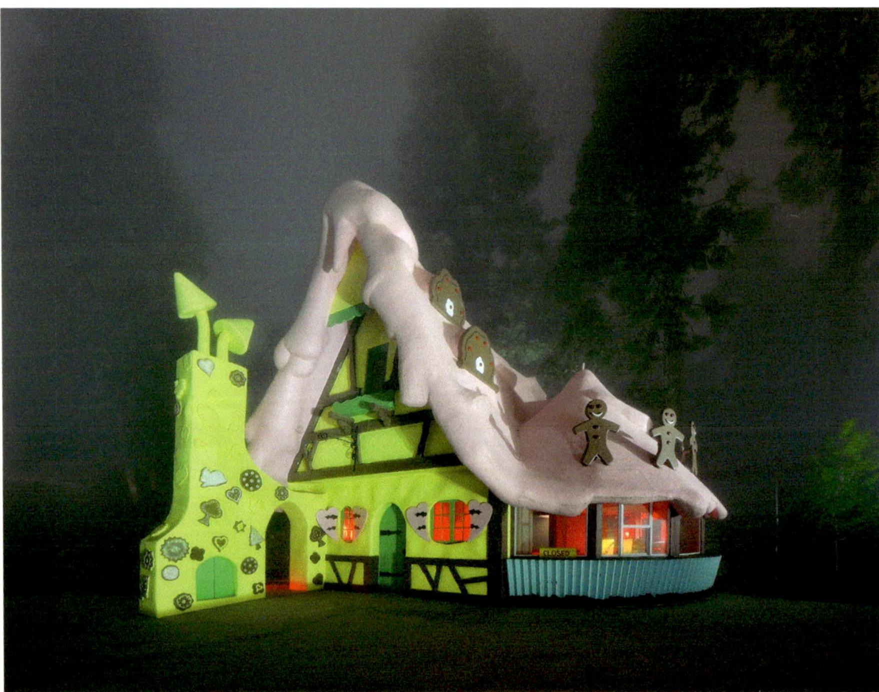

The Gingerbread House of Fog · The old Gingerbread house at Santa's Village, Skyforest, California, enshrouded in thick mountain fog · Nikon D610/14-24mm f/2.8G ED lens. 231 seconds f/8 ISO 200. May 2016 · Full moon heavily diffused through fog, ProtoMachines LED2 with warm white and red light.

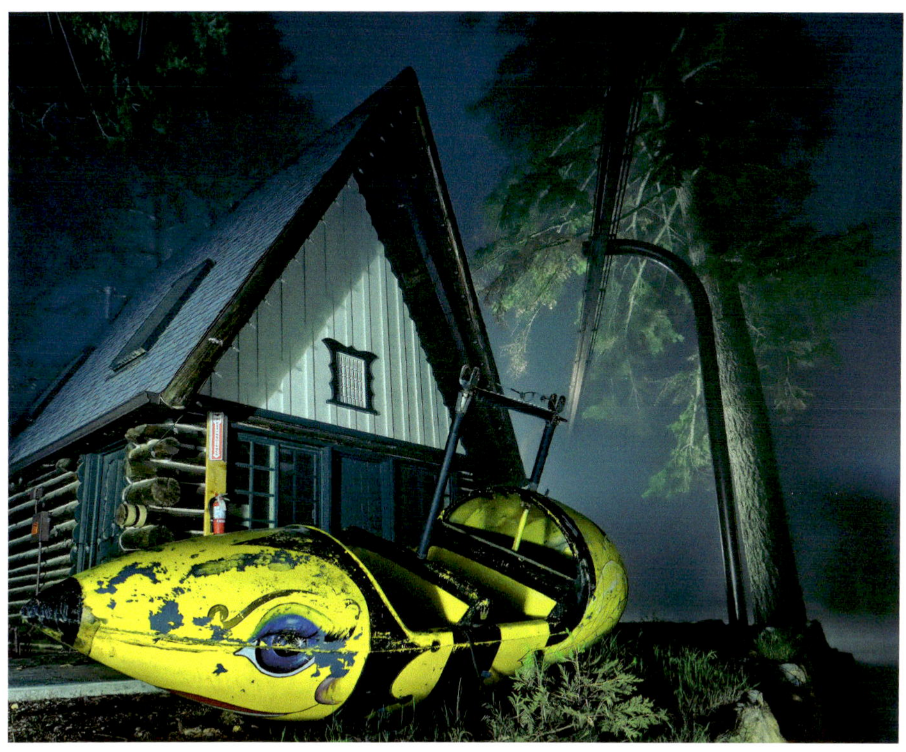

Honey and Dew · The old Bumblebee Monorail Ride at Santa's Village, Skyforest, California. When fog is present, I love lighting it for an extra dose of eeriness · Nikon D610/14-24mm f/2.8G ED lens. 111 seconds f/8 ISO 200. May 2016 · Full moon heavily diffused through fog, ProtoMachines LED2 with warm white light.

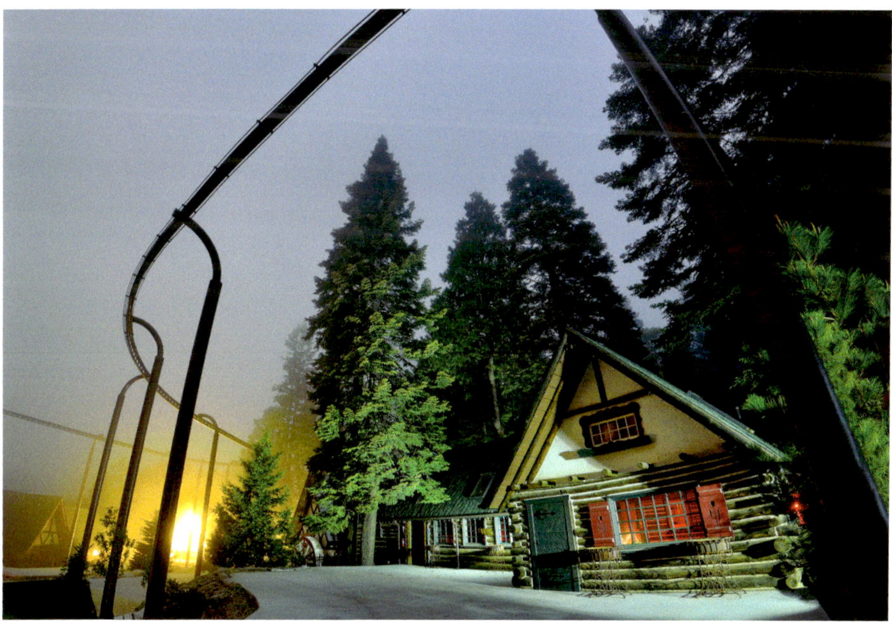

Bumblebee Woodlands · The old Bumblebee Monorail Ride at Santa's Village, Skyforest, California · Nikon D610/14-24mm f/2.8G ED lens. 368 seconds f/8 ISO 200. May 2016 · Full moon heavily diffused through fog, ProtoMachines LED2 with warm white light, worklights from construction.

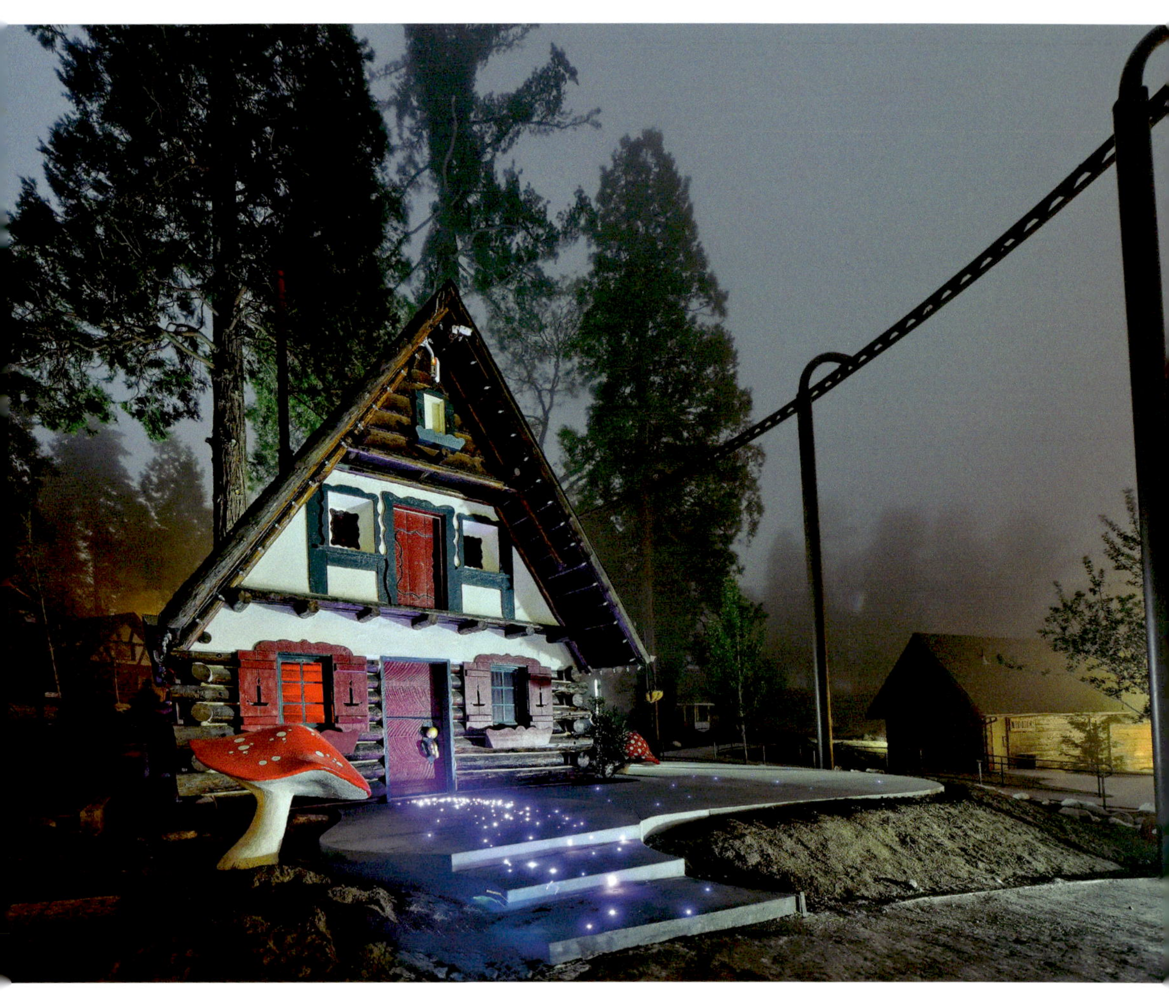

Santa's Magic Mountain Home · Santa's Village, Skyforest, California · Nikon D610/14-24mm f/2.8G ED lens. 156 seconds f/8 ISO 200. May 2016 · Full moon heavily diffused through fog, ProtoMachines LED2 with warm white and red light, tiny blue LED lights on walkway, worklights from construction.

6

NELSON GHOST TOWN, NEVADA

The allure of quick money from mines always attracts colorful characters. This certainly is what happened when the Spanish discovered gold in Eldorado Canyon in the Mojave Desert in Nevada. This drew the inevitable desperados, prospectors, deserters from the Union and Confederate armies, weirdos, murderers, and thieves, lured by visions of unimaginable riches. "El Dorado" means "the gilded one," although it is often used as a metaphor for great wealth and opportunity, serving as the name for a fabled lost gold city in South America.

Techatticup Mine was established in the middle of the canyon around 1858. The mine grew to have a dark reputation given the frequent killings over ownership and more. However, at its height, it was the largest and most productive mine in its district before closing in the mid-1940s.

A road was built in the area, benefiting the adjacent town of Nelson. The road eventually became Highway 165. A gas station sprang up. However, the town was eventually abandoned after a cataclysmic flash flood. Today, you can see some of the remnants of this former town, now a roadside attraction. Additionally, the owners offer guided tours through the Techatticup Mine.

While I was preparing to offer a night photography workshop there, I overheard a visitor asking if she should bring her dog on the mine tour.

One of the owners replied, "There's a section that's a sheer 100-foot drop over the railing."

"So, what do you think? Should I?"

Techatticup, or Nelson Ghost Town, as it's now more commonly called, now boasts quite a collection of Old Western buildings and vintage Americana. It also has an incredible, continually changing collection of vintage automobiles, trucks, buses, and more. A few of these vehicles have been reimagined as odd creations, some looking like they were yanked from a *Mad Max* movie.

The enticing combination of the collected and the abandoned has become a magnet for photo shoots, weddings, and even movies. *3000 Miles to Graceland* was filmed here. The scene in which Kevin Costner's character blows up a gas station was filmed in Nelson. The film crew also planted an airplane nose-down in the ground to simulate a crashed plane. That's still there. So is the gas station.

This is one of my favorite places to photograph at night because of its incredible collection of vintage gas pumps, airplanes, rusty vintage automobiles, old Western buildings, giant neon motel signs, and more. And for the very same reasons, it's also one of my favorite places to teach night photography workshops.

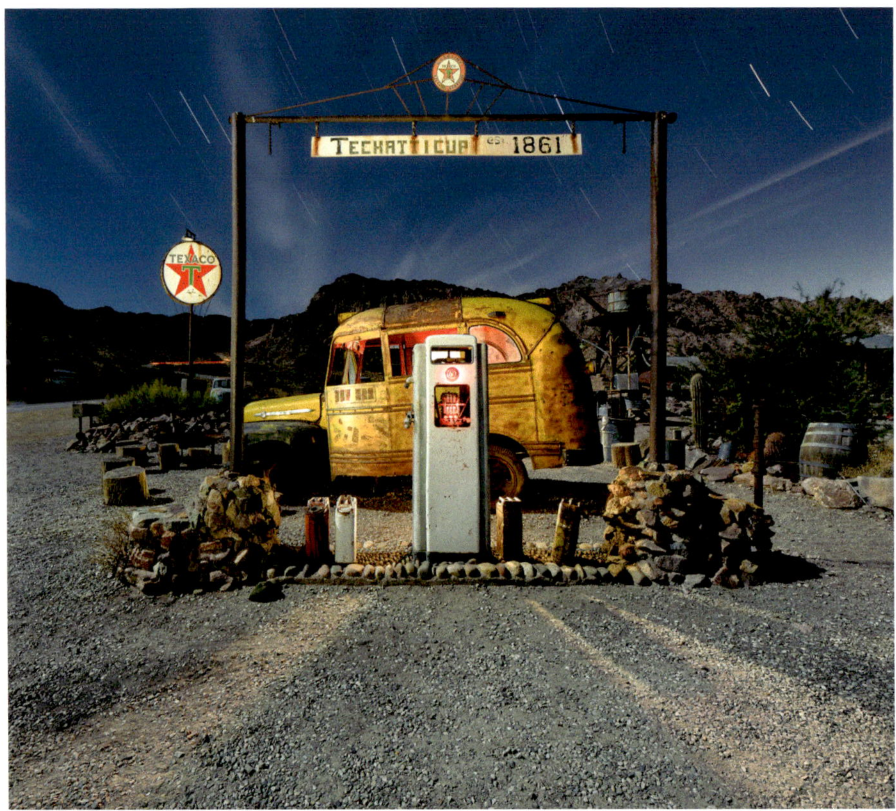

Filling Up at Techatticup · The shortest school bus I have ever seen. Still, it could be turned into a really cool RV. I created some long shadows through backlighting with my handheld light. Techatticup/ Nelson Ghost Town, Nevada · Nikon D750/14-24mm f/2.8 lens. 18 minutes total "stacked"; each photo 3 minutes f/8 ISO 320 October 2019 · Full moon, ProtoMachines LED2 with warm white light.

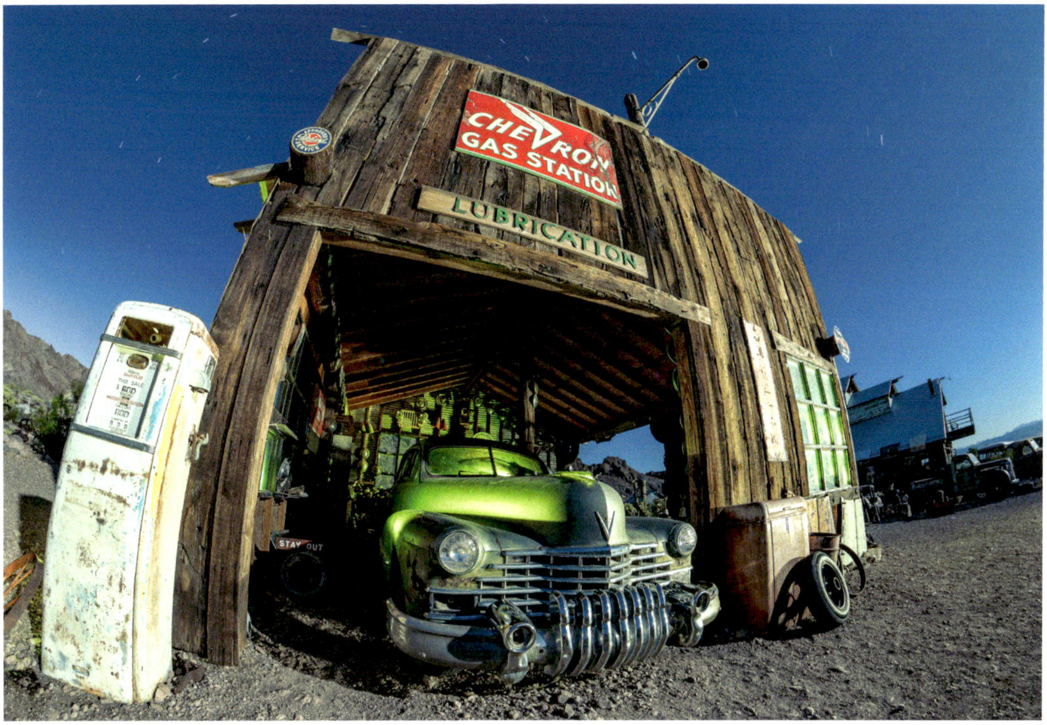

Late Night Lubrication · Fisheye night view of a 1940s Cadillac Fleetwood with a vintage Buick grille. Techatticup/Nelson Ghost Town, Nevada · Nikon D750/Rokinon 12mm f/2.8 fisheye lens. 310 seconds f/8 ISO 200. July 2019 · Full moon, ProtoMachines LED2 with warm white and green light.

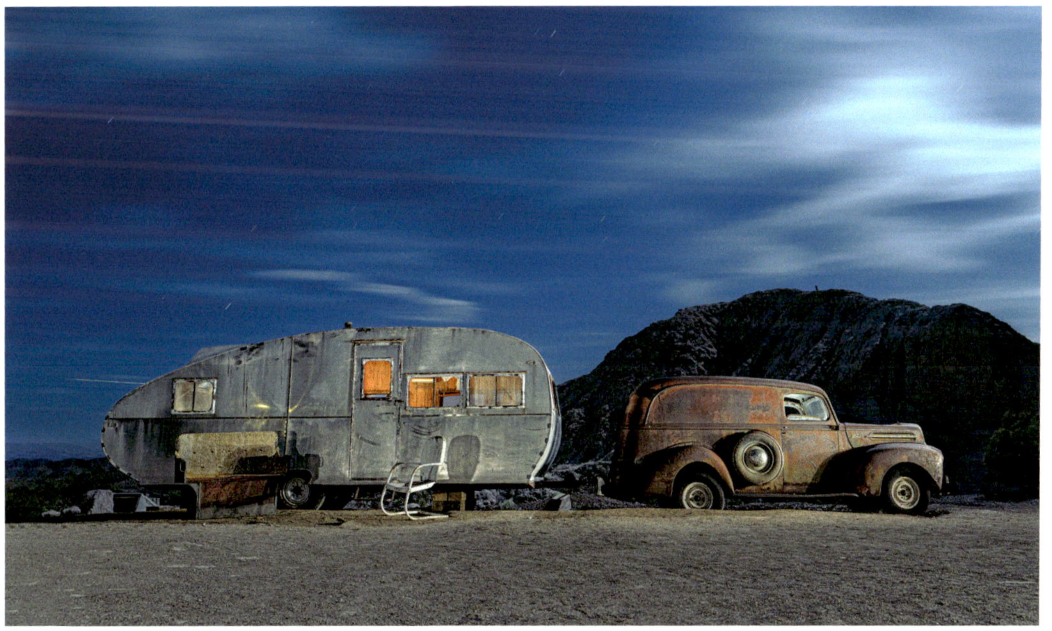

La Caravana Nocturna · Night camping with an old camper and a rusty Ford. Techatticup/Nelson Ghost Town, Nevada · Pentax K-1/28-105mm f/3.5-5.6 lens. 2 minutes f/8 ISO 200. May 2023 · Full moon, ProtoMachines LED2 with warm white light.

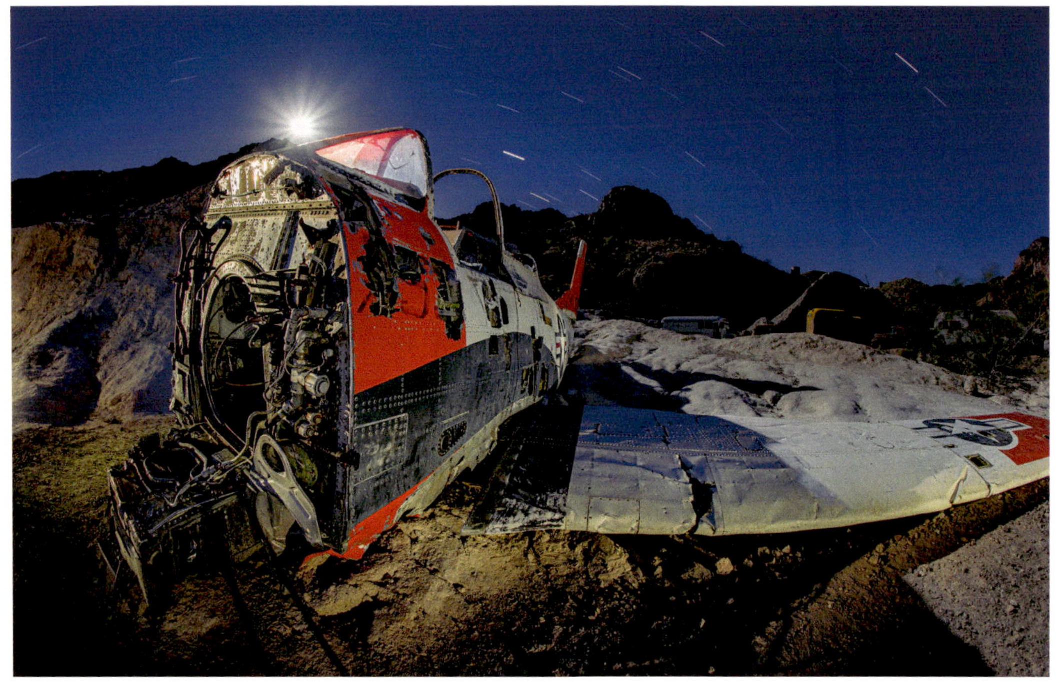

Trojan Man · Night photo of an old T-28 Trojan navy trainer. Techatticup/Nelson Ghost Town, Nevada · Nikon D610/Rokinon 12mm f/2.8 fisheye lens. 14 minutes total exposures "stacked." Each photo 2 minutes f/8 ISO 200. July 2019 · Full moon, ProtoMachines LED2 with warm white light.

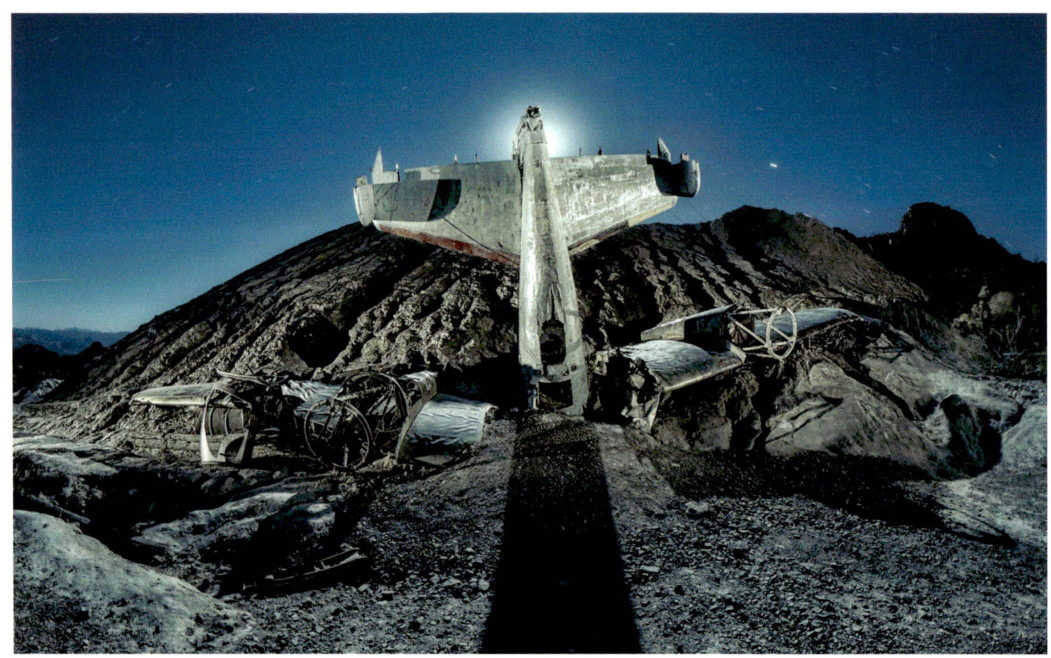

A Nose for the Dramatic · Is this the aftermath of a military plane crash? Nope. It's an old movie set built specifically for the 2001 film, *3000 Miles to Graceland*. I waited for the moon to drift behind the tail of the plane so it would cast long shadows. Techatticup/Nelson Ghost Town, Nevada · Nikon D610/Rokinon 12mm f/2.8 fisheye lens. 189 seconds f/8 ISO 200. July 2019 · Full moon, ProtoMachines LED2 with warm white light.

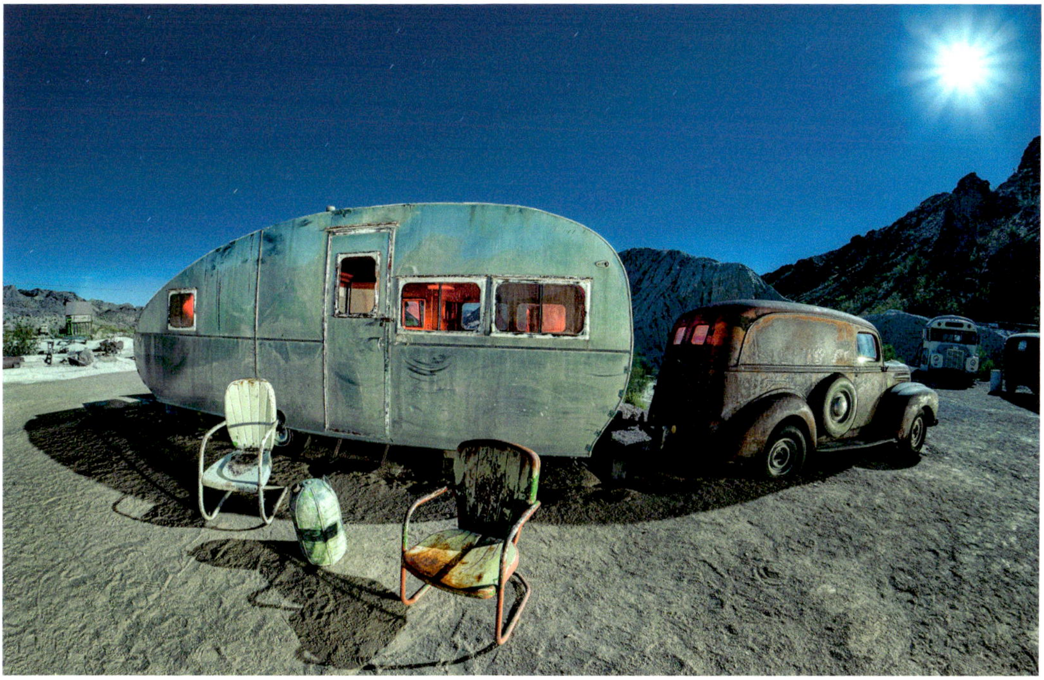

Moondocking · Night camping with an old camper and a rusty Ford, fisheye view. Techatticup/Nelson Ghost Town, Nevada · Nikon D610/Rokinon 12mm f/2.8 fisheye lens. 181 seconds f/8 ISO 200. July 2019 · Full moon, ProtoMachines LED2 with warm white light

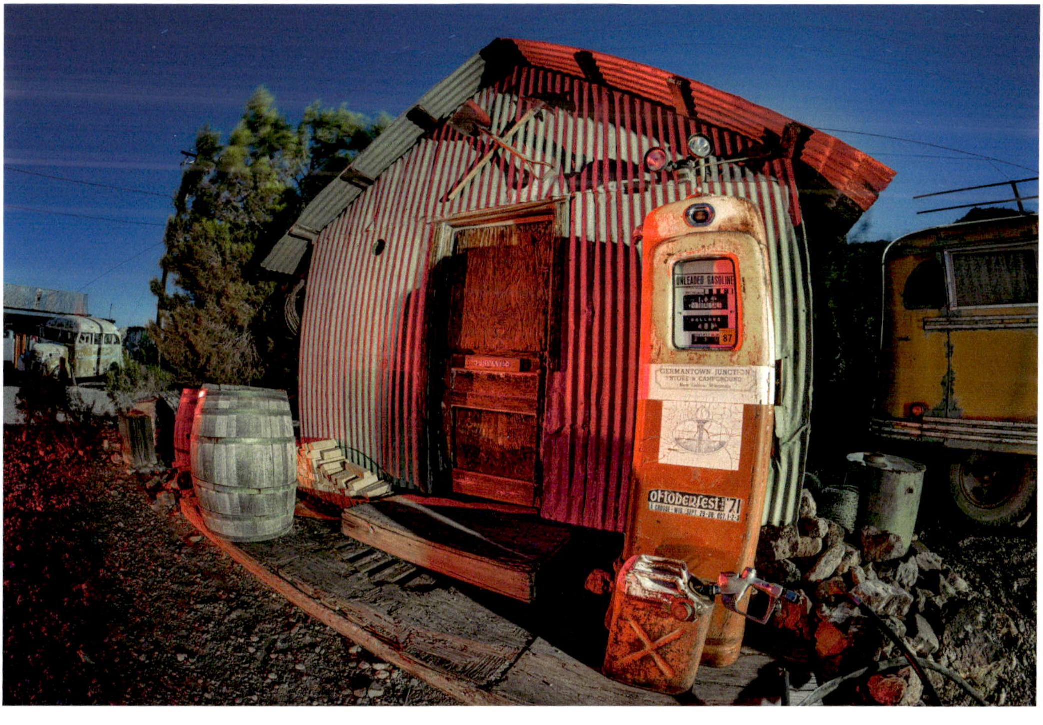

Germantown Unleaded · Techatticup/Nelson Ghost Town, Nevada · Nikon D610/Rokinon 12mm f/2.8 fisheye lens. 182 seconds f/8 ISO 200. July 2019 · Full moon, ProtoMachines LED2 with warm white and red light.

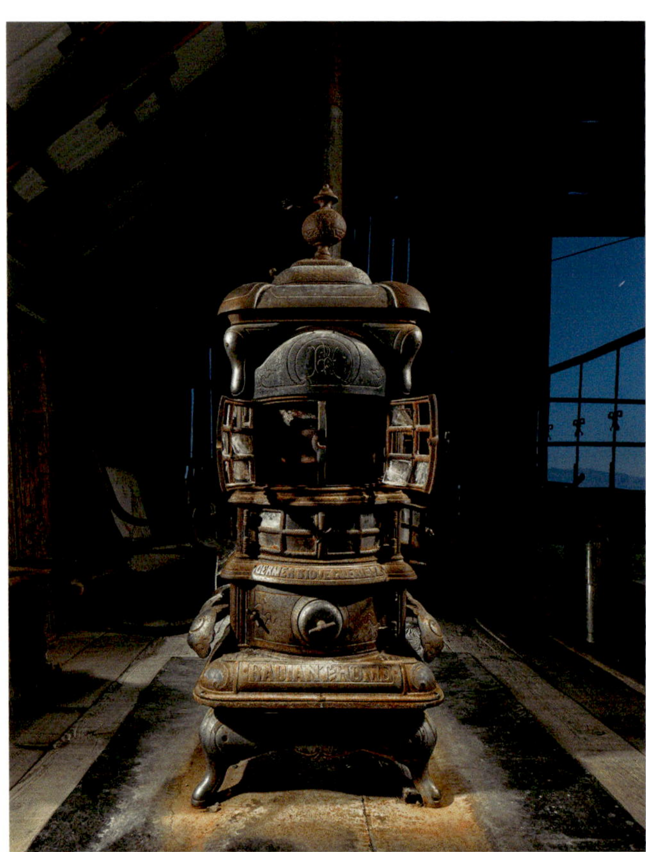

◀ **Home Sweet Radiant Home** · An exquisite cast iron Germer Radiant Stove, just as much a work of art as it is a stove. Techatticup/Nelson Ghost Town, Nevada. I lit the stove from the sides to "pull" it out from the dark interior · Nikon D610/Rokinon 12mm f/2.8 fisheye lens. 137 seconds f/8 ISO 320. July 2019 · Full moon, ProtoMachines LED2 with warm white light.

▼ **Out There** · Techatticup/Nelson Ghost Town, Nevada · Nikon D750/14-24mm f/2.8G ED lens. 10 minutes total "stacked". Each image 2 minutes f/8 ISO 200. October 2019 · Full moon, ProtoMachines LED2 with warm white and blue light.

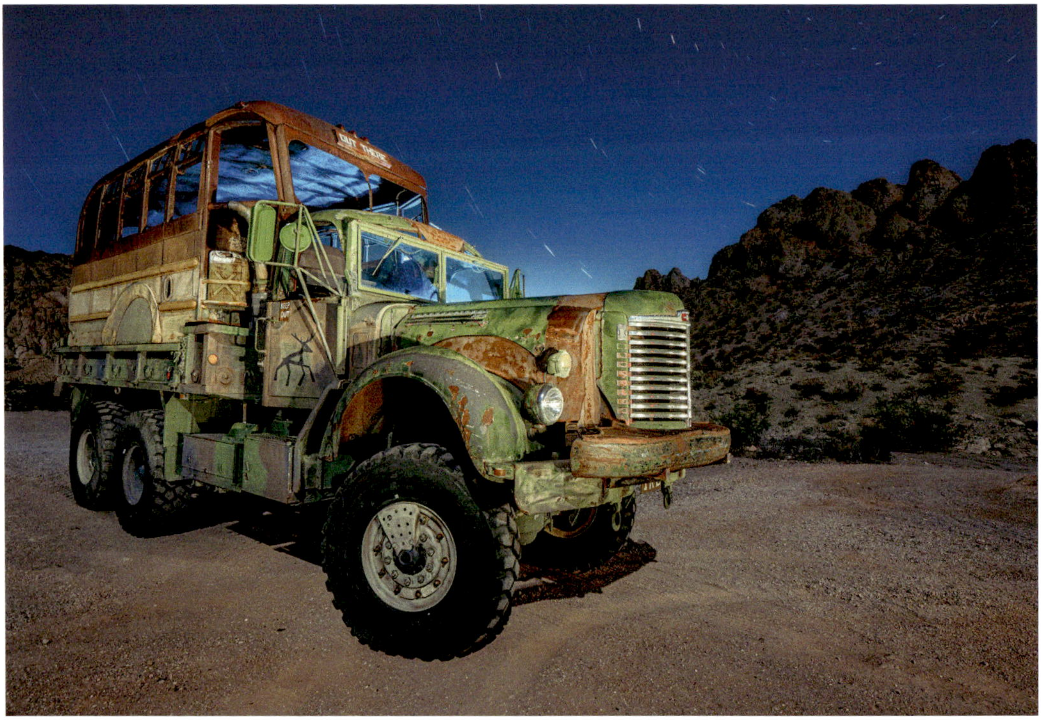

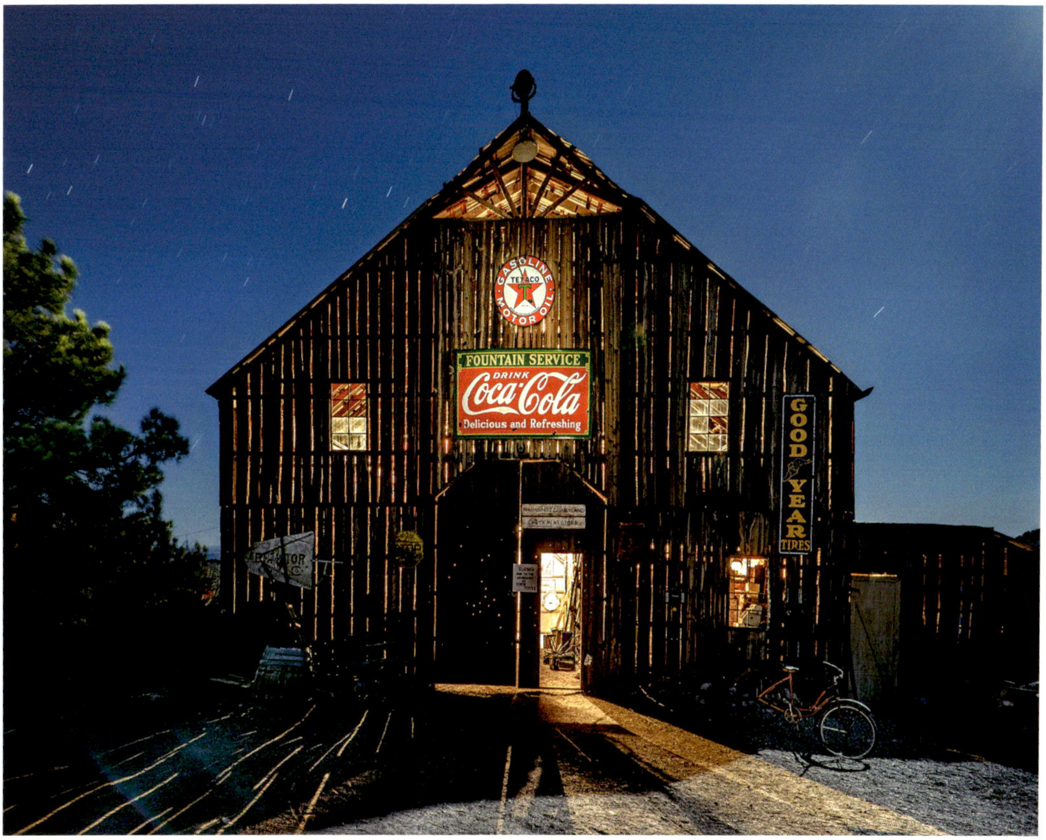

▲ **I Followed The Lights to the Mojave Barn**
· Techatticup/Nelson Ghost Town, Nevada ·
Nikon D750/14-24mm f/2.8G ED lens. 195
seconds f/8 ISO 320. October 2019 · Full
moon, ProtoMachines LED2 with warm white
light.

▶ **Phone Home** · More than phone home,
this is an all-out abduction in a lonesome
desert phone booth. Gratefully, I have no
strange marks to show for it. George Loo,
creator of the ProtoMachines light painting
devices, helped out immensely here with
lighting and suggestions. Techatticup/Nelson
Ghost Town, Nevada · Nikon D750/14-24mm
f/2.8G ED lens. 5 seconds f/4.5 ISO 4000.
October 2019 · Full moon, ProtoMachines
LED2 with warm white light.

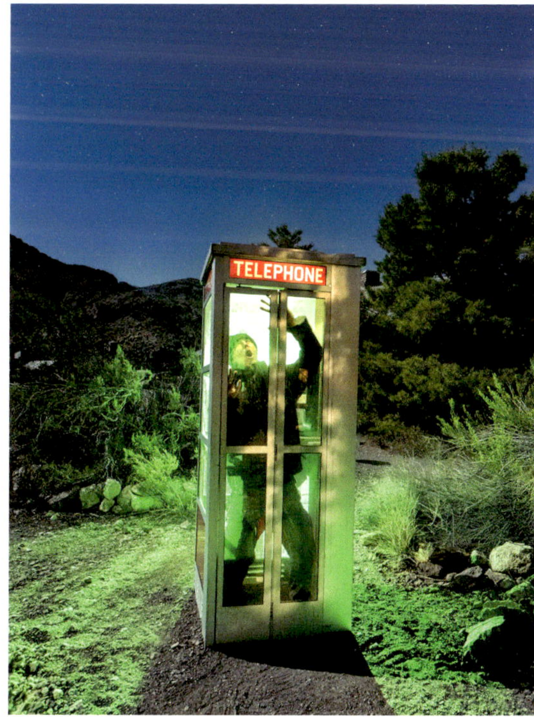

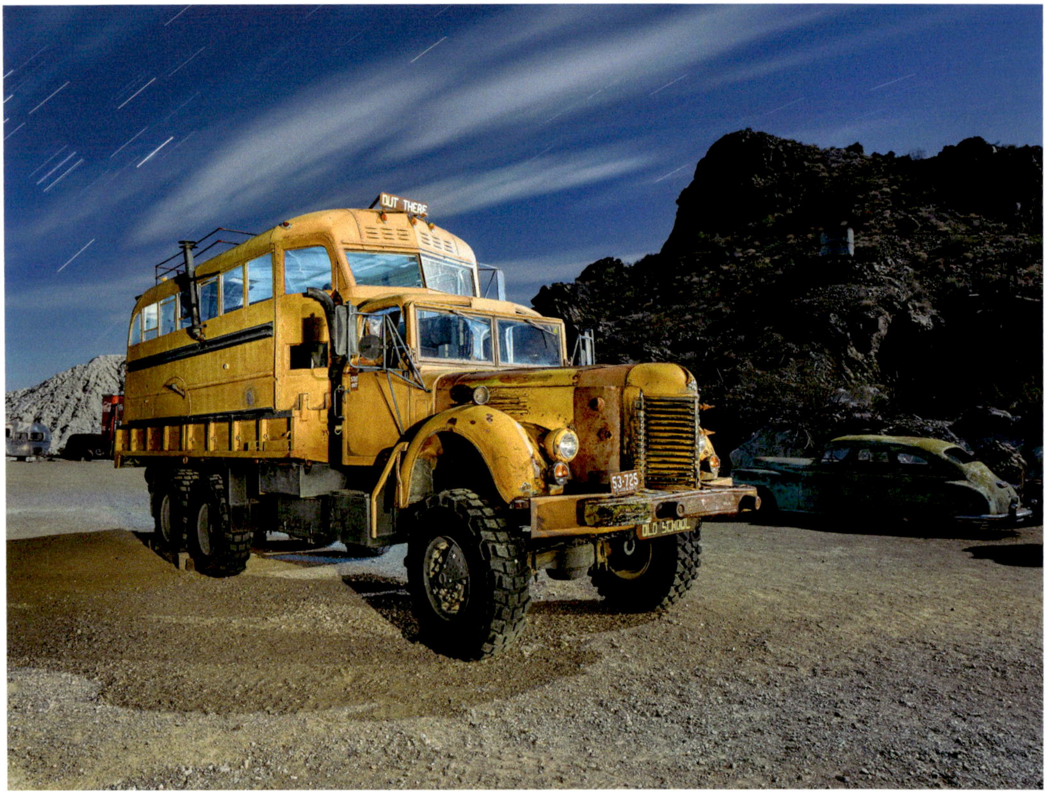

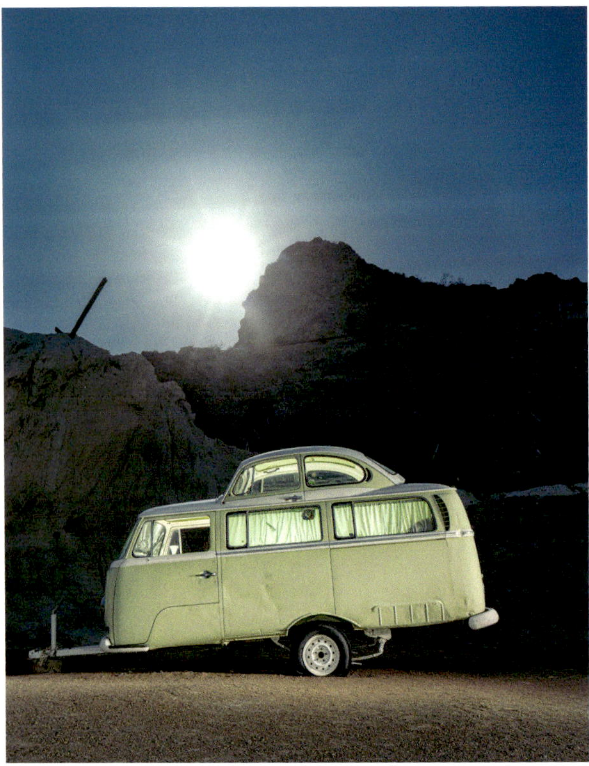

▲ **No School Is Beyond Reach ·** Two school buses in a row. However, this seems straight out of Mad Max or Wasteland Weekend. I lit the bus with warm white and blue light. Techatticup/Nelson Ghost Town, Nevada · Nikon D750/14-24mm f/2.8 lens. 9 minutes total "stacked"; each photo 3 minutes f/8 ISO 320 October 2019 · Full moon, ProtoMachines LED2 with warm white and teal light.

◄ **Ein Seltsamer Volkswagen Für Dich ·** Have you ever seen anything like this modified VW camper with a bug roof? Techatticup/Nelson Ghost Town, Nevada · Pentax K-1/28-105mm f/3.5-5.6 lens. 2 minutes f/9 ISO 200. May 2023 · Full moon, ProtoMachines LED2 with warm white light.

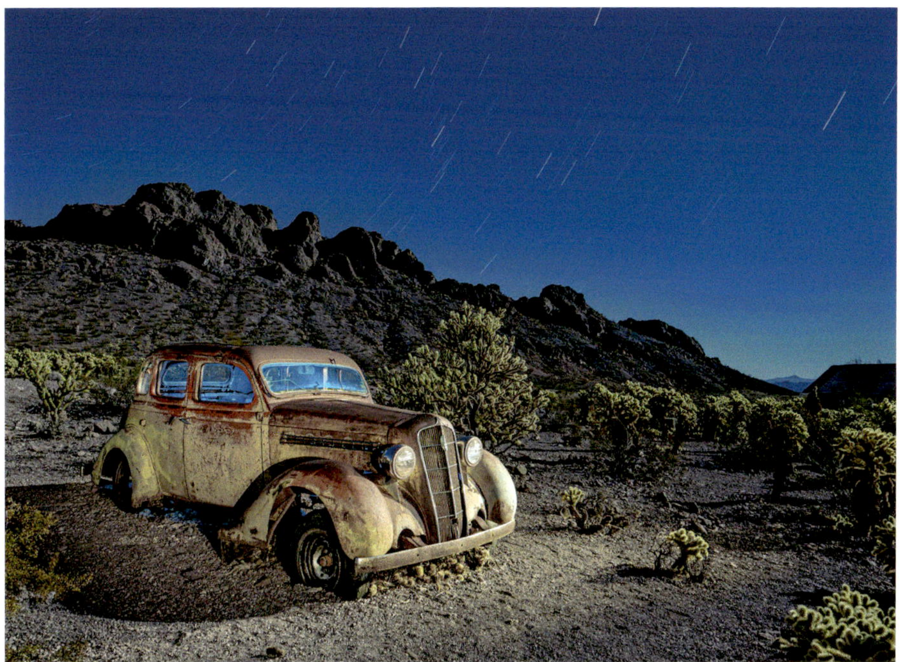

Sunday Driver · A vintage car resting among the cholla. We always warn our night photography participants about the cholla garden repeatedly. So far, so good. Techatticup/Nelson Ghost Town, Nevada · Nikon D750/Nikkor 14-24mm f/2.8 lens. 12 minutes total "stacked"; each photo 3 minutes f/8 ISO 320 October 2019 · Full moon, ProtoMachines LED2 with warm white and teal light.

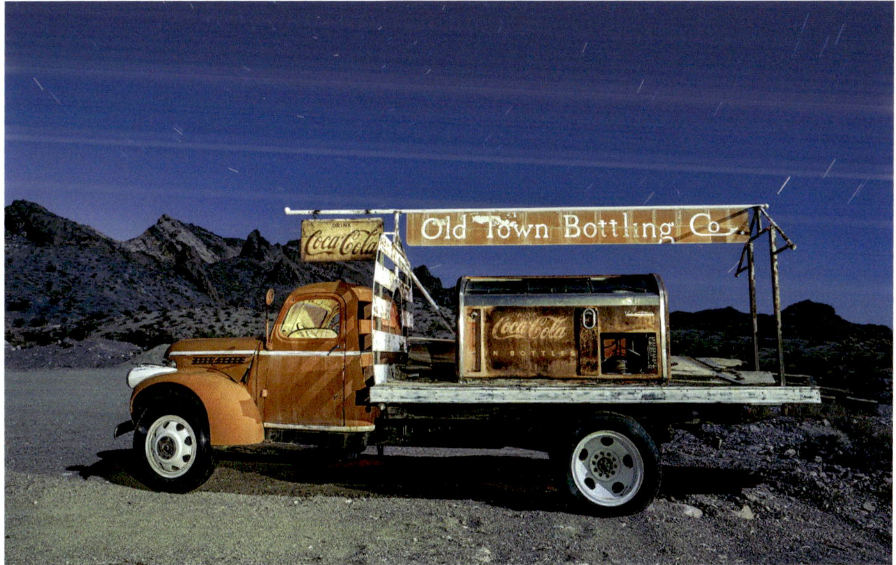

Along The Highway To Anywhere · This instantly reminded me of drinking ice-cold Coca Cola on hot, humid days in the Midwest when I was a kid, holding the cold glass bottle against my head or neck occasionally to cool off. Back then, this was my favorite drink, sort of funny since I never drink it now. "Along the Highway to Anywhere" is a 1949 Coca Cola slogan. Techatticup/Nelson Ghost Town, Nevada · Nikon D750/Nikkor 14-24mm f/2.8 lens. 9 minutes total "stacked"; each photo 3 minutes f/8 ISO 400 October 2019 · Full moon, ProtoMachines LED2 with warm white light.

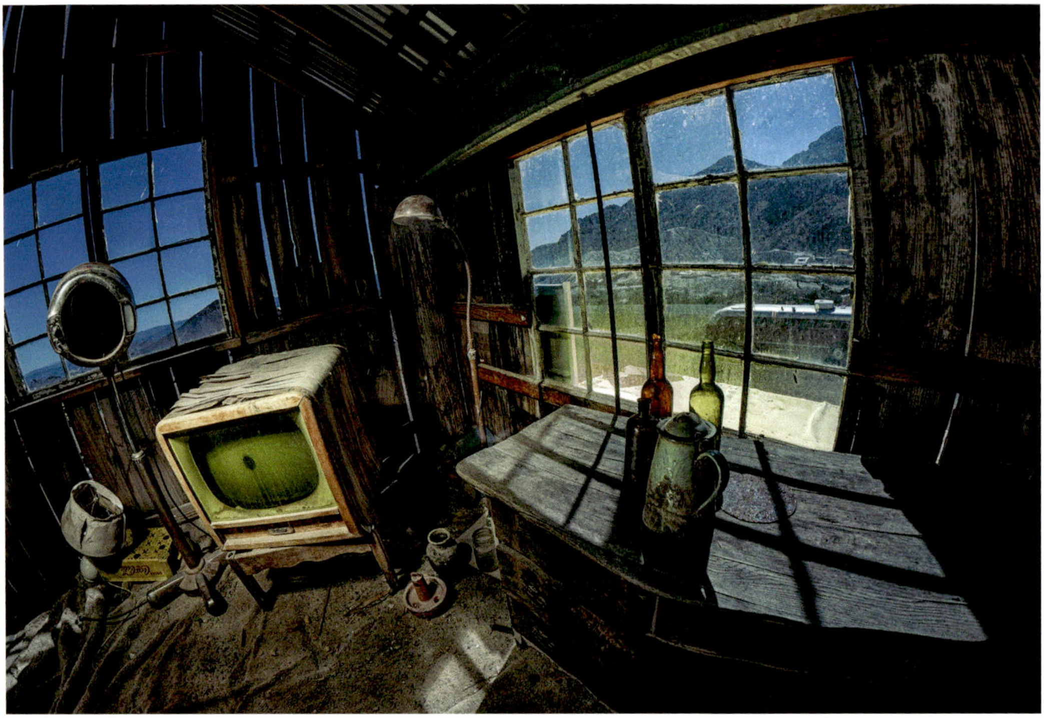

Shadow Theater · The upstairs interior of a large wooden barn. The glow from outside is from an ancient neon sign, while the shadows from the bureau are from a nearly full desert moon on a beautiful cool Mojave evening. Techatticup/Nelson Ghost Town, Nevada · Nikon D750/Rokinon 12mm f/2.8 lens. 3 minutes f/8 ISO 400 October 2019 · Full moon, ProtoMachines LED2 with warm white light.

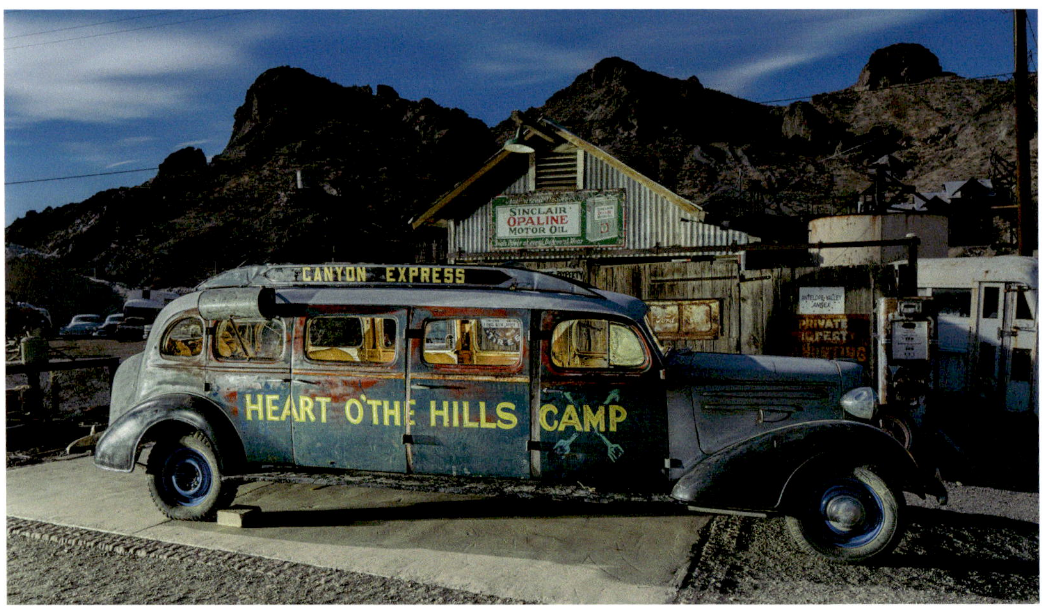

Heart O' The Hills · This must have been loads of fun back in the day, rumbling off to camp in the Canyon Express. Techatticup/Nelson Ghost Town, Nevada · Pentax K-1/28-105mm f/3.5-5.6 lens. 155 seconds f/8 ISO 200. October 2021 · Full moon, ProtoMachines LED2 with warm white light.

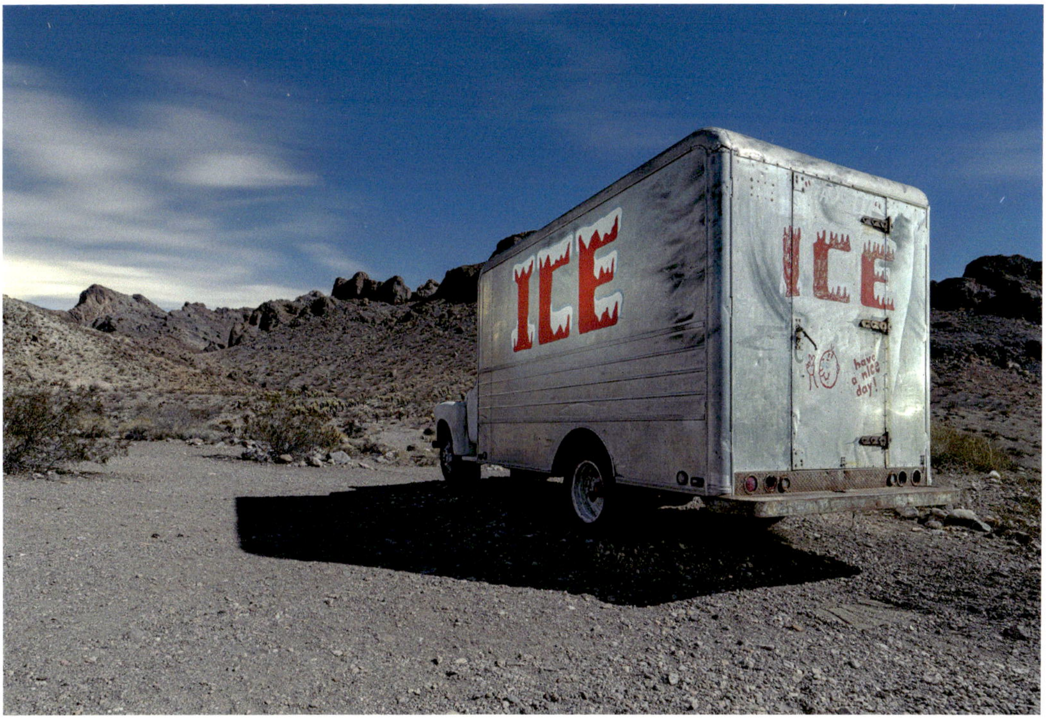

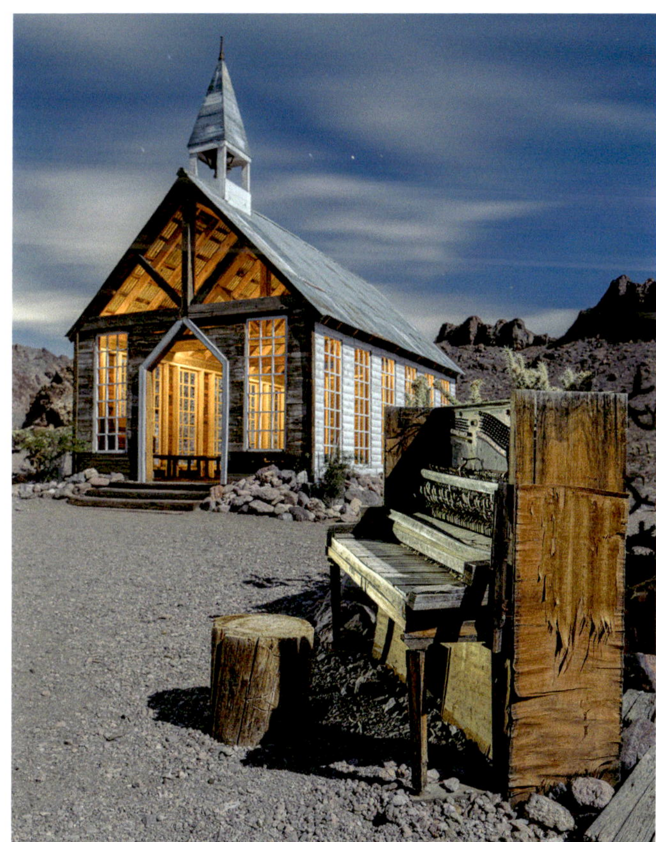

▲ **The Hills Have Ice** · Ice, ice baby. Night delivery, with an ice delivery truck cooling off the Mojave Desert in Nevada. Techatticup/Nelson Ghost Town, Nevada · Pentax K-1/15-30mm f/2.8 lens. 124 seconds f/8 ISO 200. October 2021 · Full moon, ProtoMachines LED2 with warm white light.

▶ **Caroling Mojave Style**
· A musical night winterland holiday scene, Mojave style with a rather weathered piano for accompaniment. Techatticup/ Nelson Ghost Town, Nevada · Pentax K-1/15-30mm f/2.8 lens. 139 seconds f/8 ISO 200. October 2021 · Full moon, ProtoMachines LED2 with warm white light, turning on the interior church lights for three seconds.

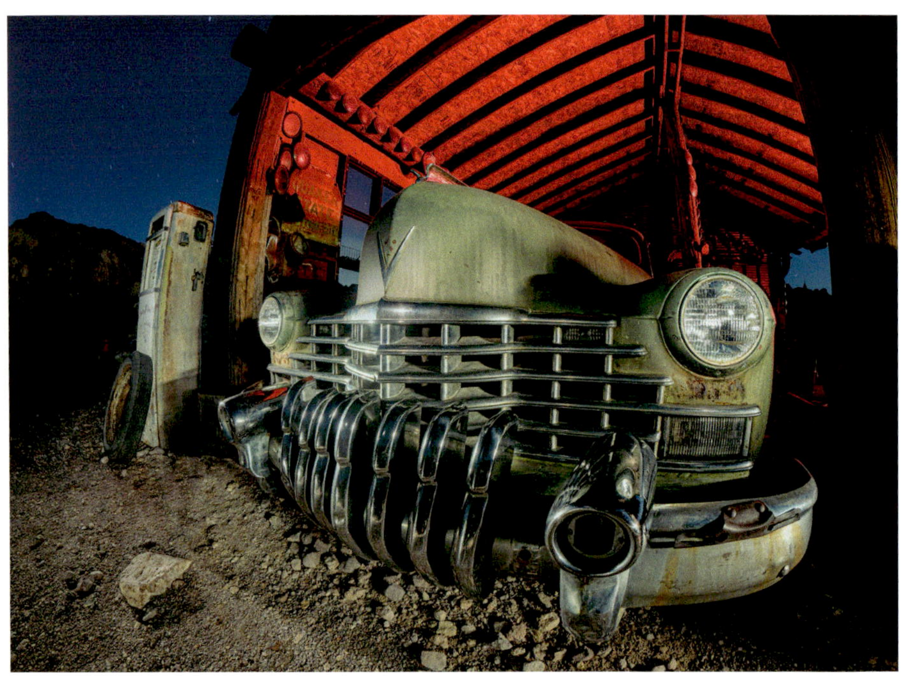

Fleetwood Cadillac-Ac-Ac · Fisheye night view of a 1940s Cadillac Fleetwood with a vintage Buick grille. Techatticup/Nelson Ghost Town, Nevada · Nikon D750/Rokinon 12mm f/2.8 fisheye lens. 111 seconds f/8 ISO 200. November 2022 · Full moon, ProtoMachines LED2 with warm white and red light.

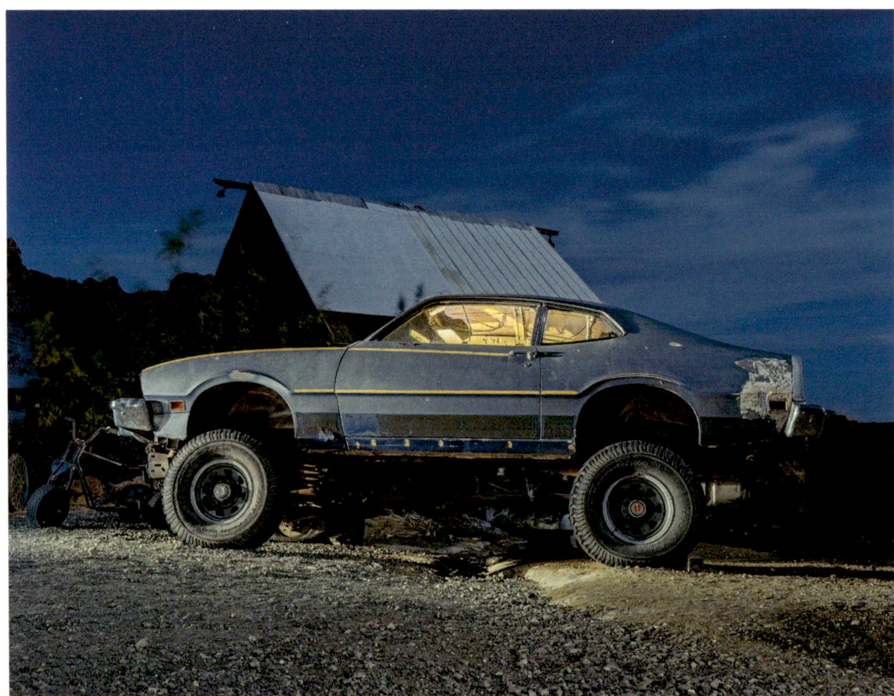

The Night Comet · A vintage Comet underneath the stars. Techatticup/Nelson Ghost Town, Nevada · Pentax K-1/28-105mm f/3.5-5.6 lens. 40 seconds f/8 ISO 200. May 2023 · Full moon, light in interior of car, ProtoMachines LED2 with warm white light.

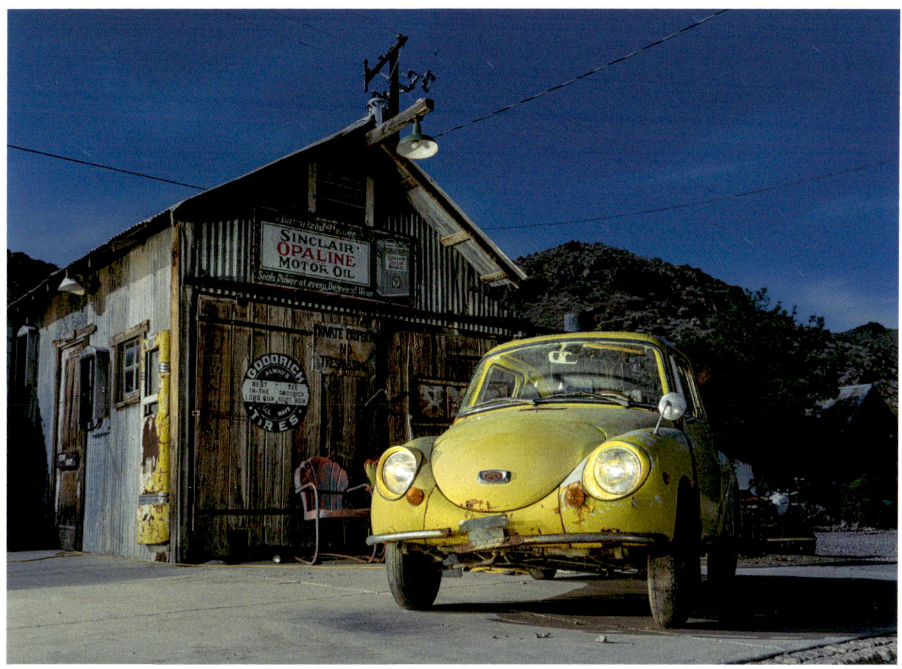

360 · My first reaction was that the diminutive Subaru 360 looked like an arcade bumper car. Turns out I wasn't too far off. This was originally manufactured in Japan as sort of a "people's car", and it was imported to the United States. However, a 1970 Consumer Reports article rated the vehicle "Not Acceptable." Not deterred, they made an attempt to use the vehicles like go-karts, modifying them somewhat. Techatticup/Nelson Ghost Town, Nevada · Pentax K-1/28-105mm f/3.5-5.6 lens. 2 minutes f/8 ISO 200. May 2023 · Full moon, ProtoMachines LED2 with warm white light.

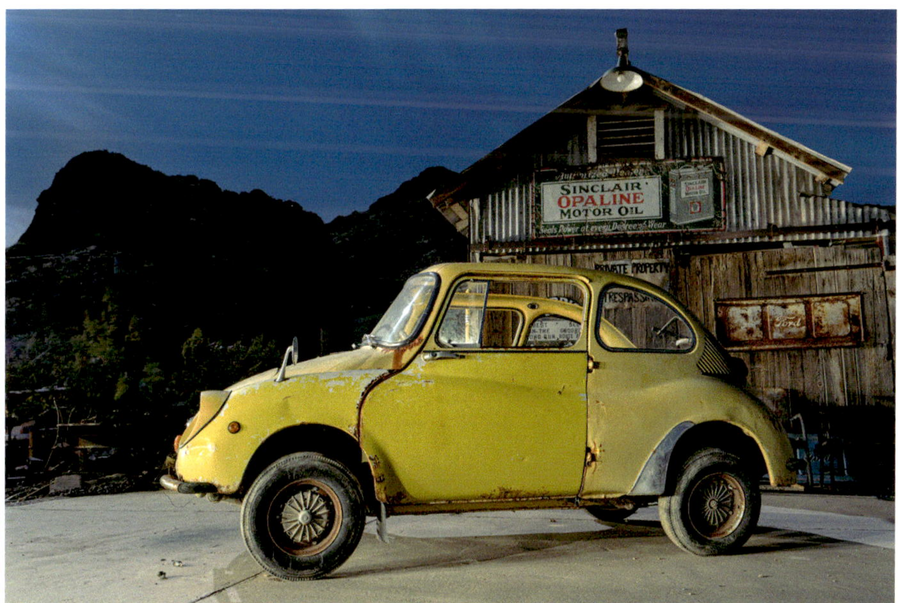

Unite · Another view of the Subaru 360. Rear engine, made from the late 1950s to the mid-1970s, and Subaru's first production car. Techatticup/Nelson Ghost Town, Nevada · Pentax K-1/28-105mm f/3.5-5.6 lens. 2 minutes f/8 ISO 200. May 2023 · Full moon, ProtoMachines LED2 with warm white light.

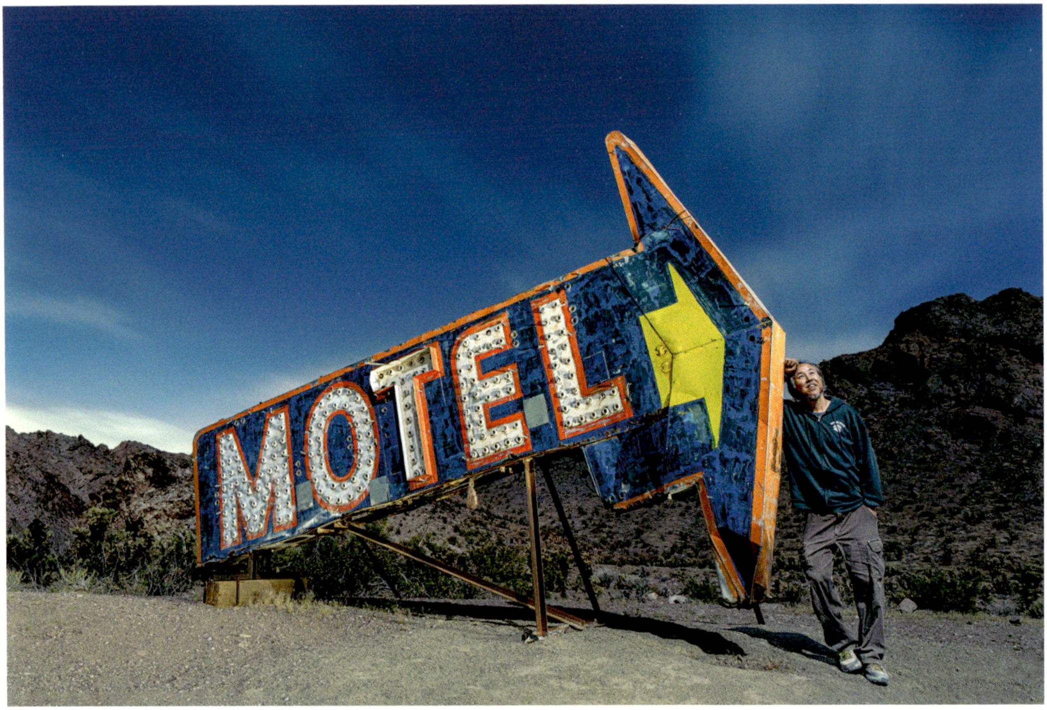

Fall in Love with the Sky · Night. Motel sign. Camera. It's all good. Techatticup/Nelson Ghost Town, Nevada · Pentax K-1/28-105mm f/3.5-5.6 lens. Blend: 2 minutes f/8 ISO 200 so I could light paint the sign and have it noise-free. 3 seconds f/3.5 ISO 3200 for me because I can't stand still for very long without blurring. May 2023.

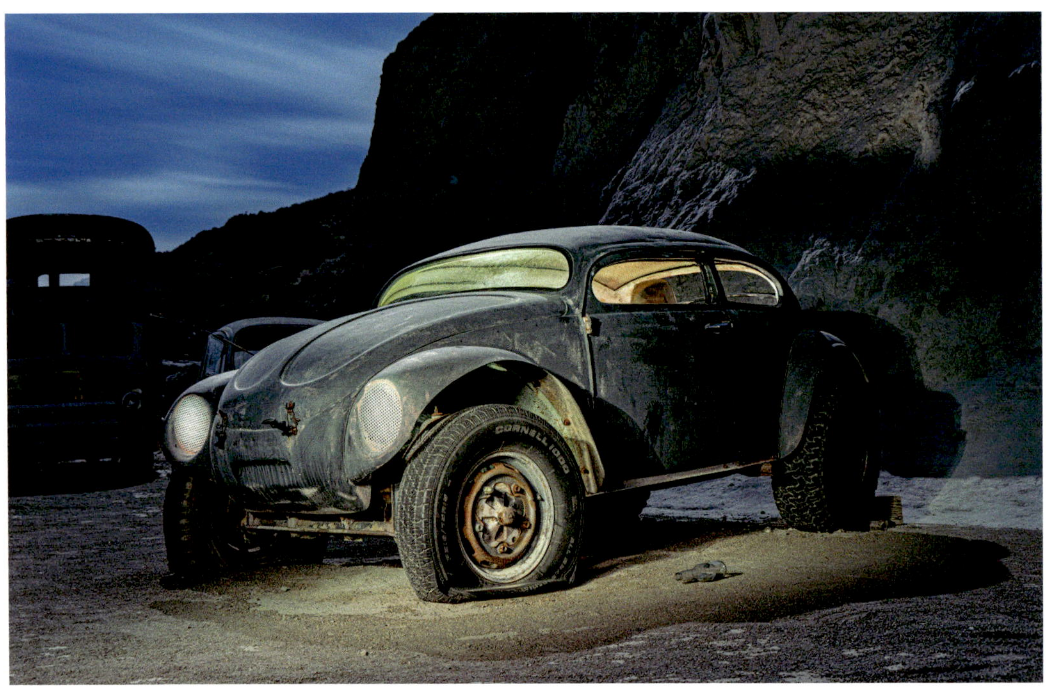

Chopped · A chopped Bug greeting the Mojave night. Techatticup/Nelson Ghost Town, Nevada · Pentax K-1/28-105mm f/3.5-5.6 lens. 2 minutes f/8 ISO 200. May 2023 · Full moon, ProtoMachines LED2 with warm white light.

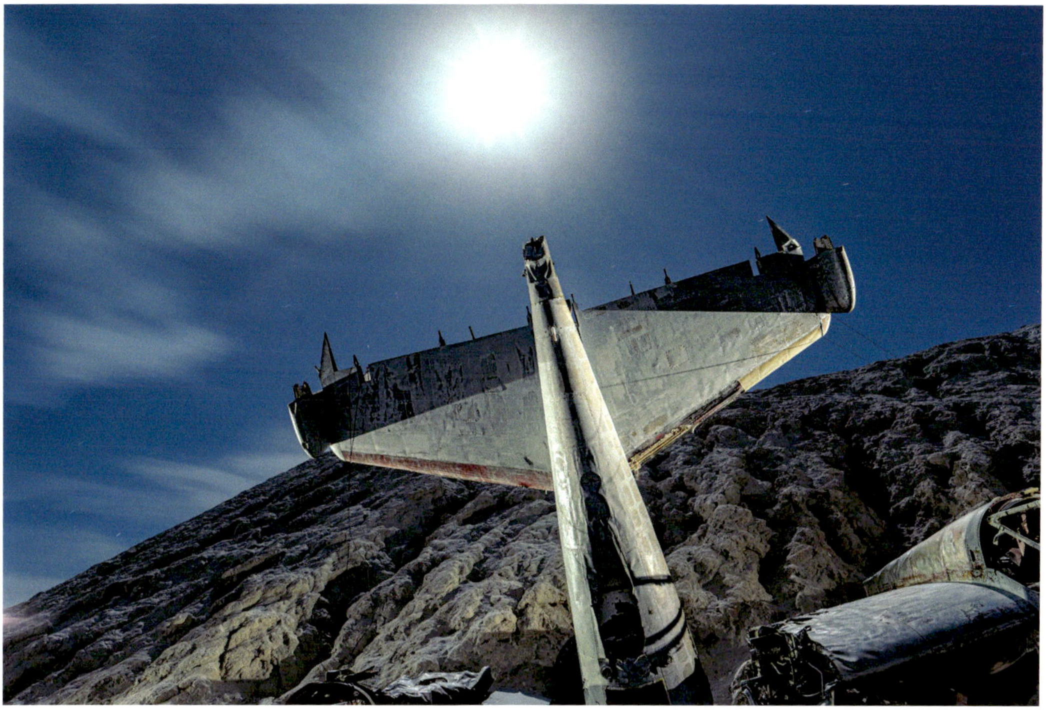

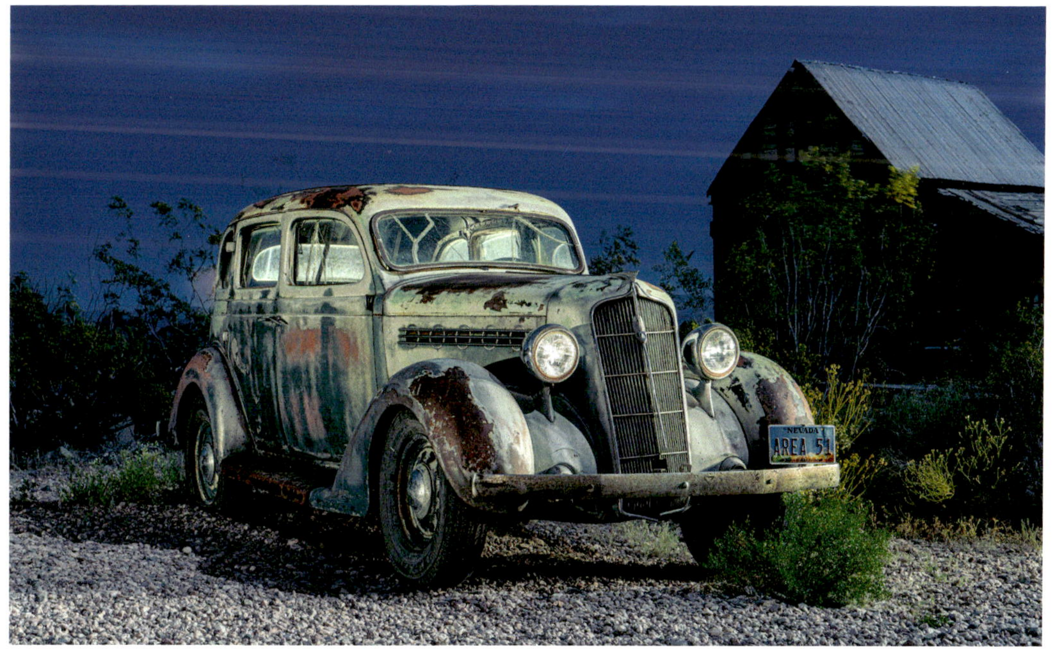

Moondial · Creative parking from a pilot? No. It's an old movie set built specifically for the 2001 film, *3000 Miles to Graceland*. I waited for the moon to drift over the tail of the plane. Techatticup/Nelson Ghost Town, Nevada · Pentax K-1/28-105mm f/3.5-5.6 lens. 81 seconds f/8 ISO 200. May 2023 · Full moon, ProtoMachines LED2 with warm white light.

Nevada Area 51 · An otherworldly vintage automobile on a beautiful Mojave Desert night. Techatticup/Nelson Ghost Town, Nevada · Pentax K-1/28-105mm f/3.5-5.6 lens. 2 minutes f/8 ISO 200. May 2023 · Full moon partially blocked by clouds, ProtoMachines LED2 with warm white light.

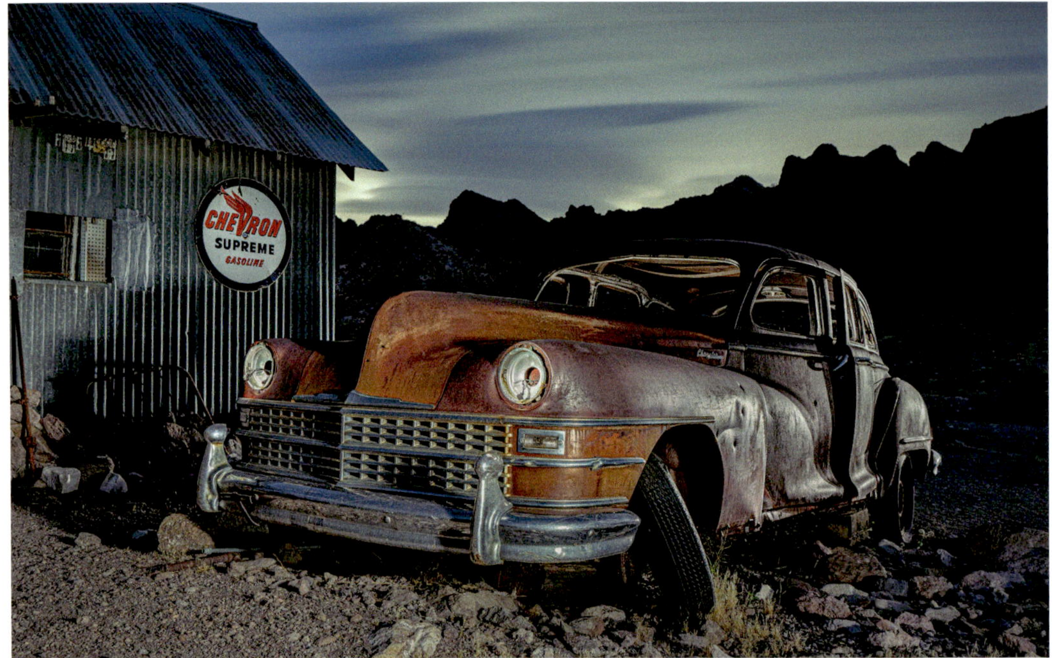

Pigeon-Toed · This car might need a front-end alignment. Techatticup/Nelson Ghost Town, Nevada · Pentax K-1/28-105mm f/3.5-5.6 lens. 2 minutes f/8 ISO 400. May 2023 · Full moon partially blocked by clouds, ProtoMachines LED2 with warm white light.

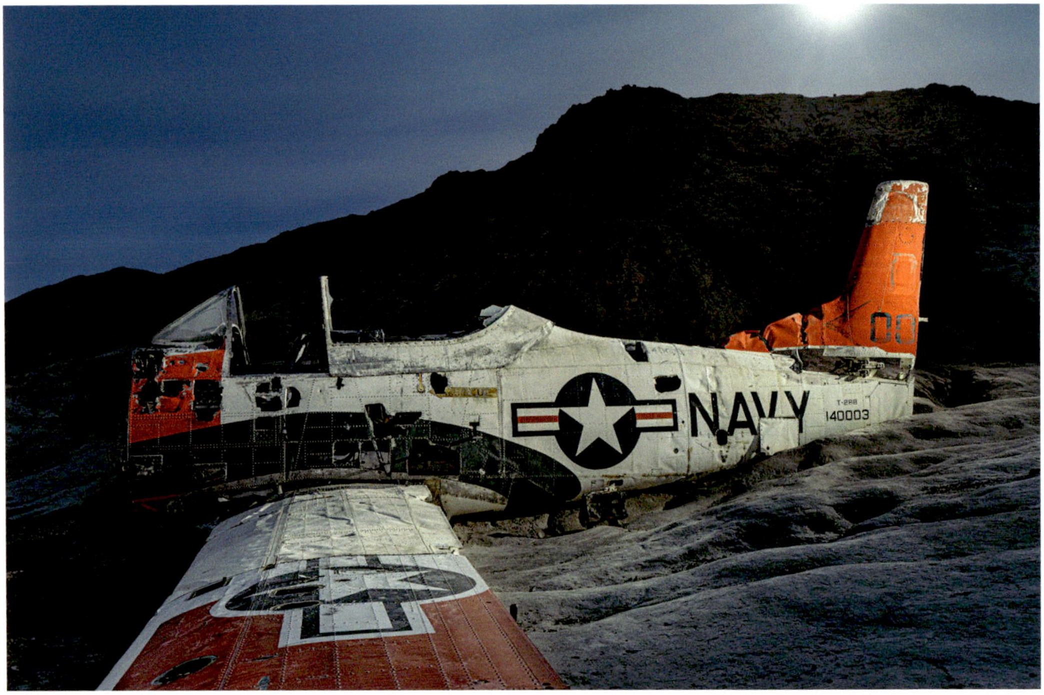

The Wings of Icarus · T-28 Trojan navy trainer, with the nearly full moon peaking in from above. Techatticup/ Nelson Ghost Town, Nevada · Pentax K-1/28-105mm f/3.5-5.6 lens. 111 seconds f/9 ISO 200. May 2023 · Full moon, ProtoMachines LED2 with warm white light.

7

MISCELLANEOUS

DESERT CHRIST PARK, CALIFORNIA

A tall, crumbling concrete statue of Christ stands tall against the rocky mountain, overlooking the town of Yucca Valley. Desert Christ Park was built on five acres owned by Reverend Eddie Garver, who envisioned a Christian-themed park as a beacon for world peace.

The Reverend was introduced to (Frank) Antone Martin, a sculptor from Inglewood, California. He had created a giant ten-foot, five-ton statue of the resurrected Christ and dreamed of placing it on the rim of the Grand Canyon. Of course, being a National Park, this was a violation of the separation of church and state. He labeled the statue "the unwanted Christ." Martin eventually took Garver up on his offer to place it on the hillside of his property.

It must have been quite a sight to haul "the unwanted Christ" up the hill from Los Angeles on the back of a truck. This fired the imagination of the nation. *Life Magazine* covered this in its April 1951 issue. Desert Christ Park was dedicated on Easter Sunday.

Martin moved to the area. In partnership with the Garvers, Martin created other Biblical concrete figures, including a three-story, 125-ton facade depicting "The Last Supper."

The partnership evaporated in the late 1950s. Any statues that could be moved were relocated to the present-day park. Garver donated his land to local parishioners, who later donated it to the Evangelical Free Church of Yucca Valley. The original statue of Christ, the tomb, and half of "The Last Supper" are still on this church property.

The Landers Earthquake shook the heads and hands off many of the statues. Vandals sometimes knocked the heads off or broke off arms from the statues. When I first began visiting Desert Christ Park many years ago, time, the elements,

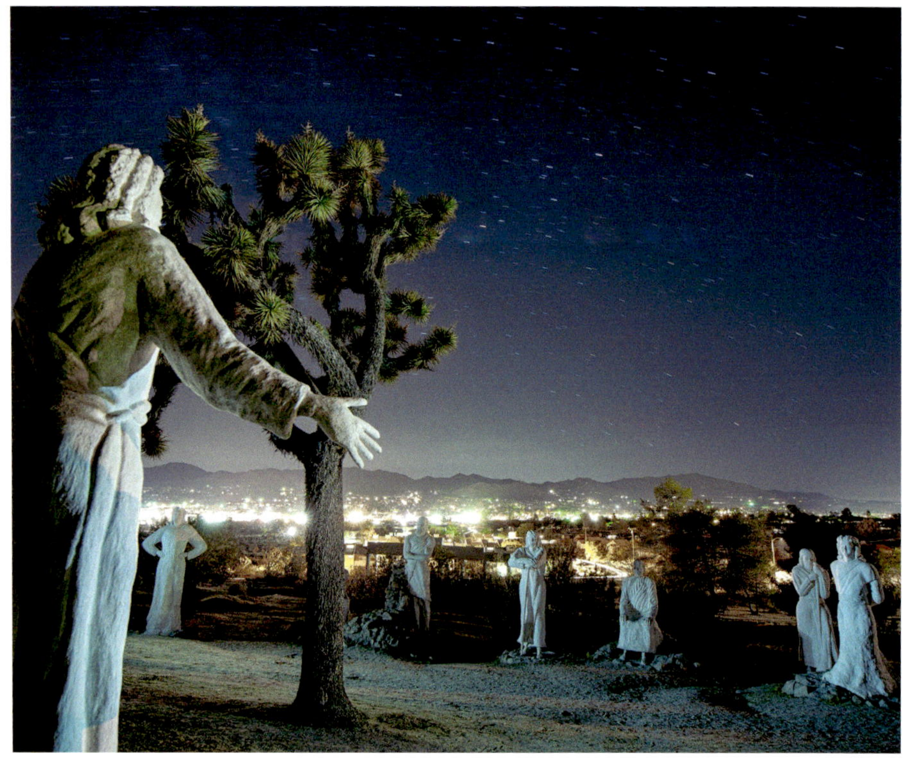

La Luz de Jesus · Looking over humankind below and beyond. Desert Christ Park, Yucca Valley, California · Nikon D610/14-24mm f/2.8G ED lens. 2 minutes 27 seconds f/4 ISO 200. July 2015 · ProtoMachines LED2 with warm white light, ambient light from nearby buildings.

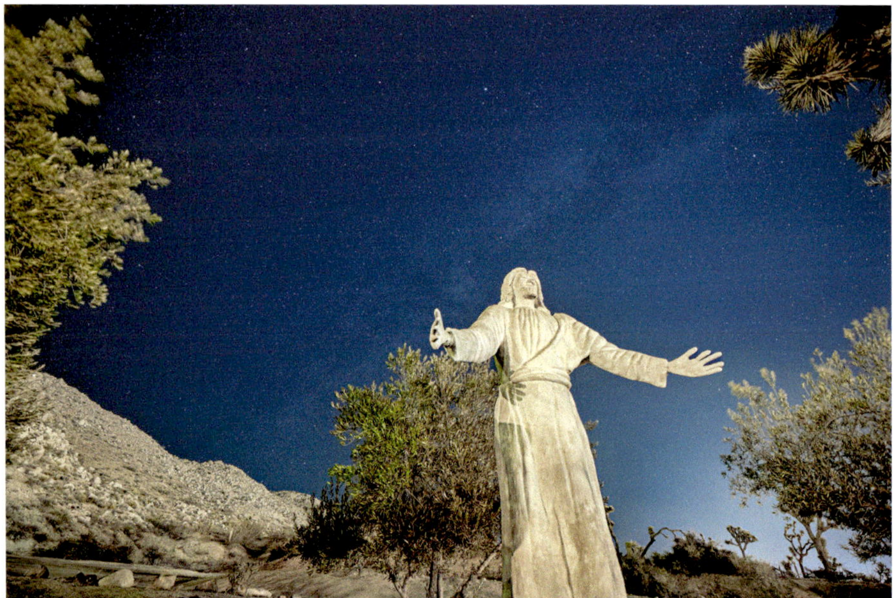

On the Fourth Day · Underneath the starry night sky, including the north part of the Milky Way. Desert Christ Park, Yucca Valley, California · Nikon D610/14-24mm f/2.8G ED lens. 15 seconds f/2.8 ISO 4000. July 2015 · ProtoMachines LED2 with warm white light, ambient light from nearby buildings.

and vandals had worn away some parts of the statues, exposing the steel rod rein-
forcements. Trash and graffiti were everywhere. More recently, however, the Desert
Christ Park Foundation has cared for the park. They operate through donations and
volunteers, who try their best to keep up with the maintenance.

METEOR CITY

As a kid, I loved watching *Starman*, finding the interplay between Jeff Bridges and
Karen Allen utterly charming. There is a scene in the 1984 movie where the two eat
Dutch apple pie, and later, Karen's character kisses the policeman to say thank you.
Starman then startles him by doing the same. The unusual dome-shaped structure
where this takes place is Meteor City Trading Post.

The first Route 66 business at this location was Sharber Texaco Service Station.
A new owner named "Lonesome Jack" Newsum expanded it to include a trading
post. He put up a faux roadside city limits sign that said, "Meteor City: Population
1." When Newsum married in 1946, he updated the sign to read "Population 2."

The geodesic dome, adorned with a bright yellow Mohawk, came later. This was
actually a curio shop that sold moccasins and shirts, not a restaurant like in *Starman*.
Consequently, the Dutch apple pie was a rather short-lived bonus.

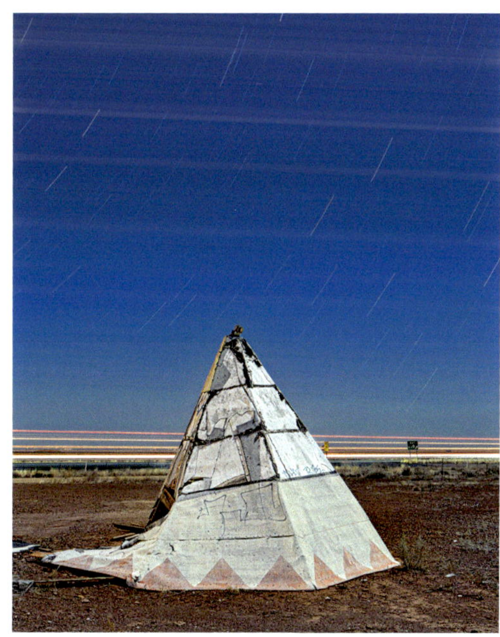

Lonesome Jack's Wigwam · An
abandoned wigwam in the once popular
dome-shaped Meteor City Trading Post
along historic Route 66. Winslow, Arizona.
Pentax K-1/28-105mm f/3.5-5.6 lens. 16.6
minutes total "stacked". Each photo 100
seconds f/8 ISO 200. February 2022 · Full
moon, ProtoMachines LED2 with warm
white light, passing lights from motorists.

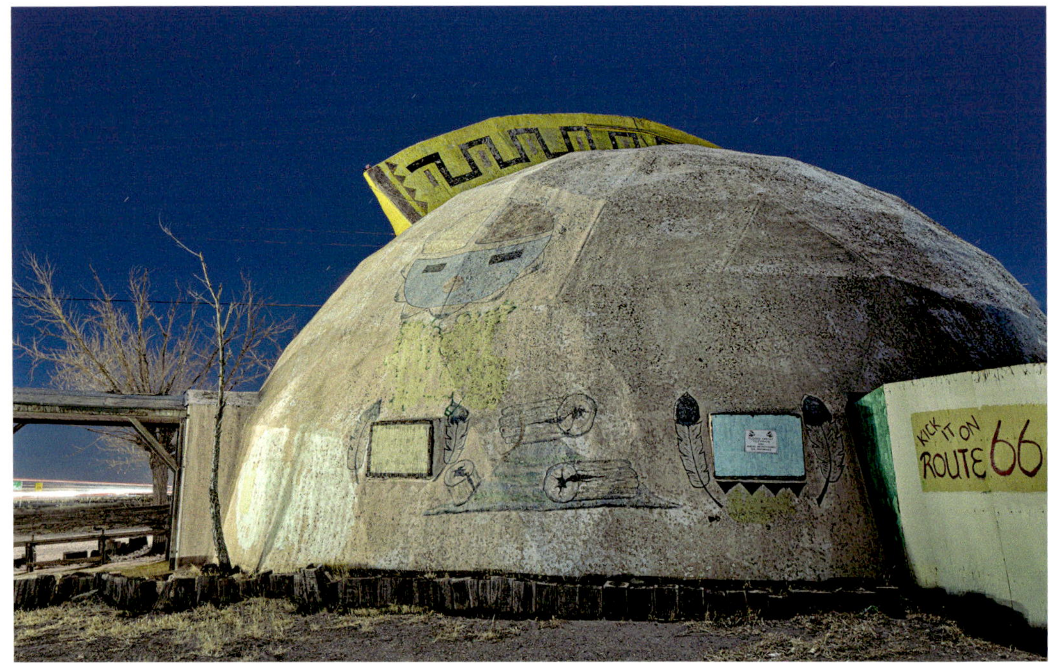

Mohawk · The streaks of headlights on I-40 zooming past the once popular dome-shaped Meteor City Trading Post along historic Route 66. Winslow, Arizona · Pentax K-1/28-105mm f/3.5-5.6 lens. 91 seconds f/8 ISO 200. February 2022 · Full moon, ProtoMachines LED2 with warm white light, passing lights from motorists.

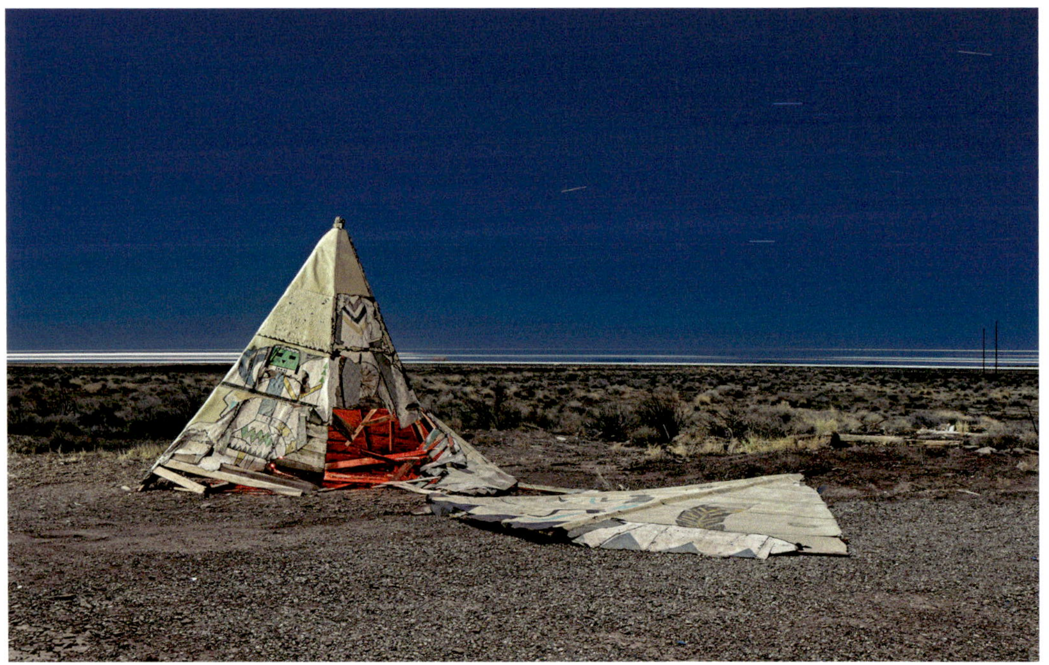

Lonely Wigwam · An abandoned wigwam in the once popular dome-shaped Meteor City Trading Post along historic Route 66. Winslow, Arizona · Pentax K-1/28-105mm f/3.5-5.6 lens. 8 minutes total "stacked." Each photo 2 minutes f/8 ISO 200. February 2022 · Full moon, ProtoMachines LED2 with warm white light, passing lights from motorists.

The 1979 dome burned down in 1990 but was replaced with another dome. Meteor City was abandoned in 2012 when no one wanted to purchase it. Of course, vandals inevitably ravaged the place. However, Joann and Mike Brown purchased Meteor City in March 2017 and have begun work on a major clean-up of the site. The outside dome and wigwams are still decaying, as most of the clean-up so far has been inside the dome or behind a tall fence.

Mike Cooper and I drove here from nearby Joseph City. We were excited to photograph the unusual dome and the abandoned wigwams in the front, still decaying in the Arizona sun.

Howdy Hank's, Arizona

Howdy Hank's Store and Cafe was built in 1941, according to the Arizona Survey Report. It originally opened as Hopi Village, operating as a motel, cafe, and trading post to attract motorists along Route 66. It has been bought and sold several times since then. In what is a familiar story, after Interstate 40 opened, business evaporated. The building has since been used as a feed store and welding shop.

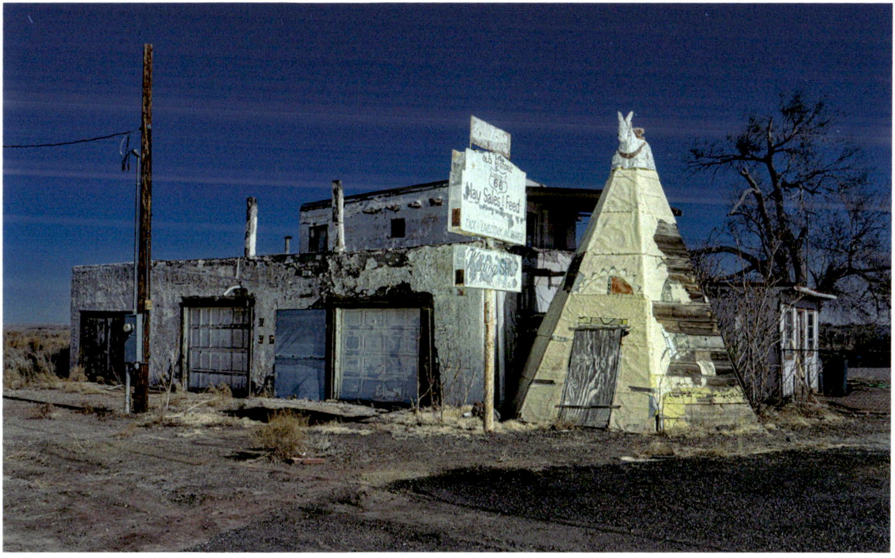

This is a Song of Hopi · The old Howdy Hank's Hopi Village Indian Store and Cafe, built in 1941 along Route 66, according to the Arizona Survey Report. New owners bought it and called it Sitting Bull Indian Stores. As you can see from the sign, there was also a motel. And they even had a swimming pool. Joseph City, Arizona · Pentax K-1/28-105mm f/3.5-5.6 lens. 2 minutes f/8 ISO 200. February 2022 · Full moon, ProtoMachines LED2 with warm white light.

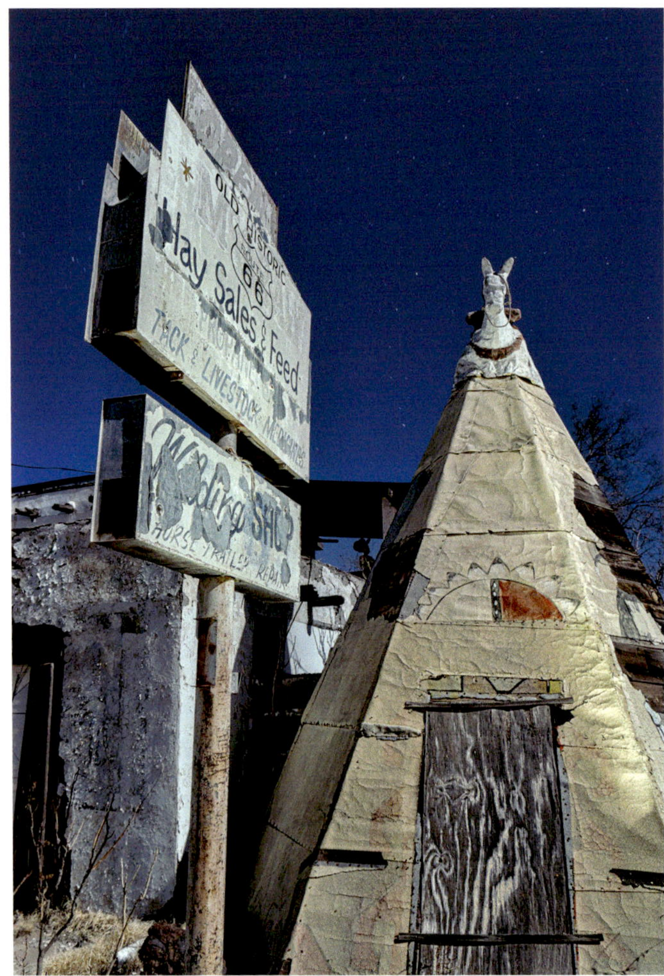

Howdy Hanks · Another view of Howdy Hank's Hopi Village Indian Store and Cafe, built in 1941 along Route 66. Joseph City, Arizona · Pentax K-1/28-105mm f/3.5-5.6 lens. 2 minutes f/8 ISO 200. February 2022 · Full moon, ProtoMachines LED2 with warm white light.

PEARSONVILLE, OWENS VALLEY, CALIFORNIA

Every time I drive past the Pearsonville Uniroyal Girl, I stop and take a photo of her. My leggy lady friend stands 18 feet tall and greets everyone who passes on Highway 395 in Owens Valley, California, faded and weathered though she may be.

International Fiberglass made several types of fiberglass statues, including the Uniroyal Girls, considerably rarer than the Muffler Men. It seems the sculptor who created the original molds had a thing for Jackie Kennedy, hence the resemblance. Ever thoughtful, he designed the Uniroyal Girls with a dress, ready for shedding or donning depending on the community climate.

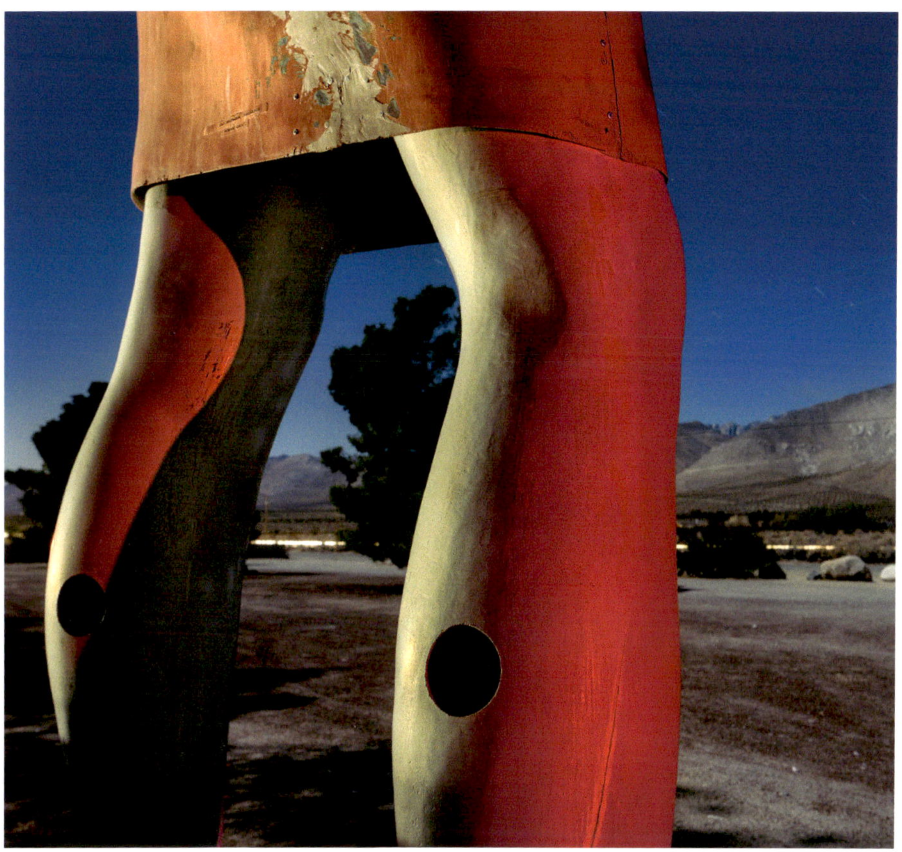

She's Got Legs · My very tall leggy lady friend. At 18 feet tall and made of fiberglass, the Uniroyal Girl greets all passersby. The sculptor apparently modeled her after Jackie Kennedy. Pearsonville, California · Pentax K-1/15-30mm f/2.8 lens. 3 minutes f/8 ISO 200. December 2019 · Full moon, ProtoMachines LED2 with warm white light, passing lights from motorists.

She stands next to a tank identifying Pearsonville as the Hubcap Capital of the World. If you wish to dispute this, you would have to find someone who had more hubcaps than Lucy Pearson, who had over 80,000. Lucy the Hubcap Queen had collected them since she and her husband Andy founded Pearsonville in 1959. For the longest time, they hung from the walls in the cafe, in Hubcap Yard, on shelves in the Hubcap Shop, and still more elsewhere. According to a 1990s *L.A. Times* article, she bought, sold, and traded them, becoming a walking encyclopedia of all things hubcaps. She even made hubcap clocks with her granddaughter.

Lucy, her hubcap collection, and just about the entire town are gone. However, my tall lady friend remains.

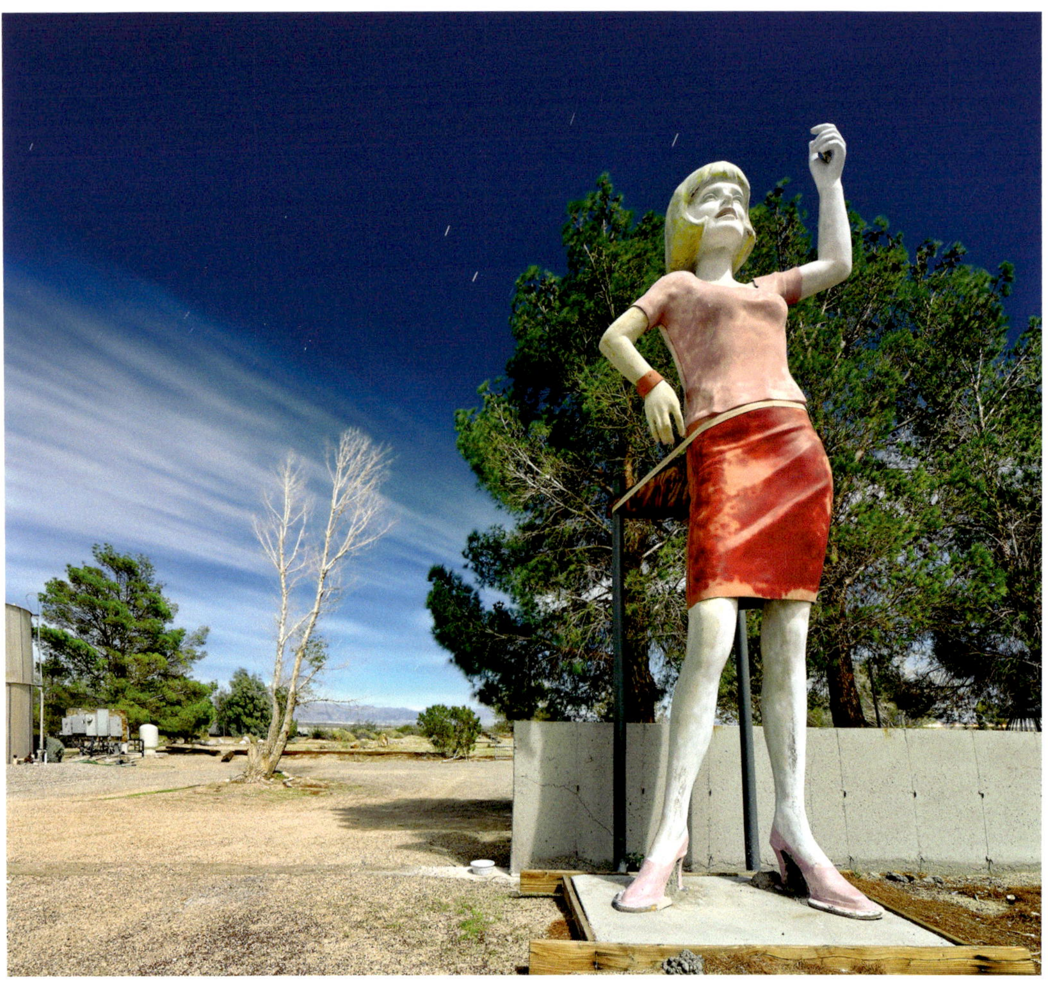

Uniroyal Girl · Even during the night, the 18-foot-tall fiberglass Uniroyal Girl warmly greets all passersby. The sculptor apparently modeled her after Jackie Kennedy. And yes, I was a gentleman. I never upskirted her. Pearsonville, California · Nikon D610/Nikkor 14-24mm f/2.8 lens. 6 minutes f/8 ISO 200. October 2015 · Full moon, ProtoMachines LED2 with warm white light.

CREATING THE IMAGES

The images in this book were created at night with long exposure photography techniques. Over the years that it took to create these images, I've used a Pentax K-1, Nikon D750, and D610 with ultra wide angle lenses and even a Lensbaby tilt-shift style lens, all mounted on a sturdy Feisol carbon fiber tripod. I typically carry one or two cameras in my backpack along with my flashlight for light painting, intervalometers, accessories, drinks, and snacks. This way, I can be extremely mobile.

On or near a full moon, which is used as the primary light source, I set the camera for long exposures that are usually between one to four minutes, often around f/8 at ISO 200. This is often long enough to show the stars streaking across the night sky, allowing the ambient light to "soak in" a bit.

Then I "light paint" the scene using a handheld ProtoMachines LED2 light painting device. Light painting involves using a handheld light to "paint" the light onto subjects, the ground, interiors, or anywhere else I wish to have light. Light painting to illuminate subjects is a beautiful, addictive art, as you can walk around the scene, deciding what to bring to light and what to keep in shadow. In this way, you are able to cumulatively add light to areas during the exposure. All the lighting is done in-camera at the time of exposure.

For most of the photos, I use a warm white light for light painting. However, there are times in which I want to add color. Fortunately, the ProtoMachines LED2 is capable of creating any color in the RGB spectrum and offers controls for brightness and saturation. Prior to owning this very flexible light, I used LED flashlights. I would attach Roscolux gels to the front of the flashlight, held on by Velcro. Sometimes, I also used colored plastic bags, which would also diffuse the light more. Although more time-consuming and cumbersome, adding color to light in this manner is still capable of producing outstanding results.

I usually walk around and light the foreground from multiple angles. I typically do not use light stands or other stationary lights. Being able to walk around and shine the light at many different and rather specific angles is quicker, more flexible, and more artistic than using stationary lights, in my opinion. I take great care in bringing out the detail and not keeping the light in one place for too long and obliterating the detail or "blowing out" the highlights. By skimming the light off the surface at a nearly 90-degree angle, I can also accentuate much of the detail. I can also backlight objects, creating long shadows that seem to reach out to the viewer. Light painting is really all about the angles. When you are unencumbered by stands, you are free to illuminate more creatively. Night photography with light painting is, in my opinion, the most actively creative form of photography.

You might notice that in many of the night photos of abandoned vehicles, it looks like their headlights are on. Sometimes, I am asked whether I somehow turned on the headlights. I did not. I held my flashlight close to the headlights and shined it on each headlight while using a light modifier called a snoot. The snoot I use is a long tube made from black ABS pipe, which I screw on to the threads of my handheld light. Prior to having a light with threads outside the front element, I simply held a cardboard packing tube in front of my LED flashlight to illuminate the headlights.

Light painting may seem odd to the uninitiated. However, when you stop and think about it, it's not so different than using a flash. The primary difference is time. With a long exposure photo that might be several minutes in length, I simply have more time to add light to an image and be creative.

You may be wondering how I am able to walk around without appearing in the photo. Generally speaking, you need to stand still for at least ten percent of the total exposure length of a photo to even begin to register. For a two-minute exposure, that's twelve seconds. If it takes two minutes to produce a properly exposed photo, you would need to stand still for most of those two minutes to be properly exposed. If you stood still for one minute, you would look like a ghost. At thirty seconds, you would appear very faintly in the image. And by twelve seconds, you might appear as a very faint smudge that might not be all that noticeable, depending on which part of the image you're in. This is all assuming, of course, that you do not inadvertently illuminate yourself with the flashlight. To prevent this, most night photographers who do light painting wear dark clothing, making it less likely to reflect light and have it mistakenly appear in the photo. It may feel like night photographers who do light painting have superpowers. However, we all possess this magical ability.

Sometimes, you might see extra-long star trails in the images. In the captions, you might see that sometimes, I write the total amount of the exposure length, saying that they are "stacked." This simply means that I took two or more photos in succession and then combined them into one image. I do this for several reasons. It reduces the amount of noise that might appear in the image, especially if it's a warm night. I also do it so I have a better chance of salvaging the photo should unexpected car lights or an errant flashlight mistakenly shine into the lens. In each caption, I give the camera equipment, camera settings, and sources of light in the hopes that it helps photographers.

Many of these night images are colorful. Some who are not familiar with night photography might regard this as odd since this isn't the way night typically appears to our eyes. As night grows darker, our eyes become increasingly monochromatic. Our retinas widen to let in more light. But while our cones function well in brighter light and see color, our rods are monochromatic. However, our camera does not have the same limitations as our eyes, registering colors in low light far more vividly.

ABOUT THE AUTHOR

I am a night photographer. I drive long hours in a dusty car listening to weird music, stay out all night creating photos, get dirty, hang out with other creative, sleep-deprived weirdos, see the stars drift across the sky, and always find the best taco stands. I have been exploring the Southwest United States as well as parts of the East Coast for over six years, brandishing a camera, tripod, and colored flashlight. I especially love creating night photos of abandoned historical places, unique features, and beautiful landscapes. These are experiences that I absolutely cherish. My images have appeared in National Geographic Books, *Omni Magazine*, *Los Angeles Times*, *Westways Magazine*, and many other publications. I am an author and on the editorial board at Photofocus.com, often writing about night photography and light painting. I also thoroughly love teaching night photography workshops as well. Keep up with me at www.kenleephotography.com and on social media.